Bring Science Alive!®

Ecosystems

TCi™

NEXT GENERATION
SCIENCE
STANDARDS
For States, By States

Chief Executive Officer
Bert Bower

Chief Operating Officer
Amy Larson

Strategic Process Director
Ellen Hardy

Director of Product Development
Maria Favata

Strategic Product Manager
Nathan Wellborne

Managing Editor
Ariel Stein

Senior Science Editor
Rebecca Ou

Senior Strategic Editor
Kim Merlino

***Ecosystems* Lead Editor**
Tanya Dewey

Science Content Developers
Karin Akre
Brennan Brockbank
Tanya Dewey
Mantissa Johnston
Douglas Le
Suzanne Lyons
Rebecca Ou
Ariel Stein
Clay Walton
Joan Westley
Jennifer Yeh

Editors
Helene Engler
Jill Farinelli
Mikaila Garfinkel
Sally Isaacs
Lauren Kent
Marlene Martzke
Tylar Pendgraft
Alex White

Writers
Sarah Martin
Linda Blumenthal
Sabre Duren
Katie Ewing
Rebecca Mikulec
Laura Prescott
Molly Wetterschneider

Illustrator/Graphic Artists
Andrew Dakhil
Martha Iserman
Aki Ruiz

Production and Design
Jodi Forrest
Jen Valenzuela
Michelle Vella

Web and Print Designer
Sarah Osentowski

Video Developer
Dominic Mercurio

Director of Operations
Marsha Ifurung

Investigation UX Testing
Davin Kunovsky

Software
Morris Thai
Robert Julius
Gabriel Redig

Software Quality Assurance
Mrudula Sarode

Art Direction
Julia Foug

TCi™

Teachers' Curriculum Institute
PO Box 1327
Rancho Cordova, CA 95741

Customer Service: 800-497-6138
www.teachtci.com

ISBN 978-1-58371-067-8
1 2 3 4 5 6 7 8 9 10 -WC- 22 21 20 19 18 17

Manufactured by Webcrafters, Inc., Madison, WI
United States of America, October 2017, Job # 133653

Welcome to *Bring Science Alive!*

Welcome to *Bring Science Alive! Ecosystems.* We've created this program to help you understand the science and engineering ideas in the Next Generation Science Standards (NGSS). The educators and scientists who created NGSS thought especially long and hard about the standards relating to ecosystems. Why? Because they believed that if you understand how our world's ecosystems function, you'll care enough to do your part in making sure those functions continue for generations to come.

In this program, you'll integrate physical, Earth, and life science knowledge to discover how the matter that makes up your body has cycled through Earth's ecosystems for billions of years, making it possible that an atom of carbon in your body was once exhaled by a dinosaur! You'll understand how changes to a wetland ecosystem can threaten nearby human communities with flooding and cause changes in biodiversity. And how the elimination of a single species can affect an entire tundra ecosystem. As a result, you'll never look at ecosystems—as large as the Amazon rainforest or as small as a local pond—in the same way.

This program is going to make you an expert on healthy ecosystems and what they do. You'll be able to dazzle your friends and family with your knowledge. Better yet, you'll develop a passion for protecting our fragile Earth. That's exactly what the educators and scientists who developed NGSS had in mind.

Enjoy the program!

Bert Bower
TCI CEO and Founder

Science Content Scholars

David Begun, Ph.D.
Professor, Population Biology and Evolution and Ecology
University of California, Davis

Gillian Bowser, Ph.D.
Research Scientist, Natural Resource Ecology Laboratory
Colorado State University

John Czworkowski, Ph.D.
Chemistry Instructor
Grossmont College
El Cajon, California

Tanya Dewey, Ph.D.
Research Scientist, Biology Department
Colorado State University

Brian W. Holmes, Ph.D.
Professor, Physics and Astronomy
San José State University
San José, California

Ehsan Khatami, Ph.D.
Assistant Professor, Physics and Astronomy
San José State University
San José, California

Charles Liu, Ph.D.
Professor, Astrophysics
The College of Staten Island
City University of New York

Michael J. Passow, Ed.D.
Adjunct Associate Research Scientist, Lamont-Doherty Earth Observatory
Columbia University

Lesilee Rose, Ph.D.
Professor, Department of Molecular and Cellular Biology
College of Biological Sciences
University of California, Davis

Paul Ruscher, Ph.D.
Dean, Science Division
Lane Community College
Eugene, Oregon
Fellow, *American Meteorological Society*

Science Teacher Consultants

Kenneth Amunrud
Science Teacher
Joseph George Middle School
Alum Rock Union Elementary School District
San José, California

Nancy Anderson
Middle School Science Teacher
Mannington Township School
Mannington Township, New Jersey

Amy Argento
Science Teacher
Jefferson Middle School
Torrance Unified School District
Torrance, California

Noel Berghout
Math and Science Teacher
Jane Lathrop Stanford Middle School
Palo Alto Unified School District
Palo Alto, California

Carla Dalfonso
Science Specialist
Joe Serna Jr. Charter School
Lodi Unified School District
Lodi, California

Nora Haddad
Science Teacher
San Martin/Gwinn Environmental Science Academy
Morgan Hill Unified School District
Santa Clara County, California

Marsenne Kendall
Chemistry Teacher
Half Moon Bay High School
Cabrillo Unified School District
Half Moon Bay, California

Ann M. Lorey
Science Department Supervisor and Instructional Coach
Jane Lathrop Stanford Middle School
Palo Alto Unified School District
Palo Alto, California

Kevin Lynch
Science Teacher
J.L. Stanford Middle School
Palo Alto Unified School District
Palo Alto, California

Michael Passow
Earth Science Teacher (ret.)
White Plains Middle School
White Plains, New York

Stephanie Ruzicka
Science Teacher
Horner Junior High School
Fremont Unified School District
Fremont, California

Michelle Serrano
Secondary Science Curriculum Specialist
Hemet Unified School District
Hemet, California

Mathematics Teacher Consultant

Kenneth Amunrud
Mathematics Teacher
Joseph George Middle School
Alum Rock Union Elementary School District
San José, California

Reading Consultant

Marilyn Chambliss, Ph.D.
Associate Professor of Education Emerita
University of Maryland

How to Read the Table of Contents

The table of contents is your guide to *Bring Science Alive! Ecosystems.* In addition to showing the parts of your Student Text, it shows the exciting science and engineering investigations you will be doing in class.

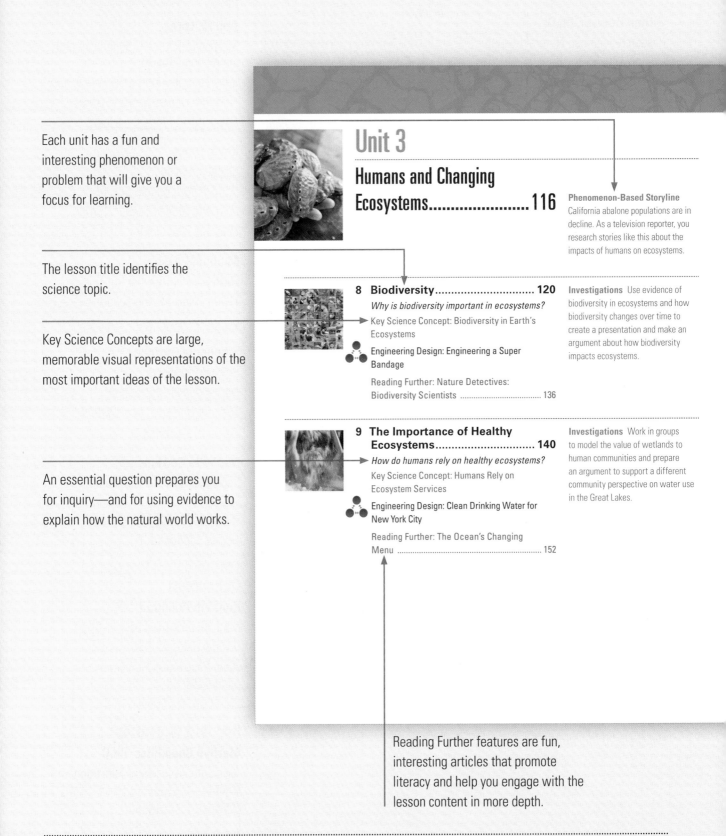

Each unit has a fun and interesting phenomenon or problem that will give you a focus for learning.

The lesson title identifies the science topic.

Key Science Concepts are large, memorable visual representations of the most important ideas of the lesson.

An essential question prepares you for inquiry—and for using evidence to explain how the natural world works.

Unit 3

Humans and Changing Ecosystems...........116

Phenomenon-Based Storyline
California abalone populations are in decline. As a television reporter, you research stories like this about the impacts of humans on ecosystems.

Investigations Use evidence of biodiversity in ecosystems and how biodiversity changes over time to create a presentation and make an argument about how biodiversity impacts ecosystems.

Investigations Work in groups to model the value of wetlands to human communities and prepare an argument to support a different community perspective on water use in the Great Lakes.

Reading Further features are fun, interesting articles that promote literacy and help you engage with the lesson content in more depth.

Engineering Design will help prepare you for success in solving engineering-focused investigations. Look for the symbol with three circles to see how engineering design is integrated into the lesson.

Investigations Examine evidence related to human resource use and its impact on ecosystems. Present an argument that describes a solution for protecting ecosystems and providing resources to human communities.

Engineering Challenge Students design and test a fishing net that protects marine biodiversity by catching only one type of sustainably harvested fish.

Performance Assessment Use a news report on abalone populations as a model for your investigation of a local interaction between humans and an ecosystem. After doing research and conducting interviews, you will put together your own news report.

Investigations integrate:

- science and engineering practices,
- crosscutting concepts,
- and disciplinary core ideas.

Engineering Challenge investigations invite you to apply science concepts and the engineering design process to solving relevant and engaging problems.

A Performance Assessment related to the unit's storyline inspires you to use science and engineering practices, crosscutting concepts, and disciplinary core ideas.

CONTENTS

The Design of the Program

Unit 1

Resources in Ecosystems 2

Phenomenon-Based Storyline
Some of the fish exhibited at the local zoo are showing signs of stress. As a zoo exhibit designer, you can help. How will you design a solution so the fish have everything they need to survive and reproduce in captivity?

1 Resources in Living Systems..... 06

How do living things get the resources they need to grow and survive?

Key Science Concept: Limited Resources Affect Populations

Reading Further: Wildlife in the City 16

Investigations Analyze data, make predictions, and construct simple models to explain the resource needs of organisms and populations in ecosystems.

2 Interactions Among Organisms... 20

How do organisms interact in ecosystems?

Engineering Design: Using Predators to Manage Ecosystems

Key Science Concept: Interactions in Ecosystems

Reading Further:
Body Snatchers and Zombies........................... 32

Investigations Explain predator/prey interactions in ecosystems. Interpret choreographed dances that illustrate patterns in interactions.

Engineering Challenge A newly constructed highway makes noise that interferes with interactions between species. Design an acoustic shield to protect these interactions from noise.

Investigations Analyze data from several case studies to explain the impact of change on populations and ecosystems. Observe how biological and physical changes affect model ecosystems.

Performance Assessment Determine why a change to a zoo exhibit is causing fish populations in the exhibit to decline. Identify resource needs and interactions of the fish and then design a solution to protect them. Present the solution as a talk at a conference.

 Engineering Design will help prepare you for success in solving engineering-focused investigations. Look for this symbol to see how engineering design is integrated into the lesson.

Unit 2

Energy and Matter in Ecosystems 50

Phenomenon-Based Storyline As animators who specialize in modeling phenomena too small to observe directly, how can you create visual models of ecosystem processes that cause rapid forest growth?

Investigations Explain the process of photosynthesis through role playing and use evidence from an experiment with plants to argue the conditions under which photosynthesis occurs.

Investigations Explain the process of cellular respiration through role playing and use experimental evidence of carbon dioxide presence to demonstrate that both snails and plants use cellular respiration.

Investigations Model the paths of energy and matter on a food web poster. Predict and explain the features of different trophic levels in a local ecosystem.

Investigations Model open and closed systems using an aquarium. Explain the path of matter between different parts of global matter cycles using an interactive card game.

Performance Assessment
Create a sequence of images that shows the path of a carbon atom through the carbon cycle. Compare this to the path of energy.

Unit 3

Humans and Changing Ecosystems....................116

10 Engineering Solutions for Protecting Ecosystems 156

How do humans affect coral reefs and other ecosystems?

Key Science Concept: Human Populations Are Changing Natural Resources

Engineering Design: Restoring Long Island Sound's Ecosystem

Investigations Examine evidence related to human resource use and its impact on ecosystems. Present an argument that describes a solution for protecting ecosystems and providing resources to human communities.

Engineering Challenge Students design and test a fishing net that protects marine biodiversity by catching only one type of sustainably harvested fish.

Performance Assessment Use a news report on abalone populations as a model for your investigation of a local interaction between humans and an ecosystem. After doing research and conducting interviews, you will put together your own news report.

Key Science Concepts

Key Science Concepts are visually exciting infographics that synthesize, summarize, and explain with enhanced features in the online subscriptions.

Figures have been crafted with care by *Bring Science Alive!* scientific illustrators and are discussed in the text.

Figures

Interdisciplinary Science makes the connections between the life, earth, and physical sciences.

Interdisciplinary Science

Mathematics Connections

Primary Sources connect science learning to real-world applications and to the history and nature of science.

Primary Sources

Bring Science Alive! Programs

Bring Science Alive! is a collection of nine middle school science programs that are 100 percent aligned to NGSS. These programs can be organized into three year-long courses for either integrated-science or discipline-specific learning progressions. Programs are well coordinated to crosscutting concepts such as patterns, energy and matter, and structure and function. Science and engineering practices are integrated with disciplinary core ideas and crosscutting concepts in engaging and challenging investigations.

Weather and Climate

Investigate the atmosphere and energy transfer, the water cycle, air pressure and air masses, weather prediction, climate factors and patterns, and Earth's changing climate.

Planet Earth

Construct explanations about Earth's natural resources, the rock and water cycles, rock layers, fossils, geologic time, plate tectonics, and natural hazards using varied time scales.

Space

Model cause and effect relationships involving Earth's rotation, revolution, and tilted axis; lunar phases and eclipses, the solar system, galaxies, and the universe.

Bring Science Alive! integrates Science and Engineering Practices, Crosscutting Concepts, and Disciplinary Core Ideas to result in Three Dimensional Learning.

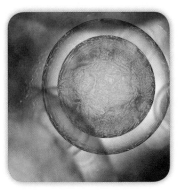

Cells and Genetics

Use evidence to explore traits, survival, and reproduction; the structure and functions of body systems and cells; genes and inheritance of traits, mutations, and engineering and genetics.

Ecosystems

Model interdependency in ecosystems, photosynthesis and cellular respiration, energy flow and cycling of matter, biodiversity, and explore the human impacts on ecosystems and biodiversity.

Adaptations

Identify cause and effect relationships between Earth's history and the fossil record, natural selection and changes in species, genes and patterns of inheritance; and humans, evolution, and heredity.

Matter

Apply the concepts of conservation of matter and energy transfer to model atoms, molecules, particle motion, state changes, and chemical reactions; and explore engineering solutions involving chemical reactions.

Forces and Energy

Solve engineering problems and plan investigations about forces, Newton's Laws of Motion; kinetic and potential energy; thermal energy, heat, and the thermal properties of matter.

Waves

Explore mechanical waves and their properties by looking at patterns in data, waves in different mediums, the wave model of light, properties of light waves, and technologies using waves to transfer information.

How to Use this Program

The components of *Bring Science Alive!* provide the tools needed for a complete learning system that integrates science and engineering practices, crosscutting concepts, and disciplinary core ideas. Designed for deep learning, *Bring Science Alive!* lessons use research-based learning strategies to reach all students.

1 Each new lesson begins with a **Lesson Guide** preview activity that teachers access through their online subscriptions. Lesson guides are the interactive guides at the heart of every TCI lesson.

2 Guided by the Lesson Guide and using the **Science Materials Kits** and their **Interactive Student Notebooks**, students conduct one or more investigations that powerfully integrate the three dimensions of NGSS. While investigating, students build understandings that they will need in order to complete the end-of-unit performance assessment.

4

The lesson concludes with students demonstrating their mastery of the science and engineering practices, crosscutting concepts, and disciplinary core ideas through a variety of paper and online **assessment tools**.

3

In their online student subscriptions, students expand their understanding by engaging with their dynamic **Student Text** and working through an **Interactive Tutorial**. Then they process what they have learned in their online **Interactive Student Notebook**.

Alternatively, students can read from the hardcover Student Edition and process their learning in a consumable Interactive Student Notebook.

Next Generation Science Standards for Three Dimensional Learning

The Next Generation Science Standards (NGSS) were written to change the way science is taught in K–12 classrooms and reflect recent advances in science, technology, and the understanding of how students learn. NGSS aims to help students prepare for college, 21st-century careers, scientific literacy needed as citizens, and competition in an increasingly global economy.

Performance Expectations

NGSS standards are called *performance expectations* and are worded to explain what students should be able to do in assessments at the completion of a unit of study. The performance expectations are built on the foundation provided by *A Framework for K-12 Science Education* (2012). Every performance expectation integrates the three dimensions described in the Framework: science and engineering practices, crosscutting concepts, and disciplinary core ideas. Also included in the performance expectations are clarification statements providing examples and other details, and assessment boundaries to guide test development. The graphic shows an example of how all the pieces result in a coherent standard to guide instruction.

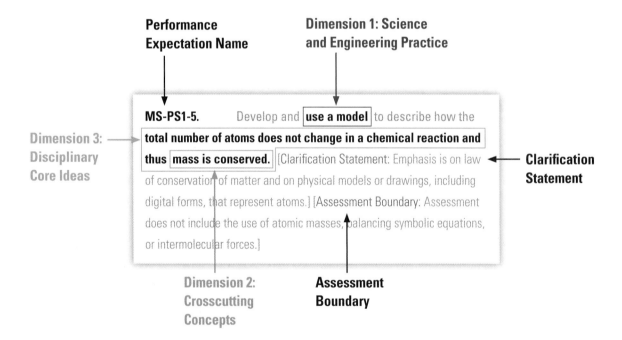

Performance Expectation Name

Dimension 1: Science and Engineering Practice

Dimension 3: Disciplinary Core Ideas

MS-PS1-5. Develop and **use a model** to describe how the **total number of atoms does not change in a chemical reaction and thus mass is conserved.** [Clarification Statement: Emphasis is on law of conservation of matter and on physical models or drawings, including digital forms, that represent atoms.] [Assessment Boundary: Assessment does not include the use of atomic masses, balancing symbolic equations, or intermolecular forces.]

Clarification Statement

Dimension 2: Crosscutting Concepts

Assessment Boundary

Dimension 1: Science and Engineering Practices

Science and Engineering Practices, such as developing and using models, describe what actual scientists and engineers do. Students develop the ability to use these practices through investigating the natural and designed worlds. While engaged in practices, students develop understandings described by the disciplinary core ideas and crosscutting concepts. The eight practices involve ways of thinking about investigations and engineering problems, the integration of mathematics, and social interactions. Without any particular order implied, these eight practices help define what has been called "scientific inquiry" and "engineering processes."

Bring Science Alive! investigations guide students to develop and reflect on their use of science and engineering practices.

Dimension 2: Crosscutting Concepts

Crosscutting Concepts, such as patterns and cause and effect, are the themes that organize students' understanding of science and engineering in the same way that scientists and engineers do. They can also be thought of as lenses all students should use as they explore and describe phenomena related to physical, earth and space, and life sciences. These "big picture" concepts are important in helping students make connections across all disciplines of science and engineering.

Each lesson focuses on a crosscutting concept that is explained in the lesson introduction and developed through the lesson.

Dimension 3: Disciplinary Core Ideas

Disciplinary Core Ideas are focused statements of content specific to the physical, earth and space, life sciences, or engineering. There are a limited number of core ideas, avoiding "mile wide, inch deep" curricula. The purpose of limiting the number of science concepts is to allow students the time they need for learning science and engineering practices through investigations. NGSS core ideas assume that students have mastered the content of previous grades and are ready for more advanced learning.

Students learn disciplinary core ideas by collecting evidence and building arguments through investigations, research, reading, and using multimedia tools.

The Next Generation Science Standards (NGSS) emphasize learning by investigating the natural world through the practices of scientific inquiry. Being able to use science understandings and practices allows students to investigate further questions about the natural world and solve meaningful engineering problems. NGSS identifies eight practices of science and engineering. Each lesson of *Bring Science Alive!* provides scaffolded instruction and reflection of one or more of these practices.

Asking Questions and Defining Problems

Science often begins by asking meaningful questions that can be answered by explanations supported by evidence. Similarly, engineering may begin with a question but always involves defining a problem that can be solved by carefully-tested solutions. Students learn to ask supporting questions that clarify and move them forward in investigations and solving engineering problems.

Developing and Using Models

Science and engineering use models to represent very large, very small, or very complicated systems. Using models helps scientists and engineers develop questions and explanations, gather data and make predictions, and communicate ideas to others. Students learn to develop, interpret, and modify models to describe scientific phenomena and test their engineering solutions.

Planning and Carrying Out Investigations

Scientific investigations are planned and carried out to describe a phenomena, test a hypothesis, or model how the world works. They are also used to test engineering solutions. Students design investigations that generate data for evidence to support their claims and learn how to be systematic in their methods so that they can obtain the most precise results.

Analyzing and Interpreting Data

All the data in the world is meaningless unless it can be presented in a form that reveals patterns and relationships and allows results to be communicated. Students analyze and interpret data by organizing their data into tables and graphs to identify overall trends and specific patterns.

Using Mathematics and Computational Thinking

Scientists and engineers use mathematics to represent physical variables and their relationships and to make quantitative descriptions and predictions. Students use mathematics aligned to the Common Core State Standards to analyze data for patterns and answer scientific questions. They also use mathematics to test and compare scientific arguments and engineering solutions.

Constructing Explanations and Designing Solutions

The goal of scientific inquiry is to construct explanations for why things happen. Likewise, the goal of engineering is to design solutions to people's problems. Students engage in constructing explanations when they make sense of the data they collect during investigations and when they propose solutions to engineering problems.

Engaging in Argument from Evidence

Argument is a process for comparing different explanations and solutions, and determining which is best. Reasoning and argument based on evidence are important for identifying the best explanation or the best solution to a design problem. Students engage in critical discussions to practice listening to, comparing, and evaluating competing explanations and solutions.

Obtaining, Evaluating, and Communicating Information

Researching, reading, interpreting, and producing scientific and technical text is an important part of science and engineering. Students learn to recognize key ideas, identify bias, distinguish observations from inferences, arguments from explanations, and claims from evidence. They communicate their findings orally, in writing, and through extended discussions.

The Next Generation Science Standards (NGSS) underscore the importance of making connections between the life, earth, physical sciences, and engineering. The seven crosscutting concepts are designed to do just this. While the seven overarching concepts are the same from kindergarten through twelfth grade, the details increase in complexity as students progress. *Bring Science Alive!* teaches crosscutting concepts in conjunction with appropriate disciplinary core ideas and science and engineering practices throughout the Student Text, Lesson Guide activities and investigations, and assessments.

Patterns

Middle school students relate macroscopic patterns to microscopic structures, identify relationships that show patterns in rates of change, analyze numerical data on graphs and charts for patterns, and identify patterns that lead to understanding cause-and-effect relationships.

Cause and Effect

Through investigations and discussion, students come to appreciate that a phenomenon may have more than one cause, that the likelihood of certain types of outcomes must be expressed in terms of probability, and that by recognizing cause-and-effect relationships they can make predictions in science and engineering. They also discover how relationships can be causal or correlational but that not all correlational relationships are causal.

Scale, Proportion, and Quantity

Phenomena involving time, space, or energy can be observed at different scales. The function of a system may change, depending on the scale at which it is observed. Students learn that some natural systems are either too large or too small to be directly observed, but they can explored using models of various scales. Mathematical reasoning becomes increasingly important to understanding and communicating scientific ideas as students learn that certain relationships can be represented as expressions or equations and that proportional relationships are useful for describing relationships between many scientific quantities.

Systems and System Models

The concept of a system as an organized group of parts is essential in all science disciplines and, certainly, for designing, building, and testing solutions to engineering problems. Throughout their investigations, students use the concept of systems to show how parts interact both within and outside a system, as well as how systems have sub-systems. Models are essential for understanding inputs and outputs and that energy and matter flow through many systems.

Energy and Matter

Energy and matter flow into, out of, and within both natural systems and designed systems. Students learn to track energy flow through both natural and designed systems. They use that understanding to describe the role energy plays in cycling of matter, and in describing the many forms energy takes as it is transferred from one part of a system to another.

Structure and Function

This crosscutting concept is closely related to systems and system models. Students learn to analyze the functions of all parts of a system by examining their shapes, properties, and their relationships to each other. Designing and building structures for particular functions also requires consideration of the parts' shapes and the materials from which they are made.

Stability and Change

Like structure and function, stability and change is a concept that directly supports the understanding of systems. Students' explanations of stability and change in systems include how changes to one part affect other parts of the system, how change can be gradual or sudden, and how equilibrium is maintained through feedback mechanisms.

The Next Generation Science Standards include a limited number of compelling scientific and engineering ideas to ensure that K–12 students learn and engage in the practices of science and engineering. Every *Bring Science Alive!* lesson allows students to build understanding of the disciplinary core ideas through the uses of these practices and the crosscutting concepts.

Core Idea ESS1: Earth's Place in the Universe

Planet Earth is part of a vast universe that has developed over a huge expanse of time and can be understood using observation, physics, and chemistry. Middle school students learn how gravitational forces hold the solar system together; explain patterns that result in lunar phases, eclipses, and seasons; and explore Earth's history by understanding rock strata and the fossil record.

Core Idea ESS2: Earth's Systems

Earth is made up of a set of dynamic systems whose interactions and processes determine how Earth changes over time. Students study the effects of energy flows and the cycling of matter in many of these systems, such as plate tectonics, the water cycle, weather systems, and changes due to weathering and erosion.

Core Idea ESS3: Earth and Human Activity

Humans depend on, are affected by, and cause changes to Earth's systems. Students learn how many natural resources are limited in quantity or distribution, the causes of natural hazards and likelihood that they will occur, and how humans impact the biosphere and can design solutions to lessen their impacts.

Core Idea LS1: From Molecules to Organisms: Structures and Processes

The functioning of all organisms is closely related to the structures that make them up, on scales ranging from individual molecules to whole body systems. Middle school students study structures such as cells, tissue, organs, and organ systems; and functions like behaviors, photosynthesis, cellular respiration, and sensory responses.

Core Idea LS2: Ecosystems: Interactions, Energy, and Dynamics

Ecosystems are dynamic systems in which organisms interact with one another and nonliving resources. They can be described by the flow of energy and cycling of matter. Students study patterns of interdependency; producers, consumers, and decomposers; and the effects of disruptions to ecosystems.

Core Idea LS3: Heredity: Inheritance and Variation of Traits

Heredity is the mechanism by which traits are passed via genes from parents to offspring. Middle school students learn that

genes control the production of proteins that affect traits, how sexual reproduction results in variation in inherited genetic information, and about the effects of mutations on traits.

Core Idea LS4: Biological Evolution: Unity and Diversity

Biological evolution explains both the similarities and differences among species and their history on Earth. Students learn how the fossil record and embryological development indicate that species are related, how natural and artificial selection result in changes to species over time, and how changes in biodiversity can affect humans.

Core Idea PS1: Matter and Its Interactions

The existence of atoms is fundamental to understanding the characteristics and behavior of matter. Middle school students apply the concepts of atoms and molecules to explain the existence of different substances, properties of matter, changes in state, and conservation of matter in chemical reactions.

Core Idea PS2: Motion and Stability: Forces and Interactions

Forces are a tool for describing the interactions between objects and for explaining and predicting the effects of those interactions. In middle school, students begin to quantitatively describe the effects of forces and learn to describe forces that act at a distance using fields.

Core Idea PS3: Energy

Energy is a tool for explaining and predicting interactions between objects. In middle school, students learn that systems often involve kinetic and potential energy. Energy concepts are extended to explain more complex interactions, such as those involved in chemical reactions, living things, and Earth systems.

Core Idea PS4: Waves and Their Applications in Technologies for Information Transfer

Waves are repeating patterns of motion that transfer energy from place to place without overall displacement of matter. Students use properties, such as wavelength, frequency, and amplitude, to understand the behaviors of wave-like phenomena, including light, sound, and water waves. Scientists and engineers also use wave properties to encode information as digitized signals for communication.

Core Idea ETS1: Engineering Design

Engineers solve problems using a design process involving specific practices and knowledge. Students in the middle grades learn the importance of defining criteria and constraints with precision, testing solutions, and using test results to improve solutions iteratively to achieve optimal designs.

Integrating Engineering with Science Learning

The Next Generation Science Standards describe engineering as a process similar to, and just as important as, scientific inquiry. The four engineering design performance expectations for middle school require students to understand how to define criteria and constraints, evaluate competing design solutions, analyze data to combine several designs, and develop models to test and refine proposed designs.

Student Text

In *Bring Science Alive!* student texts, engineering design is well integrated with the scientific core ideas of the lesson, including all the same support as other parts of the lesson: interactive tutorials, vocabulary development, and assessments.

Engineering design sections are identified by the symbol with three circles.

Engineering Design

3. Using Predators to Manage Ecosystems

The close relationship between carnivore and prey populations was the source of an ecological problem in the Yellowstone ecosystem in the western United States. During the late 1800s and early 1900s, people killed wolves in the area to prevent them from preying on livestock, such as sheep and cattle. As a result, by the mid-1900s, there were no wolves in the Yellowstone ecosystem. Without predators to keep their population in check, elk in the area grew in number and harmed plant populations through overgrazing.

In the late 1990s, conservation scientists reintroduced wolves to Yellowstone to control the elk population. They did not want this to be a temporary solution. They needed a way to ensure that the introduced wolves could survive, stay healthy, and produce offspring in the Yellowstone ecosystem. Could conservation scientists work with engineers to design a way to keep track of the wolf population?

Criteria: Monitoring a Predator Population To solve the problem, engineers first needed to precisely identify the criteria for the solution. **Criteria** are the requirements that must be met for an engineering solution to be successful. Conservation scientists needed to make sure that the tracking technology was providing them with accurate data. One of the criteria was that the technology could show whether wolves were surviving after being introduced into the ecosystem. Another was that the technology was able to observe whether the wolves were staying in Yellowstone or moving to other ecosystems. One relevant scientific fact about wolves that conservation scientists had to take into account is that they travel in packs across hundreds of square miles. The park itself has an area of more than 3,400 square miles. So, the technology needed to accurately track the movement of wolves and work well across large areas of landscape.

The introduction of wolves in the Yellowstone ecosystem affected populations of other species as well as elk. For example, wolf populations affect plant populations because wolves prey on elk, which in turn prey on grasses and other plants. When wolves eat elk, the plant populations that elk prey on will increase.

Constraints: Cost and Feasibility of Technology To design a solution, engineers must also identify the constraints of the situation. **Constraints** are the limitations on an engineering solution. Conservation scientists looked at constraints to make sure that the technology they chose to track wolves would not be too expensive or difficult to use. For example, some tracking devices use handheld signal detectors. Some require equipment flown on helicopters or airplanes. Others use GPS technology that depends on satellite communication. Another constraint was that the technology could not interfere with the natural behavior of wolves. Conservation scientists did not want their observation of the wolves to affect the outcome of the study.

Design Solution: A Successful Outcome By identifying criteria and constraints, conservation scientists arrived at a technology solution that worked to monitor wolf health and activities in the Yellowstone ecosystem. They decided to monitor the Yellowstone wolves using radio tracking. Conservation scientists fit individual animals with collars containing a device that sends out radio wave signals. Each animal's collar sends out a unique signal. To track animals, researchers use handheld antennas that can receive the signals. The radio signal is used to determine where the wolf hunts, which other wolves it interacts with, and even whether it is still alive. Using a small, removable collar means that researchers can monitor wolf activity without interfering with their natural behavior. Radio-tracking technologies have been an effective solution in this ecosystem management project.

Over time, the Yellowstone wolf population has expanded and the ecosystem has experienced a dramatic change. With the wolf population restored, elk no longer prey too heavily on plants. Other species that rely on those plant communities, such as some bird species, are on their way to returning to previous numbers. The recovery of the Yellowstone ecosystem is an example of how conservation scientists use the principles of scientific knowledge to make positive changes.

Radio-tracking technologies meet the criteria and constraints of the engineering problem faced by Yellowstone conservation scientists. To observe the movements of individual wolves and monitor the size of the wolf population, scientists place radio-tracking collars on the animals when they are sedated.

A handheld antenna can pick up radio wave signals that the collars emit, showing location and movement data.

Engineering vocabulary is developed in the same ways as science vocabulary.

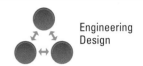
Investigations

In *Bring Science Alive!*'s engineering challenges, students use science and engineering practices to solve fun, interesting problems that have the potential to help answer scientific questions, improve lives, protect the environment, entertain, and delight.

The consistent engineering design process in *Bring Science Alive!*'s engineering challenges provides a clear road map for approaching design problems. Using it, students will decide when to define the problem, develop possible solutions, and optimize their designs.

Each engineering challenge focuses on one or two easy-to-learn engineering skills. By the time they complete the program, students will have a full set of tools for tackling any design problem.

English Language Arts & Literacy in Science

Bring Science Alive! is aligned with the Common Core State Standards for English Language Arts & Literacy (CCELA). Literacy instruction is built into the online Student Text, Interactive Student Notebook, and the Lesson Guides. The following six key points are from the grades 6–8 CCELA Standards for Literacy in History/Social Studies, Science, and Technical Subjects. They are particularly important in science instruction.

Reading Standards for Literacy

✓ **Main Ideas and Details** Identifying key ideas and details applies to reading science text, following multistep procedures for experiments, and using scientific tools and other technology.

When using the *Bring Science Alive!* online text, students have the option to see the main idea of each section highlighted. Additionally, every lesson includes one or more multistep investigations that students must follow to carry out science experiments, analyze data, and solve engineering problems.

✓ **Craft and Structure** In the middle grades, mastering new vocabulary includes understanding the meaning of scientific and mathematical symbols as well as domain-specific terms, words, and phrases.

Learning of scientific symbols and mathematical representations is scaffolded in *Bring Science Alive!* First, the concept is presented in words and phrases. Next, symbols are shown alongside these words and phrases. Finally, the symbolic notation is shown on its own.

✓ **Integration of Knowledge and Ideas** Students should be able to integrate their learning on a topic using experiments, multimedia materials, and the text.

Each *Bring Science Alive!* lesson concludes with a processing task that requires students to demonstrate their understanding of science and engineering practices, crosscutting concepts, and disciplinary core ideas as a result of carrying out investigations, manipulating simulations, and reading the text.

Writing Standards for Literacy

✓ **Purposes for Writing** The writing standards stress the use of certain conventions of good writing, including the use of previews, supporting details, appropriate transitions, domain-specific vocabulary, and an objective tone.

Bring Science Alive! students write for different purposes, including to explain scientific concepts and to record investigation procedures and results so that others can replicate and test them. Students are asked to construct written arguments to persuade others to accept an engineering design solution. They also write accounts of their investigations using precise language, scientific vocabulary, and minimal bias.

✓ **Production and Distribution of Writing** Routine writing of clear and coherent content that is appropriate to its purpose is central throughout the writing standards.

Bring Science Alive! includes regular writing opportunities in the Lesson Guides and Interactive Student Notebook. Writing, peer review, and editing are essential tools in guiding students to develop arguments and explanations that result in three dimensional learning.

✓ **Research to Build and Present Knowledge** Short research projects, using a variety of print and digital sources appropriately, should be carried out to answer broad questions that generate more specific questions.

Students build research skills using print and digital sources, including the Internet. Unit problems require students to gather and assess relevant information and to integrate this information with what they learn during hands-on investigations.

Considerate Text

Literacy is fundamental for success in science. *Bring Science Alive!* is both engaging and helps students read text that is more complex and at a higher level than other text they read. That's because our writers wrote it as "considerate text," which is another way to say that it makes readers want to read it. Considerate text is well written and well-organized. Here are some ways this Student Text is considerate of all levels of readers.

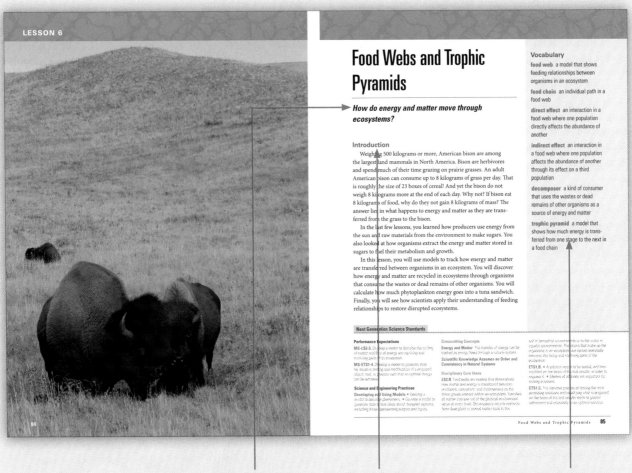

The essential question sets a purpose for reading.

The lesson introduction clearly explains the purpose and carefully-crafted organization of the lesson.

Students preview new science terms and their definitions before they read the lesson.

Short sections, each with an informative title, make it easier for readers to understand and remember the main ideas.

The paragraph that begins each section orients and engages the reader.

Scientific illustrations are carefully labeled and titled.

1. Food Webs

When coaches strategize to win a game, they might use arrows that show how players should move. Could you use a diagram with arrows to show how energy and matter move in ecosystems?

Scientists use diagrams as models to study complex systems. A **food web** is a model that shows feeding relationships between populations in an ecosystem. Food webs, like Figure 6.1A, use arrows to represent the transfer of energy and matter from one organism to another. An arrow points away from prey and toward the predator because, when a predator eats prey, the energy and matter from the prey becomes energy and matter for the predator. Food web models help scientists understand how energy and matter move among populations in ecosystems.

Some organisms have many arrows pointing toward them because they prey on many species. Organisms with multiple arrows pointing away from them are prey to many kinds of predators. Matter and energy can take more than one path in a food web. Each path is a **food chain**. To find a food chain, start with a producer and follow the arrows until you reach a top predator. Can you find a food chain that traces the transfer of energy and matter between grass and red-tailed hawks? Matter and energy in grass eventually becomes matter and energy in the red-tailed hawk.

Figure 6.1A
Scientists use food webs as models to analyze the roles organisms play in an ecosystem. Many organisms are prey to more than one species of predator. Matter and energy transferred through a food web can follow different arrows and take more than one path.

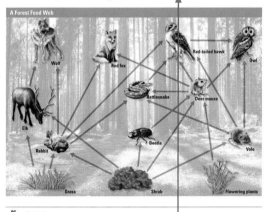

A Forest Food Web

A food chain tracks the transfer of matter and energy through a food web along a single path from prey to predators. An example food chain is shown in Figure 6.1B. Food chains always start with producers. No arrows point to producers because they get their energy and matter from their nonliving surroundings. Food chains end with top predators, such as the red-tailed hawk, because no other predators get matter and energy from hawks in this food web.

Food chains and food webs help scientists understand how populations affect one another. Rattlesnakes eat deer mice. When rattlesnakes eat deer mice, the deer mouse population decreases. This kind of interaction is a **direct effect**, an interaction in a food web where one population directly affects the abundance of another. The food web shows that a direct effect of an increase in rattlesnakes is a decrease in populations of their prey, deer mice.

Populations in a food web can also affect other populations in the food web, even if they don't interact directly. Rattlesnake populations can affect beetle populations even though rattlesnakes do not eat beetles. When rattlesnakes eat deer mice, there are fewer deer mice to eat beetles. This causes the population of beetles to increase. This kind of interaction is called an **indirect effect**, an interaction where one population affects the abundance of another through its effect on a third population.

Food webs illustrate that a change in one part of the ecosystem changes other parts through direct and indirect effects. What if the spread of a disease caused a decrease in the number of red-tailed hawks? The populations of mice, voles, and rabbits would increase as a direct effect. The populations of other predators of these prey, such as foxes, rattlesnakes, and owls, would increase as an indirect effect.

Figure 6.1B
A food chain shows the transfer of energy and matter from producers to consumers. In this food chain, the energy and matter from trees, the producers, are transferred to different consumers through feeding relationships. The matter and energy in trees find their way to red-tailed hawks.

A Forest Food Chain

Red-tailed hawk

Energy and matter

Rattlesnake

Energy and matter

Deer mouse

Energy and matter

Beetle

Energy and matter

Trees

Single-column text makes the lesson easier to read.

Captions reinforce the main idea of the section and provide supporting details.

Important new science and engineering vocabulary is in bold type, defined in the same sentence, and used throughout the rest of the text.

Resources in Ecosystems

OVERVIEW

This moray eel looks like it's about to eat a shrimp. But the shrimp will swim away from this interaction without harm. What kind of interaction allows the shrimp to survive this encounter? In this unit you will explore phenomena that allow living things to get the resources they need to grow, survive, and reproduce, even through interactions with other living things and as conditions change around them. You will propose a design that provides a species in a zoo with all of the resources and interactions it requires to live.

UNIT CONTENTS

Investigations Analyze data, make predictions, and construct simple models to explain the resource needs of organisms and populations in ecosystems.

Investigations Explain predator/prey interactions in ecosystems. Interpret choreographed dances that illustrate patterns in interactions.

Engineering Challenge A newly constructed highway makes noise that interferes with interactions among species. Design an acoustic shield to protect these interactions from noise.

Investigations Analyze data from several case studies to explain the impact of change on populations and ecosystems. Observe how biological and physical changes affect model ecosystems.

Performance Assessment Determine why a change to a zoo exhibit is causing fish populations in the exhibit to decline. Identify resource needs and interactions of the fish and then design a solution to protect them. Present the solution as a talk at a conference.

Performance Expectations

MS-LS2-1. Analyze and interpret data to provide evidence for the effects of resource availability on organisms and populations of organisms in an ecosystem.

MS-LS2-2. Construct an explanation that predicts patterns of interactions among organisms across multiple ecosystems.

MS-LS2-4. Construct an argument supported by empirical evidence that changes to physical or biological components of an ecosystem affect populations.

MS-ETS1-1. Define the criteria and constraints of a design problem with sufficient precision to ensure a successful solution, taking into account relevant scientific principles and potential impacts on people and the natural environment that may limit possible solutions.

Science and Engineering Practices

Analyzing and Interpreting Data
Analyze and interpret data to provide evidence for phenomena.

Constructing Explanations and Designing Solutions
Construct an explanation that includes qualitative or quantitative relationships between variables that predict phenomena.

Asking Questions and Defining Problems
Define a design problem that can be solved through the development of an object, tool, process, or system and includes multiple criteria and constraints, including scientific knowledge that may limit possible solutions.

Engaging in Argument from Evidence
Construct an oral and written argument supported by empirical evidence and scientific reasoning to support or refute an explanation or a model for a phenomenon or a solution to a problem.

Connections to Nature of Science: Scientific Knowledge is Based on Empirical Evidence
Science disciplines share common rules of obtaining and evaluating empirical evidence.

Crosscutting Concepts

Cause and Effect
Cause and effect relationships may be used to predict phenomena in natural or designed systems.

Patterns
Patterns can be used to identify cause and effect relationships.

Stability and Change
Small changes in one part of a system might cause large changes in another part.

Connections to Engineering, Technology, and Applications of Science: Influence of Science, Engineering, and Technology on Society and the Natural World
• All human activity draws on natural resources and has both short and long-term consequences, positive as well as negative, for the health of people and the natural environment. • The uses of technologies and limitations on their use are driven by individual or societal needs, desires, and values; by the findings of scientific research; and by differences in such factors as climate, natural resources, and economic conditions.

Disciplinary Core Ideas

LS2.A: Interdependent Relationships in Ecosystems
• Organisms, and populations of organisms, are dependent on their environmental interactions both with other living things and with nonliving factors. • In any ecosystem, organisms and populations with similar requirements for food, water, oxygen, or other resources may compete with each other for limited resources, access to which consequently constrains their growth and reproduction. • Growth of organisms and population increases are limited by access to resources. • Similarly, predatory interactions may reduce the number of organisms or eliminate whole populations of organisms. Mutually beneficial interactions, in contrast, may become so interdependent that each organism requires the other for survival. Although the species involved in these competitive, predatory, and mutually beneficial interactions vary across ecosystems, the patterns of interactions of organisms with their environments, both living and nonliving, are shared.

LS2.C: Ecosystem Dynamics, Functioning, and Resilience
• Ecosystems are dynamic in nature; their characteristics can vary over time. Disruptions to any physical or biological component of an ecosystem can lead to shifts in all its populations.

ETS1.A: Defining and Delimiting Engineering Problems
The more precisely a design task's criteria and constraints can be defined, the more likely it is that the designed solution will be successful. Specification of constraints includes consideration of scientific principles and other relevant knowledge that are likely to limit possible solutions.

Connect Your Learning

Earth is populated by living things like you! You can observe populations of plants and animals in a park, on your way to school, and even in your home. Just like you, these living things need resources to survive and interact with each other in many different ways. By understanding what living things need and how they interact, you can explain patterns and phenomena all around you.

Resources in Ecosystems

This volcanic eruption deposits ash and lava on surrounding landscapes. Disruptions like this change resources in an ecosystem. How do these changes impact living things in the ecosystem?

A dandelion grows between the cracks in a sidewalk. How does this hardy plant find the resources it needs, such as nutrients and light, even in harsh environments like a crack in the concrete?

Living things, like this chameleon, rely on many kinds of interactions to survive. The chameleon is eating a cricket. What does this chameleon get from the cricket it is eating?

Resources in Living Systems

How do living things get the resources they need to grow and survive?

Introduction

The wild horses in this photo live on the Mongolian steppe, a region of Asia characterized by its rich grasslands. How are these horses able to survive in the wild, often far away from humans? The grasslands of the Mongolian steppe provide the wild horses with all the resources they need to survive and grow.

You would not expect to find a wild horse living on ice near the North Pole, like a polar bear. You would also be surprised to see a penguin in the grassy landscape of Mongolia. That is because nonliving elements, like temperature and rainfall, have an effect on what kinds of living things can survive there. Understanding this cause and effect relationship can help you predict where living things like wild horses can survive.

In this lesson, you will discover why different places on Earth are filled with different kinds of living things. You will also discover why ecosystems are different around the world. First, you will start your journey by thinking about what living things need in order to survive and reproduce. You will then explore how living things compete with one another for the things they need. Next, you will examine how certain types of living things are found only where conditions are right for them. You will then be able to use this knowledge to explain why living things, like these wild horses and the grasses they eat, are found naturally only in places that have the right amount of water, warmth, light, nutrients, and other resources.

Vocabulary

resource any material or energy needed by living things to survive, grow, and reproduce

organism an individual living thing

species a group of living things that share traits and can breed successfully with each other, but not with other groups

competition an interaction between living things that need the same limited resource

population a group of individuals of a species that lives and reproduces in the same area

ecosystem a group of populations of living things and the nonliving parts of their environment that support them

biome a large area of Earth characterized by certain physical conditions and the living things that are found there

biosphere the parts of Earth in which organisms are able to live

---

Next Generation Science Standards

Performance Expectations

MS-LS2-1. Analyze and interpret data to provide evidence for the effects of resource availability on organisms and populations of organisms in an ecosystem.

MS-LS2-2. Construct an explanation that predicts patterns of interactions among organisms across multiple ecosystems.

Science and Engineering Practices

Analyzing and Interpreting Data Analyze and interpret data to provide evidence for phenomena.

Constructing Explanations and Designing Solutions Construct an explanation that includes

qualitative or quantitative relationships between variables that predict phenomena.

Crosscutting Concepts

Cause and Effect Cause and effect relationships may be used to predict phenomena in natural or designed systems.

Patterns Patterns can be used to identify cause and effect relationships.

Disciplinary Core Ideas

LS2.A. • Organisms, and populations of organisms, are dependent on their environmental interactions both with other living things and with nonliving factors. • In any ecosystem, organisms and populations

with similar requirements for food, water, oxygen, or other resources may compete with each other for limited resources, access to which consequently constrains their growth and reproduction. • Growth of organisms and population increases are limited by access to resources. • Similarly, predatory interactions may reduce the number of organisms or eliminate whole populations of organisms. Mutually beneficial interactions, in contrast, may become so interdependent that each organism requires the other for survival. Although the species involved in these competitive, predatory, and mutually beneficial interactions vary across ecosystems, the patterns of interactions of organisms with their environments, both living and nonliving, are shared.

Living things get the resources they need from their environment. In the wild, a horse and her young foal get their food, water, air, and everything else they need from their surroundings. These resources allow both animals to survive, grow, and reproduce.

1. Living Things Need Resources

A wild foal, or baby horse, stands up on all four legs within an hour of being born. The newborn drinks its mother's milk, which provides it with the nourishment it needs to grow and move. And move it will! The foal will walk and run in a meadow with its mother the very same day of its birth because of the nourishment it receives. But where does its mother get her nourishment?

Living things need other living things and nonliving elements in the environment in order to survive, grow, and reproduce. A mother horse gets her nourishment by eating grasses and other plants as food. Any material or energy needed by living things to survive, grow, and reproduce is called a **resource**. Resources include living things, which may be eaten as food, and nonliving things, such as sunlight, water, or oxygen.

Living things obtain the resources they need from their surroundings. Wild horses graze on grasses in meadows where they live. They get the oxygen they need by breathing in the air that surrounds them. Nearby creeks and ponds supply wild horses with water. Other species need resources that are different from those needed by the horse. The grass in the meadow needs water, carbon dioxide, and sunlight to grow. It also needs nutrients and minerals found in soil.

There are different kinds of living things. Scientists call an individual living thing an **organism**. A wild horse and her foal are the same kind of organism because they are the same species. A **species** is a group of closely related organisms. Only members of the same species can reproduce and have offspring, like the horse who gave birth to a foal. A dandelion is also a species. Its flowers produce seeds that can grow and become new dandelion plants. The grass in the meadow surrounding the horses is another species of plant.

2. Competition for Resources Affects Populations

In everyday language we use the word *competition* to describe a race or a struggle against a rival to win an event. Organisms, like wild horses, experience competition, too. They must compete to get resources that other organisms might also use. But the prize in this competition is not a trophy, it is survival. What happens when individuals of the same species compete for the same resource?

Organisms of the same species need the same resources. But there is a limit to how much of any one resource there is in an area. When living things require the same limited resource, an interaction called **competition** can arise. For example, there may be competition among wild horses for the limited amount of grass in an area. Horses that find and eat more grasses are more successful in the competition for this limited resource. They are able to get enough food to survive, to grow, and to reproduce. Individuals that are not successful go hungry and may die. In this way, competition changes the number of individuals that can survive in an area.

Unlike species, a **population** is a group of individuals of a species that lives and reproduces in the same area. Competition for limited resources can change the size of populations. When there is an abundance of a resource that a population depends on, the population can grow. For example, if a meadow has a lot of grass, it can support the survival of many horses. As a result, the horse population grows. Sparse resources cause a decrease in population size. When there is not a lot of grass, fewer horses get enough nourishment. Fewer horses survive and the population shrinks.

This link between the amount of a limited resource and the size of a population that depends on it is a cause and effect relationship. The limited resource, grass abundance, is the *cause* and the change in wild horse population size is the *effect*. Because this is a cause and effect relationship, scientists can predict whether a population will grow or shrink based on how sparse or abundant a limited resource is.

Because of competition, the amount of a limited resource in an area has an effect on how many individuals can survive in an area. Individual horses that can compete well for a limited amount of grass in a meadow will get more of that resource. They will then be more likely to survive and reproduce than other horses that do not compete as well.

Yaks and wild horses interact with each other through competition for grass.

When grazing animals use a resource in slightly different ways, such as by eating grass differently, competition is reduced.

3. Competition for Resources Affects Ecosystems

A herd of yaks grazes in a mountain meadow while wild horses look on. Every mouthful of grass eaten by a yak is a mouthful of grass that a horse cannot eat. What happens when different species compete for the same resource?

Populations of different species can compete for the same limited resources, which limits the size of both populations. Wild horses and yaks depend on grass for food. In dry years, grass populations will be low. Scientists predict wild horse and yak populations will decrease as competition for grass increases. When resources are not as limited, such as when grass is abundant, there is less competition, and populations of wild horses and yaks increase.

Different species often have different ways of using the same resource. Most grazing animals, like yaks and wild horses, are slightly different in how they eat grass. Yaks use their tongue and gums to yank out grass plants by the roots. Wild horses have sharp teeth that clip off the tops of grasses. These different ways of eating are more or less successful under different conditions, which can reduce competition and allows competing species to co-exist.

An **ecosystem** is a group of populations of living things and the nonliving parts of their environment that support them. In a grassland ecosystem, the amount of rainfall in a year will cause a change in grass populations. Changes in grass populations will have an effect on wild horses and yaks, which will cause a change in their populations.

Limited Resources Affect Populations

When the amount of a resource changes, the populations that depend on that resource also change. If the amount of a resource increases, the size of a population that uses that resource may increase. If the amount of a resource decreases, then the size of a population that uses that resource may decrease. These types of cause and effect relationships can be shown with line graphs, like these, and be used to predict what will happen to a population when a resource is limited.

Relationship Between Rainfall and Grass Population Size

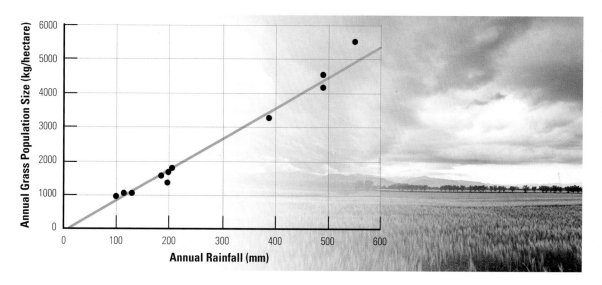

Grass population size increases when rainfall amounts increase.

Relationship Between Rainfall and Zebra Population Size

Zebra population size increases when more grass is available, so zebra populations are also influenced by amounts of rainfall.

4. Biomes are Shaped by Limited Resources

Suppose you want to observe a wild horse. Would you go to the North Pole? You're not likely to see one there. Why? What determines the kinds of organisms that live in an area?

The types of limited resources in an area determine which species can live there. Wild horses depend on grasses for food, and grasses require rich soil, a range of temperatures, and a medium amount of rainfall. These conditions are typical of grasslands, which are one type of biome. A **biome** is an area characterized by certain physical conditions that are resources for certain species. There are many kinds of biomes. Figure 1.4 shows areas of Earth where different kinds of grassland biomes are found and some of the grassland animals that live in those places.

Figure 1.4

Limited resources on Earth determine where biomes are found. Earth's grasslands are usually found at middle latitudes, between polar regions and the equator. These areas receive enough rainfall to support the growth of grasses but not so much that forests grow there. Different kinds of grassland biomes are savannas, pampas, prairies, and steppes.

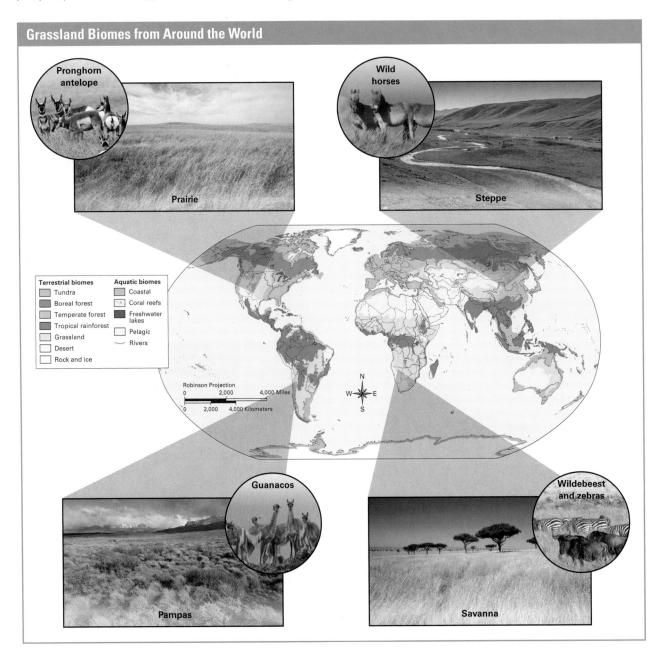

Grassland Biomes from Around the World

Pronghorn antelope — Prairie

Wild horses — Steppe

Terrestrial biomes
- Tundra
- Boreal forest
- Temperate forest
- Tropical rainforest
- Grassland
- Desert
- Rock and ice

Aquatic biomes
- Coastal
- Coral reefs
- Freshwater lakes
- Pelagic
- Rivers

Robinson Projection
0   2,000   4,000 Miles
0   2,000   4,000 Kilometers

Guanacos — Pampas

Wildebeest and zebras — Savanna

Like grassland biomes, other biomes are found in places where the physical conditions will support them. In addition to grasslands, Figure 1.4 also shows where biomes such as forests and coral reefs are found. Areas near the poles tend to be colder than areas near the equator. Some biomes are found only on land and some are found only in aquatic areas. Some areas have distinct seasonal changes in temperature, while others do not. As a result, the types of limited resources differ from place to place. These patterns of limited resources shape the patterns of biomes on Earth.

Terrestrial Biomes Some biomes are found on land. These are called *terrestrial biomes*. Each terrestrial biome experiences a particular range of temperatures and amount of rainfall. These limited resources determine which plants can survive there. Boreal forests, like the one in the photo, receive enough water to support the growth of trees. However, boreal forest trees must be able to survive cold winters with heavy snowfall. As a result, they have needle-like leaves that let snow slide off their branches.

Aquatic Biomes Aquatic biomes are areas of fresh water or salt water. As with terrestrial biomes, the limited resources in an aquatic biome determine the kinds of living things found there. In aquatic biomes, the limited resources are generally light and nutrients. The amount of sunlight that reaches into aquatic biomes decreases as the depth of the water increases. For this reason, plants that live in a lake or river biome often have leaves or other structures that float on the surface to reach the sunlight.

Boreal forest biomes on Earth

Lake and river biomes on Earth

The types of plants found in a biome are determined by the resources found there. A boreal forest biome has cold winters and plenty of snow and rainfall to support the growth of tall evergreen trees. In a lake or river biome, aquatic plants such as reeds and lilies grow because there is enough sunlight and nutrients to support their growth.

Levels of Organization in Earth's Biosphere

Organism

Population

Ecosystems

Biosphere

5. Organization of Earth's Biosphere

You are a citizen of a town, a state, a nation, and of Earth itself. Each of these levels is larger and has more people in it than the level below it. All living things on Earth can also be organized into levels. What are these levels and how are they related?

Scientists group living things into different levels of organization, or categories. Look at the young wild horse in the photo. That horse is an organism, which is one level of organization. All of the other wild horses that live in the area, including its mother, make up a larger level of organization—a wild horse population. Wild horses are all members of a single species. The next level of organization includes nonliving things and all of the populations of living things that interact in the area. This level is called an ecosystem. In this case, it is a grassland ecosystem that the horse population is a part of. What would be the level of organization that includes all ecosystems on Earth, including all of the grassland ecosystems and any other kind of ecosystem?

All Earth's ecosystems together, including all of the living things and all of the nonliving parts of ecosystems, are collectively known as Earth's **biosphere**. The parts of Earth in which organisms are able to live are part of the biosphere. Earth's biosphere extends to the highest mountaintops and the atmosphere that surrounds them. It also includes the deepest parts of the ocean and the layer of Earth's crust just beneath all aquatic and terrestrial ecosystems. And it includes every interacting living and nonliving thing from Earth's crust to the atmosphere.

Figure 1.5

Scientists organize life on Earth into different categories. Earth's biosphere is the largest category. The biosphere is made up of all ecosystems, such as this grassland. Ecosystems include many populations, like this wild horse population. Each population is made up of many individuals of one species, like this young foal.

Every organism has a role in the biosphere. Even you! Have you ever wondered where the food you eat or water you drink comes from? They come from ecosystems that are part of Earth's biosphere. When you use resources, like food and water, you are an organism that is part of an ecosystem, even if you live in a city!

When humans use resources, they affect populations of other species. For example, humans have affected wild horse populations. For centuries, humans have transformed grassland ecosystems. They grazed cattle, goats, and sheep in grasslands, increasing competition for grass. They transformed grasslands into farms and neighborhoods, causing these ecosystems to shrink. Humans also affected wild horse populations by capturing wild horses and domesticating them.

When humans use resources and impact populations, they affect ecosystems. When humans gather food and use water, they reduce the amount of resources available to other species. As the populations of those species decline, the ecosystem changes. Humans also change ecosystems by changing their structure, such as when they grow crops and build homes. Humans live in many ecosystems around the world. Because humans change ecosystems, humans have a dramatic impact on Earth's biosphere.

Humans affect both living and nonliving things that make up ecosystems in the biosphere. They also benefit from the different parts of the biosphere, including using and caring for horses that came from wild populations.

LESSON SUMMARY

Resources in Living Systems

Living Things Need Resources Living things need other living things and nonliving elements in order to survive, grow, and reproduce. Scientists call an individual living thing an organism.

Competition for Resources Affects Populations Competition over limited resources affects the number of individuals that can survive in an area. A group of living things of the same species that lives and reproduces in the same area is called a population.

Competition for Resources Affects Ecosystems Populations of different species can compete for the same limited resources. This can limit the size of both populations. Populations that compete often use resources in different ways, which can reduce competition. An ecosystem is a group of populations of living things and the nonliving parts of their environment that support them.

Biomes are Shaped by Limited Resources Patterns of limited resources shape the patterns of biomes on Earth. A biome is a large area of Earth characterized by certain physical conditions.

Organization of Earth's Biosphere All Earth's ecosystems together, including all organisms and all of the nonliving parts of ecosystems, are collectively known as Earth's biosphere, which extends from deep underground to the atmosphere above the highest mountains.

Wildlife in the City

When you think about a city, you probably picture tall buildings, concrete sidewalks, honking cars, and busy people hurrying through the streets. When you think about wildlife, you might think about tall, quiet forests or ocean shorelines. In fact, cities are home to many wild plant and animal species, too. How do these organisms survive in a place dominated by humans?

The Urban Ecosystem

Splat! There goes the tasty hot dog you just bought from the food truck parked in busy downtown. As you stand there debating whether or not to try and salvage it, you notice that a squirrel has appeared and is moving towards your lunch. You look at the squirrel; the squirrel looks at you. Suddenly it darts forward, grabs the hot dog, and runs off, leaving a trail of mustard.

This resourceful squirrel has made its home in an urban ecosystem. Like other ecosystems, an urban ecosystem provides the squirrel with all the resources it needs to live—including food, water, shelter, and mates. In an urban ecosystem, these resources come from human activities. For example, food might come from a dropped hot dog or a trash can. Drinking water might be found in an overturned hubcap or a low spot on a road. Shelter may be located inside sewer pipes, in the tall branches of a city park tree, or along the slim edge of a tall skyscraper. A mate can be found among the large population of squirrels who share the city environment.

You might think about rats and cockroaches and dandelions in cities. Although they are familiar, they are also wildlife species. Many kinds of species make a living in cities, including ones found in wild places, like peregrine falcons and coyotes. What special qualities make it possible for wild animals and plants to make a living in urban ecosystems?

Urban ecosystems provide unique resources that allow wildlife, like this squirrel, to be successful in urban areas dominated by humans. For example, squirrels dive into trash cans to find food in the city.

Cities are home to many species that are able to use different kinds of resources. Starlings are successful in urban ecosystems because they are very adaptable in their food, habitat, and nesting choices.

Adapting to City Life

Urban wildlife has to be able to get the resources needed to survive in cities. That means being able to take advantage of what is available. Urban wildlife has to be flexible in their use of resources.

Starlings are a great example of a wild bird species that thrives in cities and is flexible in its use of resources. In wild ecosystems, starlings prefer to eat insects. In cities, starlings often pick through garbage cans looking for discarded food. Using garbage for food works well because cities have plenty of garbage!

City starlings also nest in surprising spots. Starlings build their nests in cavities, such as those found in tree trunks. In cities, those cavities are found in the cracks of buildings and openings of vents and drainage pipes. Flexibility in food choices and nesting locations allows starlings to live successfully in cities.

Animals are not the only wild organisms living in cities. While much of the city is covered in concrete, hearty plants like dandelions find homes in small cracks in the sidewalk. Just like animals, plants adapt to city life to get the resources they need.

Many urban plants grow wherever there is space available, even with just a tiny bit of soil. This dandelion has adapted to grow in a crack where just enough soil and water was present to allow the seed to germinate.

Coyotes in the City?

It is dawn in the city. As a bus makes its way down the empty streets, a dog suddenly appears from behind a park bench. It stands perfectly still and sniffs the air. But wait, this is no dog, it's a coyote! Coyotes are becoming more common in cities across the United States. What is bringing them to our cities, and why are they staying?

Scientists agree that there are many reasons coyotes are making their homes in cities. Growing populations of coyotes in wild ecosystems means that some coyotes must move into new areas. When they find the resources they need, including food to eat and places to live, they move in, even if their new home is an empty city lot.

Coyotes do well in urban ecosystems because, like starlings, squirrels, and dandelions, they are adaptable. In addition to hunting prey like rabbits and rats, they eat fruits and even insects. Coyotes take advantage of secluded parks and empty lots to build dens and care for their young. Because coyotes are active in the early morning or at night, few urban residents even know they are there.

Coyotes are rarely seen by humans in the city. But there is evidence that coyotes are living there, such as a footprint like this.

Young coyotes come to the city in search of new territories. Coyotes are adaptable and can easily find resources such as shelter and food within city limits.

Pigeons are very well adapted to city life. By studying the habits of urban pigeons, scientists hope to learn more about this popular city dweller and maybe even help humans.

An Urban Laboratory

While coyotes are relative newcomers to urban ecosystems, pigeons, or rock doves, have been living in cities around the world for centuries. In fact, pigeons have adapted so well to city life that their population worldwide is now estimated to be over 120 million.

Because pigeons are among the most numerous of wild urban dwellers, scientists would like to know more about their habits, such as where they nest and what routes they use to fly around town. But there are so many pigeons to study! How can a small team of scientists do all this work? Fortunately, scientists have identified another urban population that can help gather data—people!

Citizen scientists are regular people who gather data that are used in scientific research. Because anyone can be a citizen scientist with some training, many people can be involved and collect a lot of data. Citizens involved in these scientific projects learn about their local wildlife and about the scientific process.

Perhaps you want to learn more about the pigeons in your neighborhood. You can become involved in a citizen science project in which you share your own observations on pigeons near you. You then share your observations with scientists by posting them online. Your observations are combined with those of thousands of other people around the world. The result is data that professional scientists can use to learn more about the habits of pigeons.

How can scientists use this information to help people? Scientists are using pigeons to track air pollution in London. Scientists capture pigeons and fit them with tiny backpacks, which hold sensors that record data on air pollution levels. That information is sent back to a lab through cellular connections, where the sample is analyzed. People can use an app on a smartphone or computer to see the data and avoid areas with polluted air. Some day, maybe you will use a pigeon app to avoid air pollution and protect your health! ◆

Scientists are always looking for volunteers to make observations for citizen science projects. Do you want be a citizen scientist?

Interactions Among Organisms

How do organisms interact in ecosystems?

Introduction

The green tentacles of the anemone look harmless, but they are venomous and paralyze small fish! How do clown fish nestle safely among them? Other fish avoid the tentacles, but clown fish are immune to the venom. Anemones benefit because clown fish chase off other animals that might eat anemones. Not all interactions among species are so friendly. In many interactions, one organism may not survive!

You have learned that there is a cause and effect relationship between limited resources and the size of the populations of different organisms. For example, you learned that competition for limited resources between species can harm both.

In this lesson, you will explore other ways that species interact with one another. You will learn that some species get resources by eating other species. Others interact in ways that benefit both species. Sometimes one species is not affected at all. Still others live on or in the bodies of other species and eat their tissues as a source of nutrition. After learning about these interactions, you will explore how patterns in interactions can help scientists predict changes in populations and design ways to manage ecosystems.

Vocabulary

predation a relationship in which one organism, the predator, benefits by eating another organism, the prey

carnivore an organism that mainly eats animals

herbivore an organism that mainly eats plants or plant parts

omnivore an organism that eats both plants and animals in similar amounts

criteria the requirements that must be met for an engineering solution to be successful

constraint a limitation on an engineering solution

mutualism a relationship between two species in which both species benefit

commensalism a relationship between two species in which one species benefits and the other is unaffected

parasitism a relationship in which one species benefits while the other is harmed but not usually killed

---

Next Generation Science Standards

Performance Expectations

MS-LS2-1. Analyze and interpret data to provide evidence for the effects of resource availability on organisms and populations of organisms in an ecosystem.

MS-LS2-2. Construct an explanation that predicts patterns of interactions among organisms across multiple ecosystems.

MS-ETS1-1. Define the criteria and constraints of a design problem with sufficient precision to ensure a successful solution, taking into account relevant scientific principles and potential impacts on people and the natural environment that may limit possible solutions.

Science and Engineering Practices

Analyzing and Interpreting Data Analyze and interpret data to provide evidence for phenomena.

Constructing Explanations and Designing Solutions Construct an explanation that includes qualitative or quantitative relationships between variables that predict phenomena.

Asking Questions and Defining Problems Define a design problem that can be solved through the development of an object, tool, process or system and includes multiple criteria and constraints, including scientific knowledge that may limit possible solutions.

Crosscutting Concepts

Cause and Effect Cause and effect relationships may be used to predict phenomena in natural or designed systems.

Patterns Patterns can be used to identify cause and effect relationships.

Influence of Science, Engineering, and Technology on Society and the Natural World

Disciplinary Core Ideas

LS2.A • Organisms, and populations of organisms, are dependent on their environmental interactions both with other living things and with nonliving factors. • Similarly, predatory interactions may reduce the number of organisms or eliminate whole populations of organisms. Mutually beneficial interactions, in contrast, may become so interdependent that each organism requires the other for survival. Although the species involved in these competitive, predatory, and mutually beneficial interactions vary across ecosystems, the patterns of interactions of organisms with their environments, both living and nonliving, are shared.

ETS1.A The more precisely a design task's criteria and constraints can be defined, the more likely it is that the designed solution will be successful. Specification of constraints includes consideration of scientific principles and other relevant knowledge that are likely to limit possible solutions.

Predation is a relationship between a predator, like this eagle owl, and prey, like this deer mouse. The eagle owl gets resources that it needs to survive, grow, and reproduce from the prey.

1. Predators

A kitten crouches low. It waits for the right moment and then, playing at being a lethal hunter, it pounces on a toy. Kittens practice this hunting behavior because, when they are adult cats, they may need to sneak up on their food. Pet cats do not have to hunt, but cats in the wild must be able to capture and kill other animals to eat so that they have the resources they need to survive. How do scientists describe the relationship between the organism that eats and the organism being eaten?

Predation is a relationship in which one organism, the predator, benefits by eating another organism, the prey. An eagle owl is a predator that feeds on prey, such as a mouse. The mouse provides resources that allow the eagle owl to survive, grow, and reproduce.

There are countless examples of feeding relationships across ecosystems on Earth, but scientists have observed patterns to these relationships. One pattern scientists have observed in feeding relationships is that predators can be organized into three large categories depending on the type of organism that they eat. Some predators eat animals, others eat plants, and still others eat both animals and plants.

Carnivores Wild cats, eagle owls, and panther chameleons are examples of a type of predator called a carnivore. A **carnivore** is an organism that mainly eats other animals. Eagle owls and panther chameleons are good examples of carnivores because they rarely, if ever, eat anything other than animals. Most carnivores are animals or unicellular organisms, but even plants can be carnivores. Venus flytraps are plants that catch insects to eat.

This panther chameleon is using its long, sticky tongue to capture a cricket to eat. Panther chameleons are carnivores, predators that eat mainly animals as prey.

Herbivores are predators that eat mainly plants as prey. These cows are herbivores and spend the greater part of every day grazing on grasses and other plants. Through their predation on grasses, herbivores, like these cows, impact grass populations.

Herbivores In everyday speech, we use the word *predator* to mean an animal that hunts and eats other animals. However, scientists include plant eaters in this category as well. An **herbivore** is an organism that mainly eats plants or plant parts. Their prey may not be able to run away, but plants often have strategies that make it more difficult for a predator to eat them. A white-tailed deer might prefer to feed on a plant that does not have thorns, so having thorns is a survival strategy of some plants that deer prey on. Familiar herbivores include grazing animals that feed on grasses, such as zebras, wildebeests, and cows.

Omnivores Most humans and many other animal species eat both plants and animals. Such predators belong to another category: omnivores. An **omnivore** is an organism that eats both plants and animals in similar amounts. Mona monkeys, like the one shown here, eat many kinds of fruit from plants, such as bananas. They also eat animals, such as insects. Because of their diverse diet, Mona monkeys are considered omnivores. Raccoons are also omnivores. In cities and suburbs, raccoons often go through people's garbage in search of discarded meat and vegetable scraps. In the wild, they eat a variety of prey, including frogs, mice, eggs, insects, fruits, and nuts. Most humans are omnivores because they eat both plant foods, like grains and vegetables, and animal foods, like eggs or fish.

Omnivores eat both animals and plants. This Mona monkey is enjoying a banana, but it also eats insects. Mona monkeys are omnivores. You may also be an omnivore!

Predators in Ecosystems In nearly every ecosystem on Earth, you will find every kind of predator: carnivores, omnivores, and herbivores. The species that occupy those roles are different between ecosystems, but patterns in feeding relationships are similar. Because patterns are similar across ecosystems, scientists can make predictions about a population based on its feeding relationships with other populations. For example, the populations of both predators and prey change as a result of their interaction. How do populations of predators impact populations of their prey?

A carnivore population will reduce the size of the prey population that it feeds on. When lions eat zebras, they reduce the size of the zebra population. The lion population will increase, because lions use the resources they get from zebras to grow and reproduce.

2. Interacting Populations Affect One Another

Squeak! A stray cat gobbles up a mouse. Every stray cat needs to get enough resources to survive, and it does this by hunting and eating prey, such as mice. If the stray cat population increases, then what happens to the mouse population? If mice become rare and stray cats cannot find enough prey, what happens to the cat population?

Predators Affect Prey Populations Like stray cats and mice, predator and prey populations affect one another. Carnivores reduce the size of prey populations because they usually kill their prey. When a lion eats a zebra, the zebra population is reduced by one. When herbivores and omnivores eat plants they often do not kill the prey. When a cow nibbles on a grass plant, it is only eating part of the plant. Because of this, it can be difficult to predict the impact of an herbivore or omnivore on their prey populations. However, it is possible to predict patterns of interaction between populations of carnivores and their prey.

When scientists look at populations of carnivores and their prey, they often see a pattern that results from a cause and effect relationship. When there are carnivores in an area, prey populations decrease. The cause is that carnivores, like lions, are eating prey. The effect is a decrease in prey, like zebras. Sometimes, carnivores can reduce prey populations until they are eliminated entirely.

A Scarcity of Prey Reduces Carnivore Populations What happens to carnivore and prey populations as they interact? One ecosystem that scientists have studied to understand these interactions is Isle Royale, an island in the middle of Lake Superior. Moose came to the island in the early 1900s by swimming or walking across frozen lake ice. Wolves, which are predators of moose, walked to the island when the lake was frozen in the 1940s. Michigan's Isle Royale is an isolated ecosystem, so scientists can see how moose and wolf populations affect one another without the influence of other factors.

Scientists have found that changes in the population of wolves have effects on the population of moose prey on Isle Royale, but the moose population also affects the wolf population. In the early 2000s, the moose population on the island was shrinking. Many moose weakened and died because they were infected with ticks. When the moose population decreased, there was less food for the wolves. By 2007, the wolf population had also decreased. There were fewer prey to support so many wolves. By observing populations of predators and prey over time, scientists gather data on population size. The numbers show a pattern observed in many ecosystems. When prey become a limited resource, predator populations decrease.

A Scarcity of Carnivores Increases Prey Populations A scarcity of carnivores also has an effect on prey populations. It causes them to increase. As the wolf population on Isle Royale decreased, dropping to only three wolves in the spring of 2015, the moose population grew. There were fewer predators killing them off, so more moose survived each year and their population increased.

Carnivore and prey populations are closely linked so that their populations grow and decline together. Because of this cause and effect relationship between populations, scientists can analyze population data in ecosystems and make predictions. The graph in Figure 2.2 shows this pattern in wolf and moose populations. In the graph, you see that an increase in the moose population causes the wolf population to increase a little later. With this increase in the wolf population, the moose population will decrease after a period of time. The wolf population then decreases as well, which causes an increase in the moose population. This pattern happens over and over again in a cycle. Each rise in the moose population is followed by a rise in the wolf population. Also each rise in the wolf population is followed by a fall in the moose population. This is because living things in an ecosystem are affected by each other. Scientists see this pattern between carnivore and prey populations all over the world.

A change in the size of the carnivore population affects its main prey population in an ecosystem. Each time a wolf eats a moose, the moose population decreases. Scientists track the number of wolves and the number of moose to observe how these populations affect one another.

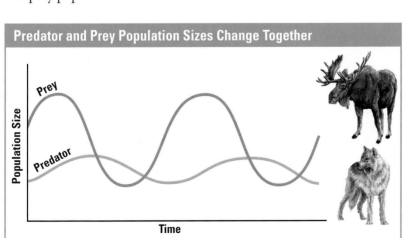

Predator and Prey Population Sizes Change Together

Prey

Predator

Population Size

Time

Figure 2.2
When scientists graph the size of carnivore and prey populations in an ecosystem, they observe a repeating pattern. Wolf population size is affected by the size of the moose population, increasing when moose are abundant and decreasing when moose are scarce.

3. Using Predators to Manage Ecosystems

The close relationship between carnivore and prey populations was the source of an ecological problem in the Yellowstone ecosystem in the western United States. During the late 1800s and early 1900s, people killed wolves in the area to prevent them from preying on livestock, such as sheep and cattle. As a result, by the mid-1900s, there were no wolves in the Yellowstone ecosystem. Without predators to keep their population in check, elk in the area grew in number and harmed plant populations through overgrazing.

In the late 1990s, conservation scientists reintroduced wolves to Yellowstone to control the elk population. They did not want this to be a temporary solution. They needed a way to ensure that the introduced wolves could survive, stay healthy, and produce offspring in the Yellowstone ecosystem. Could conservation scientists work with engineers to design a way to keep track of the wolf population?

Criteria: Monitoring a Predator Population To solve the problem, engineers first needed to precisely identify the criteria for the solution. **Criteria** are the requirements that must be met for an engineering solution to be successful. Conservation scientists needed to make sure that the tracking technology was providing them with accurate data. One of the criteria was that the technology could show whether wolves were surviving after being introduced into the ecosystem. Another was that the technology be able to observe whether the wolves were staying in Yellowstone or moving to other ecosystems. One relevant scientific fact about wolves that conservation scientists had to take into account is that they travel in packs across hundreds of square miles. The park itself has an area of more than 3,400 square miles. So, the technology needed to accurately track the movement of wolves and work well across large areas of landscape.

The introduction of wolves in the Yellowstone ecosystem affected populations of other species as well as elk. For example, wolf populations affect plant populations because wolves prey on elk, which in turn prey on grasses and other plants. When wolves eat elk, the plant populations that elk prey on will increase.

Radio-tracking technologies meet the criteria and constraints of the engineering problem faced by Yellowstone conservation scientists. To observe the movements of individual wolves and monitor the size of the wolf population, scientists place radio-tracking collars on the animals when they are sedated.

Constraints: Cost and Feasibility of Technology To design a solution, engineers must also identify the constraints of the situation. **Constraints** are the limitations on an engineering solution. Conservation scientists looked at constraints to make sure that the technology they chose to track wolves would not be too expensive or difficult to use. For example, some tracking devices use handheld signal detectors. Some require equipment flown on helicopters or airplanes. Others use GPS technology that depends on satellite communication. Another constraint was that the technology could not interfere with the natural behavior of wolves. Conservation scientists did not want their observation of the wolves to affect the outcome of the study.

Design Solution: A Successful Outcome By identifying criteria and constraints, conservation scientists arrived at a technology solution that worked to monitor wolf health and activities in the Yellowstone ecosystem. They decided to monitor the Yellowstone wolves using radio tracking. Conservation scientists fit individual animals with collars containing a device that sends out radio wave signals. Each animal's collar sends out a unique signal. To track animals, researchers use handheld antennas that can receive the signals. The radio signal is used to determine where the wolf hunts, which other wolves it interacts with, and even whether it is still alive. Using a small, removable collar means that researchers can monitor wolf activity without interfering with their natural behavior. Radio-tracking technologies have been an effective solution in this ecosystem management project.

A handheld antenna can pick up radio wave signals that the collars emit, showing location and movement data.

Over time, the Yellowstone wolf population has expanded and the ecosystem has experienced a dramatic change. With the wolf population restored, elk no longer prey too heavily on plants. Other species that rely on those plant communities, such as some bird species, are on their way to returning to previous numbers. The recovery of the Yellowstone ecosystem is an example of how conservation scientists use the principles of scientific knowledge to make positive changes.

A mutualism is when two species interact with one another in a relationship that benefits both organisms. Green sea turtles benefit when cleaner fish eat the algae that grow on their carapaces because it keeps them clean. The fish benefit by getting a satisfying meal.

4. Mutually Beneficial Interactions

So far, you have analyzed relationships that involve predators and prey and populations that compete with each other. Both kinds of relationships harm an organism's chances of survival. But not all relationships in ecosystems are harmful. Some interactions among organisms in an ecosystem are helpful. How could one species help another species survive?

Sometimes two species have a relationship in which they help one another survive, grow, or reproduce. A **mutualism** is a relationship between two species in which both species benefit. In a mutualism, the organisms are called *mutualists*. The green sea turtle and the fish pictured on this page are mutualists. Their interaction benefits both species. The fish benefit by getting nutrients when they eat algae and other organisms that live on the sea turtle's shell, or carapace. The sea turtle benefits because the fish "clean" the sea turtle as they eat. Having a clean carapace helps the sea turtle stay healthy and avoid disease and injury. Without mutualism, both organisms would have a more difficult time surviving. The relationship between the clown fish and the sea anemone described at the beginning of this lesson is another example of a mutualism.

Some mutualisms are between species that are completely dependent on one another for survival. Lichen may look like single organisms, but they are actually formed by two species: an alga that uses sunlight to produce food and a fungus that can attach to hard surfaces and provide protection.

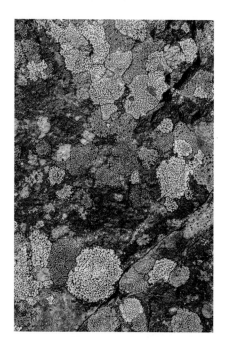

Because mutualists depend on one another, changes in the population size of one species in the relationship can affect the population size of the other. The interaction helps both populations grow because both populations benefit. If another factor, such as disease or an increase in predators, causes one population to shrink, the other population may also shrink as a result. The mutualism between the two species that make up the colorful patches of lichen you might see on a rock is so strong that, in some interactions, neither can survive without the other. Each lichen is not an individual, but a pair of organisms: an alga and a fungus. The alga acts as a plant does and uses sunlight to produce food for both organisms, while the fungus provides structure and shelter for the pair and also helps absorb water from the surroundings. Their populations are linked such that when the fungus population increases, so does the algae population.

5. Other Kinds of Interactions

A kitten scratches behind its ear. Oh no, it has fleas! What is the interaction between the kitten and the fleas that live on it? You have learned that species interact with other species in different ways. Sometimes one species benefits from an interaction and the other is harmed, such as when a wolf preys on a moose. Sometimes both species benefit, such as when cleaner fish eat things growing on a sea turtle's shell. What other types of interactions are there between species?

Commensalism Some interactions between organisms in an ecosystem help one organism and have no effect on the other. **Commensalism** is a relationship between two species in which one species benefits and the other is unaffected. One example of commensalism involves barnacles. Barnacles are sea creatures that have hard shells. Some species spend their lives stuck to rocks and other hard surfaces, where they wait for passing bits of food to float by. Other species of barnacles stick to a surface that moves from place to place—such as the body of a whale—in order to consume bits of food. The barnacle benefits from being stuck to the whale, but the whale is mostly unaffected by the relationship.

Parasitism A barnacle does not harm the whale, nor does it compete for resources, but some organisms do cause harm. **Parasitism** is a relationship in which one species benefits while the other is harmed but not usually killed. Parasitism is similar to predation in that one species benefits while the other is harmed. A parasite lives on or in a living organism called a *host*. A parasite usually does not kill the host, although it may weaken it. Instead, it takes small amounts of resources from the host that, over time, can weaken the host. The kitten is a host for its fleas. The fleas drink small amounts of blood and live on the kitten but do not kill it.

Barnacles have cemented themselves to the body of a humpback whale. The whale is unaffected by their presence, but the barnacles gain access to a constantly replenishing source of food as the whale moves from place to place.

Parasites obtain resources from other organisms but do not kill them. Many insect parasites, such as a tick or this flea, live off of the blood of mammals. They do not need to kill their hosts to eat, but their bites and the resulting blood loss can harm the host's health.

Interactions in Ecosystems

Interactions between species can be organized by whether the impact on each species is positive (+), negative (–), or neutral (0). In mutualism, there is a positive impact on both species. In commensalism, one species is unaffected and the other benefits. In competition, both species are harmed through the interaction. In predation and parasitism, one species benefits and the other is harmed. These patterns of interaction between species is found in ecosystems around the world and can be used to predict how different interactions can impact these species.

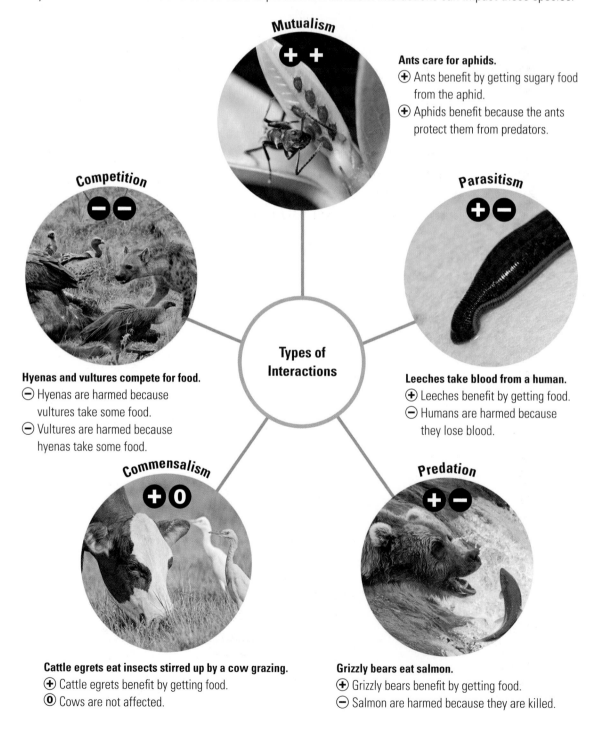

Mutualism

Ants care for aphids.
⊕ Ants benefit by getting sugary food from the aphid.
⊕ Aphids benefit because the ants protect them from predators.

Competition

Hyenas and vultures compete for food.
⊖ Hyenas are harmed because vultures take some food.
⊖ Vultures are harmed because hyenas take some food.

Parasitism

Leeches take blood from a human.
⊕ Leeches benefit by getting food.
⊖ Humans are harmed because they lose blood.

Types of Interactions

Commensalism

Cattle egrets eat insects stirred up by a cow grazing.
⊕ Cattle egrets benefit by getting food.
⓪ Cows are not affected.

Predation

Grizzly bears eat salmon.
⊕ Grizzly bears benefit by getting food.
⊖ Salmon are harmed because they are killed.

6. Scientists Predict Interactions

Suppose you are in charge of a wildlife preserve that is designed to protect snow leopards, a wild cat species that is found in only a few places on Earth. Although the preserve is designed to protect snow leopards, their population is declining. What can you do to maintain or increase the snow leopard population?

If you know how snow leopards interact with other species, you can predict how those interactions impact snow leopards. You can find ways to increase populations of snow leopard prey or decrease populations of snow leopard competitors.

Scientists can make predictions like this because there are patterns in how different interactions affect populations in ecosystems. Patterns of interactions can help scientists predict and manage changes in populations. To understand why a population is growing or shrinking, scientists look at its interactions with other populations. Each interaction is rated as beneficial (+), harmful (−), or having no effect (0) on the population's growth. These patterns of interactions are found in ecosystems everywhere on Earth.

Armed with this information, scientists can manage populations of snow leopards in their unique ecosystem. For example, they can reduce the negative impacts of a parasite species or increase the positive impacts of a larger prey population on snow leopards.

LESSON SUMMARY

Interactions Among Organisms

Predators Predation is an interaction in which one organism, the predator, benefits by eating another organism, the prey. Predators include carnivores, herbivores, and omnivores.

Interacting Populations Affect One Another Predator populations impact their prey populations through a cause and effect relationship.

Using Predators to Manage Ecosystems Conservation scientists use their understanding of interactions between predators and prey to manage ecosystems.

Mutually Beneficial Interactions Sometimes two species have a relationship in which they help one another.

Other Kinds of Interactions There are other kinds of interactions between species, including commensalism and parasitism.

Scientists Predict Interactions Populations of organisms can interact in ways that are beneficial (+), harmful (−), or have no effect (0).

Body Snatchers and Zombies

In the 1956 zombie movie classic—*Invasion of the Body Snatchers*—beings from outer space land on Earth and take over the bodies of humans. But zombies and body snatchers are only in movies, right? Wrong.

Invasion of the Spider Snatcher

This brown spider doesn't know it, but it is about to have its body snatched. A female spider wasp has landed on the spider and stung it with her powerful venom. The venom paralyzes the spider so that the wasp can drag it back to her nest. There, she deposits an egg on the spider and buries it alive. The living spider's body provides a food source for the wasp larva after it hatches from the egg.

The spider wasp is a parasitoid, a special kind of parasite that uses a host as a food source during development. Unlike most parasites, parasitoids kill their hosts—in this case, the brown spider.

This orange and black spider wasp has paralyzed a brown spider with her venom. She will drag her prey to her nest, where it will be a source of food for her developing larva.

This black wasp is a parasitoid wasp that is using this caterpillar as a host for her developing larva. She is dragging a caterpillar that she paralyzed into her nest, where she will deposit her egg on it.

How to Snatch a Body

Some female wasps use the bodies of spiders and other species, such as caterpillars, as hosts for their developing larvae. This process could be a scene right out of a horror movie. How do they do it?

Find and Paralyze a Host Once a female wasp has a fertilized egg, she must find the right host for it. A nice, plump spider is a good choice. Attacking it can be dangerous work. As she approaches to sting the spider, the female wasp must be careful to avoid being trapped in a web or bitten by the spider. Otherwise, she may end up as the food source in this relationship!

Deposit the Egg After the wasp stings the spider, the spider is paralyzed by the wasp's venom. At this point, the wasp deposits her egg in the spider's abdomen.

Consume the Host Soon after the egg is deposited, a hungry wasp larva emerges and slowly feeds on the body of the immobilized spider. Because the spider is still alive, its flesh has not rotted and can provide the growing larva with the nutrients it needs to develop. By the time the larva turns into a pupa and emerges as an adult wasp, the spider host is dead.

This spider is serving as a host for a wasp larva, which is attached to it along its back. The larva is feeding on the body fluids of the spider and will kill it eventually.

Zombie Mind Control

Parasitoids can also make zombies—mindless creatures they control. Let's look at one parasitoid and her zombie: the female jewel wasp and the American cockroach. Like the spider wasp, the jewel wasp depends on a host to feed her larvae. Like the spider, the cockroach is consumed by wasp larvae and eventually dies. Rather than paralyzing her host, the jewel wasp creates a zombie whose movements she can control.

First, she stings the cockroach around its middle, paralyzing its front legs. As the cockroach struggles, the wasp injects venom into its brain. There, the venom blocks an important brain chemical called octopamine. This chemical is responsible for regulating the cockroach's ability to move and eat. The cockroach can still move, but with the brain chemical blocked, it won't flee from the wasp. The wasp is able to guide the cockroach to its burrow simply by gently tugging on it.

Scientists studying these zombie cockroaches found something else interesting: by injecting an octopamine-like chemical into the cockroach's brain, they could reverse the effects of the venom and release the cockroach from its zombie state. Scientists hope that studying the interactions between wasp venom and brain chemicals may lead to medical breakthroughs for humans as well.

The emerald jewel wasp uses venom injected into the cockroach brain to control her zombie prey. After the second sting, she is able to guide the cockroach into her burrow so that her offspring will have a steady supply of food as they develop.

Useful Parasitoids

Are there other ways that parasitoid hosts can be useful to people? If the host happens to be a garden pest, then parasitoid wasps can be beneficial to gardeners.

Take, for example, the tomato hornworm. This larval form of the hawk moth is a voracious eater and can consume large sections of a ripe tomato in a single night of feeding. Fortunately for gardeners, the hornworm is a favorite host of the *Cotesia* wasp.

The female *Cotesia* wasp stalks her prey among the green leaves of the tomato plant. Once the wasp has landed on the hornworm, she deposits up to 65 eggs just under its skin. At the same time, she injects the hornworm with a virus that prevents its immune system from attacking the egg invaders. As the hornworm continues to move around the garden and eat, wasp larvae emerge from the eggs and slowly eat its insides. Once the wasp larvae have grown, they bore holes through the hornworm's skin. There, they turn into pupae and spin little cocoons on its surface.

After adult wasps emerge from the cocoons, the weakened hornworm soon dies. In this way, the *Cotesia* wasp serves as a form of biological control—an organism used to control pests. By using a biological control, gardeners are able to apply less chemical pesticides to their crops.

You may not be used to the idea of parasitoids all around you— yet. But they can be as close to you as your neighborhood park, and they can be useful in protecting the food that you eat. ◆

Parasitoid wasps can be used to naturally control crop-eating pests. This tomato hornworm has many white *Cotesia* wasp cocoons hanging from its body. As the developing larvae feed on the tissues of this hornworm, the hornworm will eat less and soon die.

Biological controls are useful in gardens in urban areas, where pesticides could negatively affect the health of people. While chemical pesticides may be dangerous to humans, parasitoid wasps that prey on caterpillars are not.

Changing Ecosystems

How do ecosystems change over time?

Introduction

As the thick ice of this glacier melts away, it leaves behind bare rock and soil. Small flowering plants and mosses are the first organisms to settle and grow on the gravel left behind by the glacier. As these organisms grow, others move in. Bumble bees visit the flowers and beetles eat the dead leaves and other organic matter. As the small plants and mosses grow and die, they form rich layers of soil that can support larger plants. This process continues until what was once snow and ice has become a wet meadow filled with flowers. Which organisms will move in next? How will those new organisms change the ecosystem even more?

All ecosystems change naturally over time. Natural changes in climate have been transforming ecosystems since life first appeared on Earth. Sometimes natural changes are slow, such as a glacier receding. Other times they are rapid, like an avalanche destroying a hillside full of trees. Ecosystems can also change because of human activities, such as people clearing a forest to plant a field. Whether natural or human-caused, small changes in one part of an ecosystem can cause changes throughout the ecosystem.

In previous lessons, you learned how resources limit populations and how populations interact in ecosystems. In this lesson, you explore the impacts of slow and rapid changes on populations in ecosystems. First, you will consider how changes in interactions and resources affect populations. Then, you will look at how engineers use scientific understanding of changing resources and interactions to restore damaged ecosystems.

Vocabulary

dynamic system any system that is characterized by constant change

ecological succession the predictable way that ecosystems change from one type to another over time

evidence information obtained by observation or experimentation

---

Next Generation Science Standards

Performance Expectations

MS-LS2-4. Construct an argument supported by empirical evidence that changes to physical or biological components of an ecosystem affect populations.

MS-ETS1-1. Define the criteria and constraints of a design problem with sufficient precision to ensure a successful solution, taking into account relevant scientific principles and potential impacts on people and the natural environment that may limit possible solutions.

Science and Engineering Practices

Engaging in Argument from Evidence Construct an oral and written argument supported by empirical evidence and scientific reasoning to support or refute an explanation or a model for a phenomenon or a solution to a problem.

Asking Questions and Defining Problems Define a design problem that can be solved through the development of an object, tool, process, or system and includes multiple criteria and constraints, including scientific knowledge that may limit possible solutions.

Scientific Knowledge is Based on Empirical Evidence

Crosscutting Concepts

Stability and Change Small changes in one part of a system might cause large changes in another part.

Influence of Science, Engineering, and Technology on Society and the Natural World

Disciplinary Core Ideas

LS2.C. Ecosystems are dynamic in nature; their characteristics can vary over time. Disruptions to any physical or biological component of an ecosystem can lead to shifts in all its populations.

ETS1.A. The more precisely a design task's criteria and constraints can be defined, the more likely it is that the designed solution will be successful. Specification of constraints includes consideration of scientific principles and other relevant knowledge that are likely to limit possible solutions.

1. Ecosystems Change Over Time

In a pond full of aquatic plants and animals, decayed matter from these organisms sinks to the bottom. Over time, this layer gets thicker and the water gets shallower until there is no longer a pond. What happens to populations of aquatic organisms as the pond disappears?

The living and nonliving parts of the pond are always changing, because ecosystems are dynamic. A **dynamic system** is any system characterized by constant change. These can be small or large changes, and they can happen gradually or suddenly. However, there is always something changing in a dynamic system, like an ecosystem.

Gradual Change Change in ecosystems often takes place gradually as resources fluctuate, and populations rise and fall as a result. Look at Figure 3.1. Without a constant source of water, like a stream, the pond can become shallower over time. Populations of aquatic organisms, like fish and ducks, decline. Meanwhile, cattails and other wetland plants thrive. A wetland is an ecosystem that is saturated with water, like a swamp or marsh. Wetland plants, like reeds and cattails, support populations of wetland animals, such as dragonflies, frogs, and turtles. Over many years, the wetland continues to fill in, and new plants colonize the area, such as grasses, shrubs, and trees. The ecosystem transforms into a meadow, which attracts animals like voles, rabbits, and foxes. As meadow plants grow and die, they create thicker layers of soil. The ecosystem now supports the growth of large trees and attracts forest animals, such as deer and birds that nest in trees. Over many years, a pond ecosystem can turn into a tall forest.

This pattern of change is called **ecological succession,** the predictable way that ecosystems change from one type to another over time. This process does not happen overnight. It can take thousands of years for a pond to change into a forest. The particular changes that happen and how long they take depends on the ecosystem, but this pattern is seen in ecosystems around the world over time.

Figure 3.1

Ecosystems can change in predictable ways. One pattern of change in ecosystems is the gradual change from a pond to a wetland to a meadow and then to a forest. As the physical conditions change in an area, so do the populations of organisms that live there.

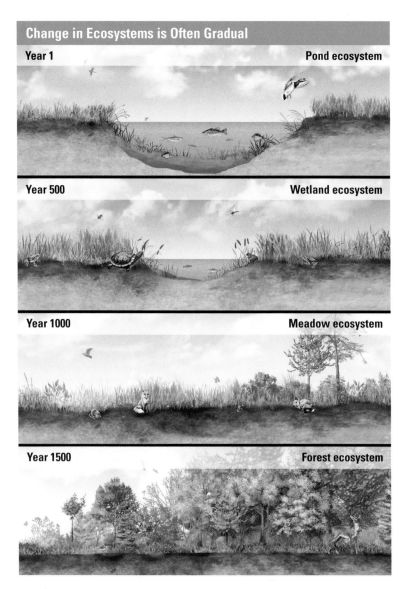

Change in Ecosystems is Often Gradual

Year 1 — **Pond ecosystem**

Year 500 — **Wetland ecosystem**

Year 1000 — **Meadow ecosystem**

Year 1500 — **Forest ecosystem**

Sudden Change Some changes to ecosystems happen very quickly. A catastrophic event, such as a volcano erupting, can change an ecosystem dramatically. An eruption can kill all of the living things in the area as hot lava flows down the slopes of the volcano and toxic clouds of ash and dust cover everything within miles. This kind of change can rapidly and completely wipe out an ecosystem.

Over long periods of time, the ecosystem undergoes ecological succession, just like the pond that turned into a forest. Afterwards, a new ecosystem will be found where once there was just cooling lava. After a volcanic eruption, the land is often covered with thick layers of lava and ash. Over time the ash and lava cool and become hard. Small living things, like plant seeds and small insects, float in on the wind or are transported by animals and settle into the small air pockets in the lava on this new, empty landscape. Some plants, like the one pictured here, can survive on the hardened lava. As they grow, they create homes for insects and other small organisms. Over time this old lava develops a layer of soil, and more organisms move in as they find the resources they need to survive there. This is similar to the glacier example at the beginning of this lesson.

Sudden changes can transform ecosystems rapidly, but ecosystems usually recover after long periods of gradual change. Sometimes the ecosystem that results after this long period of recovery resembles the ecosystem that was there before the sudden change. Other times, the ecosystem is different after the period of recovery.

Sudden changes to ecosystems can be natural or human-caused. Volcanic eruptions are natural events, as are hurricanes, droughts, fires, landslides, and floods. Human activity can also cause sudden changes to ecosystems. Humans clear large areas of land for farming and construction, generate pollution during industrial accidents and oil spills, and introduce new species to an area, sometimes unintentionally. All of these events can cause rapid changes that disrupt ecosystems and change them temporarily or permanently.

Ecosystems change suddenly during catastrophic events, such as a volcanic eruption. Lava may kill organisms, but it also cools and forms new land—a valuable resource for organisms that move to the area after the eruption.

Ecosystems recover from sudden events, such as volcanic eruptions, through ecological succession. Hardy plants that don't need soil can sprout in the cracks and holes of cooled lava.

2. Changes to Living Parts of Ecosystems

A prairie dog pokes its head out of a hole in the ground and watches for predators. Prairie dogs are small animals, but their presence can change grassland ecosystems dramatically, including the populations of other organisms that rely on that ecosystem. How can one species cause changes in so many other species in an ecosystem?

Prairie dogs are ground dwelling squirrels that live in large groups. They dig elaborate tunnels that provide shelter for sleeping, hiding from predators, and raising young. They eat grasses and other plants. Because prairie dogs depend on grassland ecosystems, the destruction of these ecosystems for farming and other human uses has had a negative impact on them. Some data suggest their numbers have decreased to 2 percent of what they were 100 years ago.

Scientists have observed that these changes in prairie dog populations have caused changes in the populations of other species. When scientists compare grasslands with prairie dogs to grasslands without prairie dogs, they observe a pattern. When prairie dogs are absent, the populations of other species, like burrowing owls and rabbits, are absent or are much lower. These changes in different populations are **evidence,** or information scientists obtain through observation or experimentation, that the living parts of ecosystems affect one another. When evidence from many different grasslands is compared, patterns in the evidence emerge and help scientists understand how prairie dogs impact grassland ecosystems.

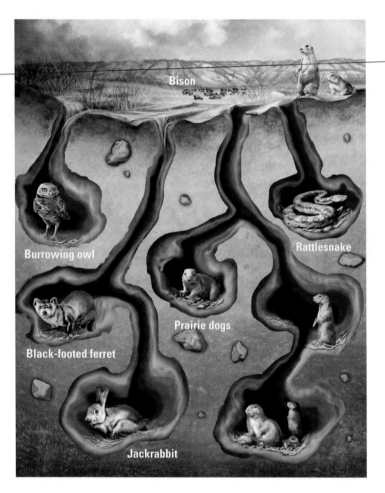

Prairie dog populations impact other populations. Prairie dog burrows provide homes for rabbits, burrowing owls, rattlesnakes, and black-footed ferrets. Burrows also change the grassland, making more abundant grass for bison and for prairie dogs to eat. Prairie dog populations themselves also create an important resource—prey for black-footed ferrets and rattlesnakes to eat!

Some Species Benefit from Prairie Dogs Many organisms rely on prairie dogs because of the way that their burrows and feeding activities affect the ecosystem. The burrows of prairie dogs allow water to seep into the ground and mix air into the soil. These effects on the soil benefit grassland plants, causing more grass growth. Bison benefit from this because they eat this abundant grass. Other organisms, like burrowing owls, rattlesnakes, and black-footed ferrets, use the burrows as shelters. Prairie dogs change grassland ecosystems in ways that have a positive impact on bison, rattlesnakes, burrowing owls, rabbits, and black-footed ferrets. Populations of those species decrease when prairie dog populations decrease.

Prairie dogs thrive in grassland ecosystems, forming large colonies. There are many animals that prey on prairie dogs, including black-footed ferrets, badgers, coyotes, eagles, and hawks. When prairie dogs are present, they form an important and abundant resource for these predators. Black-footed ferrets prey almost exclusively on prairie dogs. As prairie dog populations have declined, populations of their predators, especially black-footed ferrets, have also declined. This is evidence that populations of many species in grassland ecosystems are dependent on the presence of prairie dogs.

Some Species Do Not Benefit from Prairie Dogs Not all species benefit from prairie dogs. When prairie dog populations increase, they reduce the population of the flowering plants and shrubs because prairie dogs eat them. This means there are fewer flowering plants and shrubs for pronghorn antelope to eat, and pronghorn antelope populations decrease.

Prairie Dog Populations Change Prairie Ecosystems By gathering evidence from grassland ecosystems under different conditions, scientists have observed a pattern. When prairie dog populations are found in an ecosystem, they change the resources available in the ecosystem. This then changes populations of other living things in the ecosystem. Prairie dogs illustrate that changes in the living parts of ecosystems cause changes in the available resources in the ecosystem. These changes impact other populations of organisms in the ecosystem. Some species, like prairie dogs, are linked through interactions to so many others that the stability of the entire ecosystem depends on them.

The many ways that prairie dogs change grassland ecosystems and the resources that are available in those ecosystems affect many other species. Prairie dog populations change ecosystems in ways that benefit bison, burrowing owls, and rattlesnakes. Prairie dogs change the ecosystem in a way that does not benefit pronghorn antelope.

Changes to the nonliving parts of ecosystems cause changes to populations in ecosystems. When beavers build a dam, the dam slows down the flow of water, changing the area upstream into a pond. The pond supports species that cannot live in the fast-flowing water of the stream.

3. Changes to Nonliving Parts of Ecosystems

Whiskered "engineers" chop down trees and use them to build dams. These dams cause flooding and change how streams flow. As a result, the ecosystem changes dramatically. These busy builders are not humans, they are beavers! How do beavers change the nonliving parts of ecosystems?

Upstream from a new beaver dam, the area floods and creates a pond. The water in the pond is deeper than the river and it moves more slowly. This slow-moving, deep water attracts populations of aquatic plants and animals that could not survive in the shallow, fast-moving water of the river.

When beavers cut trees down to build a dam, more light reaches the forest floor along the river. As a result, the populations of smaller plants there grow faster and better. The increase in small plant populations provides food for populations of herbivores, such as moose and elk.

When a beaver builds a dam across a stream, it also changes how water flows through the ecosystem far downstream. Scientists have studied how beaver ponds impact plant communities downstream. In those areas, there is more water available to plants. This promotes abundant plant growth. These lush plant communities provide resources to populations of other organisms. Without beaver ponds upstream, these plant communities and the populations of other organisms that they support do not have the resources they need.

When beavers build dams, they change the amount of light that reaches lower levels of the forest and the speed of water in the river, turning it from a fast-flowing stream into a calm, slow pond. Scientists have observed that these changes to the nonliving parts of the ecosystem change populations of organisms in the ecosystem, even far downstream from the beaver dam. When scientists observe ecosystems with and without beavers, they find evidence that beaver dams change nonliving resources, such as light and water, in an ecosystem. These changes then change other populations that live there.

Ecosystem Changes Shift Populations

When resources in ecosystems change, populations of organisms that live there also change. About 200 years ago, in the Gulf of Mexico, there were healthy populations of native species, including black bears, manatees, and pocketbook mussels. After humans modified Gulf of Mexico landscapes, populations changed; for example, cattle egrets were introduced and populations of some native species disappeared. These changes can be visualized on a graph. What patterns do you see in population sizes before and after ecosystem changes?

Gulf of Mexico wetland before changes:
The ecosystem is characterized by populations of species found there. The ecosystem is functioning normally.

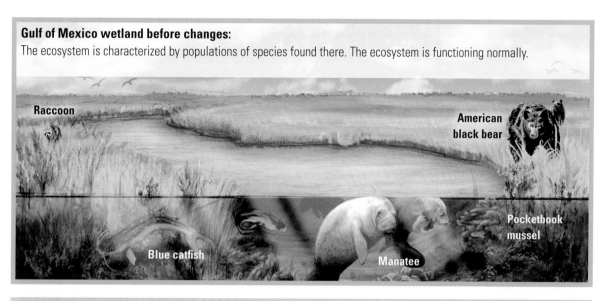

Gulf of Mexico after changes:
Some populations have increased and some have decreased because of changes in limited resources. Ecosystem functions have changed as a result.

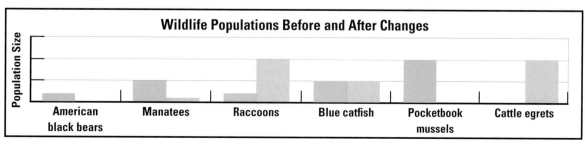

4. Rebuilding Wetland Buffers

Most years, storms in the Gulf of Mexico cause flooding in coastal cities like New Orleans. Floods can force people to evacuate their homes and can cause extensive damage. Under natural conditions, the Mississippi River brings sediments from hundreds of miles away and deposits them where the river enters the Gulf of Mexico. These sediments form large coastal wetlands. Healthy coastal wetlands act to protect communities from storms. But people have changed the path of the river, and some places do not receive those sediments anymore.

In the early 1990s, engineers were looking for a way to rebuild nearby wetlands to protect New Orleans from flooding and provide habitats for wildlife populations. Part of solving any complex problem is to precisely determine the criteria. Criteria are the standards against which the success of the solution is judged. In this case, the solution is successful if it restores healthy wetlands. There are also constraints on the solution. For example, if rebuilding the wetlands is too expensive, or causes additional flooding, then the city may decide that a concrete barrier would be better than natural wetlands.

Sediment Diversions Rebuild Wetlands A successful solution to rebuild wetlands is found at Wax Lake Delta in Louisiana, shown in Figure 3.4. In the early 1940s, workers dug a channel to divert water from the Atchafalaya River into the Gulf. The purpose of the channel was to divert the river away from nearby communities and avoid flooding. However, the river diversion provided a surprise benefit. After digging the diversion, the river deposited sediment into the Gulf, and new wetlands formed at a rate of 2.8 square kilometers per year! Soon, wetland plants were growing on newly formed islands. In Figure 3.4 you can see that wetlands continue to expand and form healthy wetland ecosystems that protect local human communities against flooding more effectively than the original channel.

Figure 3.4

Engineers use river diversions to encourage the growth of coastal wetlands. Coastal wetlands provide valuable resources, such as homes for local wildlife and important food sources for local communities. They also protect people that live on nearby land by reducing damage caused by flooding and hurricanes.

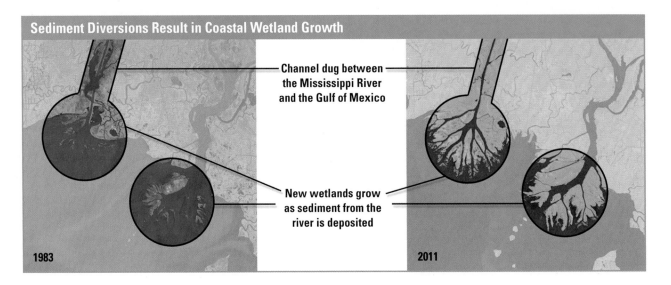

Sediment Diversions Result in Coastal Wetland Growth

Channel dug between the Mississippi River and the Gulf of Mexico

New wetlands grow as sediment from the river is deposited

1983

2011

Protecting Local Communities from Flooding The solutions that engineers decided on for Wax Lake would not work well in New Orleans. A permanent river diversion is difficult to construct in densely populated communities on low coastal lands, such as those around New Orleans. People in this region use levees, reinforced river banks, that prevent high waters from flooding neighborhoods during storms. Levees prevent the natural flow of water and sediment that build wetlands. Opening up a hole in a levee to divert river water would restore wetlands but could also lead to dangerous flooding of surrounding communities.

To ensure that their solution is successful, engineers consider both criteria and constraints as they develop their design. In New Orleans, engineers constructed a different kind of diversion to address flooding issues. The Caernarvon Freshwater Diversion is built into a levee and acts as a door to open or close it as needed. This controls how much river water enters the surrounding wetland. The door is opened when there is no risk of flooding and closed when there is a risk of flooding. Engineers have collected data on the impact of the diversion on the ecosystem. Since its construction, surrounding coastal wetlands have started to form again as sediments from the river are deposited. Solutions that re-create wetlands may be different, depending on local conditions. Taking into consideration the specific criteria and local constraints can help engineers design an effective solution.

The people of New Orleans depend on engineering efforts like the Caernarvon Freshwater Diversion. It allows them to preserve and rebuild coastal marshes while also protecting their communities during storms and floods.

LESSON SUMMARY

Changing Ecosystems

Ecosystems Change Over Time Changes in ecosystems often take place gradually, but they can also be rapid. As resources in ecosystems change, populations of organisms rise and fall as a result.

Changes in Living Parts of Ecosystems Changes in the living parts of ecosystems can cause changes in available resources in the ecosystem. These changes impact other populations of organisms in the ecosystem, either increasing or decreasing those populations.

Changes in Nonliving Parts of Ecosystems Change in the availability of nonliving resources can change the populations of organisms that live there by changing the structure of the ecosystem.

Rebuilding Wetland Buffers Engineers identified criteria and constraints that permitted them to design a successful solution for rebuilding wetlands that protect communities from flooding.

Into the Deep Blue Ocean

In the 1960s and 1970s, science was dominated by men. But Sylvia Earle dared to join the ranks of her fellow male scientists. While astronauts like Neil Armstrong explored the vastness of outer space, she explored the deepest parts of Earth's ocean. What did she find there, and how did she work to protect it?

A Historic Dive

In September 1979, Sylvia Earle stood on a boat off the coast of Oahu, Hawaii, and looked around at the open ocean. She was about to descend 381 meters (1,250 feet) below the ocean surface to explore the seafloor. Ready for her solo adventure, she steadied her nerves and climbed into the 450 kg metal JIM suit that would protect her from the extreme pressure at that depth. The suit was attached to a submersible that would push her to the ocean floor.

Once on the ocean floor, the weight of the JIM suit kept her feet firmly on the sediment. She disconnected from the submersible and began her two-and-a-half-hour walk. That is about the same amount of time the first astronauts walked on the moon! Bright lights from the submersible revealed crabs with vibrant colors. Many of the organisms actually glowed in the darkness! She found herself drawn to some corals. When she touched them, the coral emitted a fiery blue light. Earle fell in love with deep ocean ecosystems. Finding a way to explore the deep ocean would become her life's work.

Sylvia Earle was the first person to deep-sea dive in a pressurized JIM suit to a depth of over 381 meters below the sea surface. The opportunity allowed her to observe deep sea creatures, including ones that glowed in the darkness.

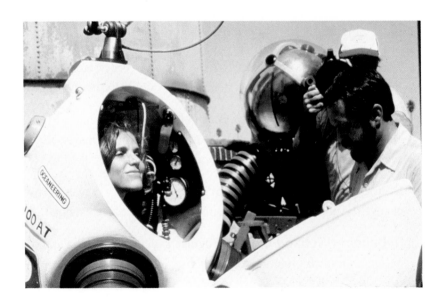

Nothing Got in Her Way

Exploring the unknown can be scary, but for Sylvia Earle, it was nothing new. Growing up on the Gulf of Mexico, she was encouraged by her parents to explore nature on her own. She loved the algae and seaweed that washed up onto the shore in her backyard and wanted to know about the ocean that it came from. When asked how she became an explorer, she said, "I started out as a kid and never did grow up. The best scientists and explorers have the attributes of kids!"

When Earle entered Florida State University in the early 1950s, she was often the only female in her science classes. Because female scientists were rare at the time, Earle missed out on several opportunities. A project called Tektite I allowed scientists to live in an enclosure 15 m below the ocean surface and study ocean ecosystems. Earle was told she could not participate because the enclosure did not have separate sleeping rooms for females.

But Earle did not give up. In 1970, she was asked to lead an all-female team in the same underwater enclosure for the Tektite II project. For two weeks, the team used SCUBA gear to study the ecology and impact of pollution on coral reef ecosystems. The work was strenuous, but the team of women was successful.

Earle became a leading scientist in the study of algae and corals in deep ocean ecosystems. Her special passion for pushing the limits of exploration led to many scientific discoveries. Earle was named the first "Hero for the Planet" by *Time Magazine* in 1998, a National Geographic Explorer-in-Residence, and was inducted into the National Women's Hall of Fame in 2000.

Sylvia Earle led an all-female team for the Tektite II project. To conduct their research in the deep ocean, the women used SCUBA gear to dive for long periods of time.

Sylvia Earle, a leading marine biologist and advocate for Earth's oceans, continues to explore new ways to design submersibles for deep sea exploration.

Earle studied algae and seaweeds in ocean ecosystems. Here, she shares a sample of seaweed with another scientist as they study the impact pollution has on changing ocean ecosystems.

Sylvia Earle sits at an albatross nesting site where human impact on this marine ecosystem is obvious. Trash litters this nesting site, and the seabirds unintentionally feed their young plastic, which causes their death.

A Witness to Change in the Ocean

Earle said, "Fifty years ago, when I began exploring the ocean, no one . . . imagined that we could do anything to harm the ocean by what we put into it or by what we took out of it." Unfortunately, we now know that humans are changing populations of ocean organisms, which could change ocean ecosystems permanently.

Through her many years of research, Earle has witnessed a dramatic decline in populations of ocean organisms, like fish, algae, and corals. New technologies allow humans to catch massive amounts of fish. This has resulted in a 90 percent decline in some fish populations in the last 50 years. Fertilizers and pesticides used in agriculture travel through rivers into the ocean. There they have created hundreds of "ocean dead zones" around the world. And the worldwide use of disposable plastics, like water bottles and grocery bags, is threatening many ocean species and the ocean ecosystems they inhabit. Marine animals, like albatrosses, sometimes accidentally ingest plastic trash, mistaking it for squid or fish. Thousands of albatrosses die each year after eating plastic and feeding it to their young.

Watching these changes in her beloved oceans inspired Earle to use her position as an influential scientist to advocate for ocean health. Earle has raised awareness of the issues of intense fishing, pollution, and plastic trash in ocean ecosystems.

Fighting for the Oceans

Sylvia Earle's observations of changing marine ecosystems led her to become an advocate for ocean health. An advocate is someone who publicly works to raise awareness around an issue. In order to make a real impact on ocean ecosystems, Earle focuses on research, education, and conservation.

In 2009, Earle founded the organization Mission Blue. The goal of the organization is to generate public support for protected marine areas around the globe. The Mission Blue team explores and researches various marine ecosystems to determine which need to be protected. Then, they use all means necessary—the Internet, speaking engagements, films—to drum up financial and moral support to protect what she calls "Hope Spots."

Hope Spots may be areas where a rare species is found. Or, they may be in an area negatively impacted by humans. In all cases, Hope Spots have been deemed worthy of conservation.

A true pioneer in her field, Sylvia Earle helped us discover the wonders and diversity of deep water ocean ecosystems. Her work helped us see that ocean ecosystems can be destroyed by human activity unless we protect them. She has vowed to keep working to protect oceans, one Hope Spot at a time. ◆

As part of her Mission Blue Campaign, Sylvia Earle prepares for a dive to collect data on the health of an area of the ocean. She will use this data to identify locations for Hope Spots and fight to protect them.

Energy and Matter in Ecosystems

OVERVIEW

These caterpillars are sharing a tasty leaf for lunch. They use the energy they get from the leaf to fuel their activities. They use the matter from their lunch to build their bodies. But where did the leaf get the energy and matter that the caterpillars will use? And what happens to the energy and matter in the caterpillars if a bird eats them? In this unit you will explore the transfer of energy and matter through ecosystems on Earth. You will trace the path of energy and elements of matter to see what happens to them and then compare the two paths.

UNIT CONTENTS

Investigations Explain the process of photosynthesis through role playing and use evidence from an experiment with plants to argue the conditions under which photosynthesis occurs.

Investigations Explain the process of cellular respiration through role playing and use experimental evidence of carbon dioxide presence to demonstrate that both snails and plants use cellular respiration.

Investigations Model the paths of energy and matter on a food web poster. Predict and explain the features of different trophic levels in a local ecosystem.

Investigations Model open and closed systems using an aquarium. Explain the path of matter between different parts of global matter cycles using an interactive card game.

Performance Assessment
Create a sequence of images that shows the path of a carbon atom through the carbon cycle. Compare this to the path of energy.

UNIT 2

Performance Expectations

MS-LS1-6. Construct a scientific explanation based on evidence for the role of photosynthesis in the cycling of matter and flow of energy into and out of organisms.

MS.LS1-7. Develop a model to describe how food is rearranged through chemical reactions forming new molecules that support growth and/or release energy as this matter moves through an organism.

MS-LS2-3. Develop a model to describe the cycling of matter and flow of energy among living and nonliving parts of an ecosystem.

MS-ETS1-2. Evaluate competing design solutions using a systematic process to determine how well they meet the criteria and constraints of the problem.

MS-ETS1-4. Develop a model to generate data for iterative testing and modification of a proposed object, tool, or process such that an optimal design can be achieved.

Science and Engineering Practices

Developing and Using Models
• Develop a model to describe unobservable mechanisms.
• Develop a model to describe phenomena. • Develop a model to generate data to test ideas about designed systems, including those representing outputs and inputs.

Engaging in Argument from Evidence
Evaluate competing design solutions based on jointly developed and agreed-upon design criteria.

Constructing Explanations and Designing Solutions
Construct a scientific explanation based on valid and reliable evidence obtained from sources (including the students' own experiments) and the assumption that theories and laws that describe the natural world operate today as they did in the past and will continue to do so in the future.

Connections to Nature of Science: Scientific Knowledge is Based on Empirical Evidence
Science knowledge is based upon logical connections between evidence and explanations.

Crosscutting Concepts

Energy and Matter
• Matter is conserved because atoms are conserved in physical and chemical processes. • Within a natural system, the transfer of energy drives the motion and/or cycling of matter. • The transfer of energy can be tracked as energy flows through a natural system.

Connections to Nature of Science: Scientific Knowledge Assumes an Order and Consistency in Natural Systems
Science assumes that objects and events in natural systems occur in consistent patterns that are understandable through measurement and observation.

Disciplinary Core Ideas

LS1.C: Organization for Matter and Energy Flow in Organisms
• Within individual organisms, food moves through a series of chemical reactions in which it is broken down and rearranged to form new molecules, to support growth, or to release energy. • Plants, algae (including phytoplankton), and many microorganisms use the energy from light to make sugars (food) from carbon dioxide from the atmosphere and water through the process of photosynthesis, which also releases oxygen. These sugars can be used immediately or stored for growth or later use.

LS2.B: Cycle of Matter and Energy Transfer in Ecosystems
Food webs are models that demonstrate how matter and energy is transferred between producers, consumers, and decomposers as the three groups interact within an ecosystem. Transfers of matter into and out of the physical environment occur at every level. Decomposers recycle nutrients from dead plant or animal matter back to the soil in terrestrial environments or to the water in aquatic environments. The atoms that make up the organisms in an ecosystem are cycled repeatedly between the living and nonliving parts of the ecosystem.

PS3.D: Energy in Chemical Processes and Everyday Life
• Cellular respiration in plants and animals involves chemical reactions with oxygen that release stored energy. In these processes, complex molecules containing carbon react with oxygen to produce carbon dioxide and other materials. • The chemical reaction by which plants produce complex food molecules (sugars) requires an energy input (i.e., from sunlight) to occur. In this reaction, carbon dioxide and water combine to form carbon-based organic molecules and release oxygen.

ETS1.B: Developing Possible Solutions
• A solution needs to be tested, and then modified on the basis of the test results, in order to improve it. • There are systematic processes for evaluating solutions with respect to how well they meet the criteria and constraints of a problem. • Models of all kinds are important for testing solutions.

ETS1.C: Optimizing the Design Solution
The iterative process of testing the most promising solutions and modifying what is proposed on the basis of the test results leads to greater refinement and ultimately to an optimal solution.

Connect Your Learning

Energy and matter are essential for life on Earth. Where does energy on Earth come from? And how do living things get the matter that builds their cells? Where does your energy and matter come from? Where do you fit into global transfers of energy and matter? Observing and evaluating phenomena related to living things, including you, will help you answer these questions.

This aquatic plant doesn't eat food like you do, but it somehow gets energy and matter and stores them in its body. Where does this energy and matter come from? Where does it go?

Energy and Matter in Ecosystems

A manatee searches for its favorite food, aquatic plants. How does the manatee use the energy and matter from food? Where do the atoms and molecules of matter that pass into and out of the manatee go?

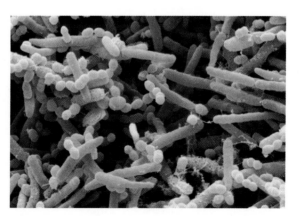

Though too small to see with the unaided eye, bacteria are all around you in every ecosystem. Their role in ecosystems is to recycle matter. What would happen to ecosystems if there were no bacteria?

Capturing the Sun's Energy

How do producers capture energy and matter?

Introduction

Sequoia trees, like this one, are some of the largest organisms on Earth, but where do they get the resources they need to grow so large? Like nearly all plants, sequoias capture the energy they need from the sun and store that energy in sugars and other substances. They get the matter that builds their bodies from the surrounding air and from water absorbed from soil. But how do plants use energy from sunlight and matter from their surroundings to grow?

Plants and some other organisms are able to use a chemical process that can capture energy from sunlight and use that energy to transform nonliving parts of ecosystems, like air and water, into living parts of ecosystems, like the leaves of a sequoia tree or the wings of a moth on a tree. This process is the source of nearly all of the energy and matter used by all other organisms on Earth! Have you ever wondered where you get the resources you need to grow and survive? The energy your body uses comes from the sun, too.

This lesson will introduce you to the variety of organisms that capture the sun's energy and transfer it to molecules that store energy. You will then explore how these molecules provide energy to support life processes or how they store this energy for later use. These molecules are also the building blocks that make up the bodies of all organisms on the planet. You will then consider how engineers use stored energy to create sources of energy for human use, such as fuels.

Vocabulary

matter anything that has mass and volume

producer an organism that captures energy and matter from its surroundings to produce sugars and other molecules

photosynthesis the process of using energy from the sun and matter from the environment to produce sugars that store energy in chemical bonds

chloroplast a cell structure that uses the sun's energy to make sugar through the process of photosynthesis

chlorophyll a green pigment that is important in photosynthesis

cellulose the material that forms the rigid walls and support for plant cells

biomass the combined mass of the bodies of organisms, which collectively represents stored energy

biofuel a material that is made from biomass and releases energy when it is burned

Next Generation Science Standards

Performance Expectations

MS-LS1-6. Construct a scientific explanation based on evidence for the role of photosynthesis in the cycling of matter and flow of energy into and out of organisms.

MS-ETS1-2. Evaluate competing design solutions using a systematic process to determine how well they meet the criteria and constraints of the problem.

Science and Engineering Practices

Constructing Explanations and Designing Solutions Construct a scientific explanation based on valid and reliable evidence obtained from sources (including the students' own experiments) and the assumption that theories and laws that describe the natural world operate today as they did in the past and will continue to do so in the future.

Engaging in Argument from Evidence Evaluate competing design solutions based on jointly developed and agreed-upon design criteria.

Scientific Knowledge is Based on Empirical Evidence

Crosscutting Concepts

Energy and Matter Within a natural system, the transfer of energy drives the motion and/or cycling of matter.

Disciplinary Core Ideas

LS1.C. Plants, algae (including phytoplankton), and many microorganisms use the energy from light to make sugars (food) from carbon dioxide from the atmosphere and water through the process of photosynthesis, which also releases oxygen. These sugars can be used immediately or stored for growth or later use.

PS3.D. The chemical reaction by which plants produce complex food molecules (sugars) requires an energy input (i.e., from sunlight) to occur. In this reaction, carbon dioxide and water combine to form carbon-based organic molecules and release oxygen.

ETS1.B. There are systematic processes for evaluating solutions with respect to how well they meet the criteria and constraints of a problem.

Evergreen Trees

Deciduous Trees

Mosses

Ferns

Producers are organisms that capture energy from the sun to store in molecules of sugar. Plants, such as these trees, ferns, and mosses, are producers.

1. Producers Capture Energy and Matter

Whether it is a cow eating grass or a lion eating a zebra, a predator must eat other organisms to live. What about a plant? Plants are not predators, but they need food to live. How do plants get food?

All organisms need matter and energy to survive, grow, and reproduce, but they get this matter and energy in different ways. **Matter** is anything that has mass and volume. Your body, its cells, and the bodies and cells of other organisms are made up of matter. The matter all around you is made of tiny units called atoms. These atoms make up larger units called molecules. Molecules make up even larger structures, like your cells. When your body grows, matter is added to it in the form of new cells and body structures. It takes energy to move your body when you walk or run. It also takes energy to change the molecules in your body into new cells and body structures through the chemical reactions involved in growth and other life processes. You get matter and energy from the food that you eat, but not all organisms need to eat food to get energy.

Some organisms are able to produce their own food—they are called producers. A **producer** is an organism that captures energy and matter from its surroundings to produce sugars and other molecules. Most producers capture energy from sunlight to make their food. They get the matter they need from gas molecules captured from air and water absorbed from the environment. Without access to sunlight, air, and water, a producer cannot make its own food and may die.

Producers in Terrestrial Ecosystems All ecosystems contain producers of many kinds. In terrestrial ecosystems the most familiar producers are plants, which include trees, mosses, and ferns. Many have leaves that absorb energy from sunlight. Some absorb water from soil through roots. Some of the largest producers in terrestrial ecosystems are trees, such as pines and maples. Grasses are the main producers found in grassland ecosystems.

Some producers in terrestrial ecosystems are not plants. Instead they are single-celled organisms that can capture energy from the sun. For example, cyanobacteria are single-celled producers that are found nearly everywhere on the planet.

Producers in Aquatic Ecosystems Aquatic ecosystems also have producers. There are some aquatic plants, such as eelgrasses, which inhabit both marine and freshwater ecosystems. Most producers in aquatic ecosystems are algae, which can be multicellular or single-celled. *Volvox* are a group of single-celled green algae that live in spherical colonies of thousands of cells in freshwater ecosystems. Single-celled algae called phytoplankton are the main producers in the open ocean. Phytoplankton, such as the diatom pictured here, survive only in the topmost layer of the ocean where sunlight penetrates. Cyanobacteria are single-celled producers found in many different aquatic ecosystems. Some live in frozen lakes, while others live in hot springs that have boiling-hot temperatures!

Producers are found in ecosystems all over the world, converting the sun's energy into molecules of sugar, which store energy for later use.

There are many kinds of producers in aquatic ecosystems. Some, like eelgrass, are aquatic plants. Others are not plants. *Volvox* are colonies of single-celled algae. Diatoms are microscopic single-celled algae. Cyanobacteria are single-celled producers.

Eelgrass

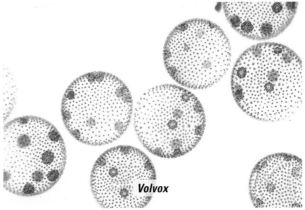
Volvox

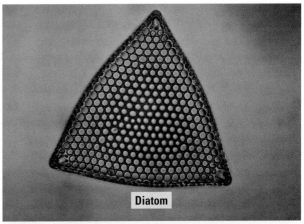
Diatom

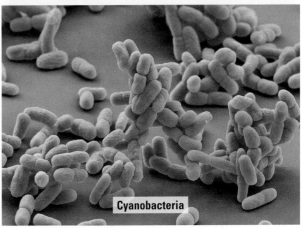
Cyanobacteria

2. Producers Use Photosynthesis

You may have noticed a lot of green in the photographs in this lesson. That is because this lesson is about producers, and most producers are green. What does the color green have to do with capturing energy to make food?

Photosynthesis Takes Place in Chloroplasts In almost all ecosystems on Earth, producers capture energy from sunlight and use it to produce food through photosynthesis. **Photosynthesis** is the process of using energy from the sun and matter from the surroundings to produce sugars that store energy in chemical bonds. In most producers, such as the plant shown in Figure 4.2A, this process happens in chloroplasts. **Chloroplasts** are cell structures that use the sun's energy to make sugar through the process of photosynthesis. The middle panel of Figure 4.2A shows the cells of a plant leaf. Each cell contains many chloroplasts, shown in the right hand panel of the figure. One striking characteristic of chloroplasts is that they are green.

Chlorophyll Absorbs Energy from Light The green color of a chloroplast comes from a molecule that absorbs energy from sunlight. The molecule, **chlorophyll,** is a green pigment that is essential for photosynthesis. Chlorophyll absorbs energy when light shines on it. Like other pigments, chlorophyll absorbs only certain colors of light. It reflects any colors of light that it does not absorb. One color of light that chlorophyll does not absorb is green light. When you study waves and light, you learn that the light reflecting off an object is what allows you to see it. That is why green plants look green. Their leaves are made up of cells that have many chloroplasts. Chloroplasts contain chlorophyll, and chlorophyll reflects mostly green light. Thus, plants appear green in color.

Figure 4.2A

Producers have structures that function to capture energy and matter through the process of photosynthesis. Chlorophyll is an energy-absorbing molecule found in chloroplasts. Chloroplasts are found in leaf cells. Leaf cells make up the leaves of producers, like this plant.

Photosynthesis in Chloroplasts

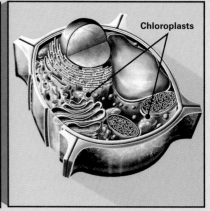

Producer

Producer cells

Chloroplasts in cells

Producers Get Matter from Air and Water Producers also need matter, which they get from their surroundings. Photosynthesis requires water, which many plants absorb through their roots. It also requires carbon dioxide, a gas found in air. Aquatic plants use carbon dioxide dissolved in water. With carbon dioxide, water, and sunlight, producers have everything they need for photosynthesis.

Light Causes a Chemical Reaction The process of photosynthesis begins when chlorophyll absorbs the energy of sunlight. This input of energy causes a chemical reaction to occur in the chloroplast. Chlorophyll can transfer the sun's energy to the bonds of molecules of sugar through a chemical reaction.

In photosynthesis, energy is captured from sunlight and is used to produce sugar molecules from water and carbon dioxide. The chemical equation representing this process is:

carbon dioxide + water + energy → sugar + oxygen

The equation in Figure 4.2B is a model that describes the reaction as a chemical formula. Chemical formulas have reactants, or the molecules used in the reaction on the left side. Products, the molecules produced in the reaction, appear on the right side. The reactants in this chemical equation are carbon dioxide (CO_2) and water (H_2O), and the products are sugar ($C_6H_{12}O_6$) and oxygen (O_2). Notice how energy is placed on the left side of the arrow. That is because this chemical reaction requires an input of energy, which is then transferred to the molecules of the products. The chemical bonds that hold together the atoms in the sugar molecule store that energy. Notice that in Figure 4.2B the reaction is balanced on each side. Because sugar has six carbon atoms in it ($C_6H_{12}O_6$), the reaction requires six carbon dioxide molecules on the reactant side. Review the reaction. Are all of the atoms balanced on each side?

Figure 4.2B

Photosynthesis is a chemical reaction that captures energy from the sun to convert carbon dioxide and water into sugars and oxygen. The energy from sunlight is stored in the chemical bonds of the sugar molecule.

The Chemical Equation for Photosynthesis

carbon dioxide + water + energy ⟶ sugar + oxygen

$$6CO_2 + 6H_2O + energy \longrightarrow C_6H_{12}O_6 + 6O_2$$

Matter and Energy in Photosynthesis

Photosynthesis is a process that producers use to transfer energy from the sun to stored chemical bonds of sugar. The sun's energy is captured by chlorophyll pigments in the chloroplasts of plants and other producers. Photosynthesis uses the matter in carbon dioxide and water and transforms it into matter in sugars and oxygen. Photosynthesis stores the energy from sunlight in the chemical bonds in sugars.

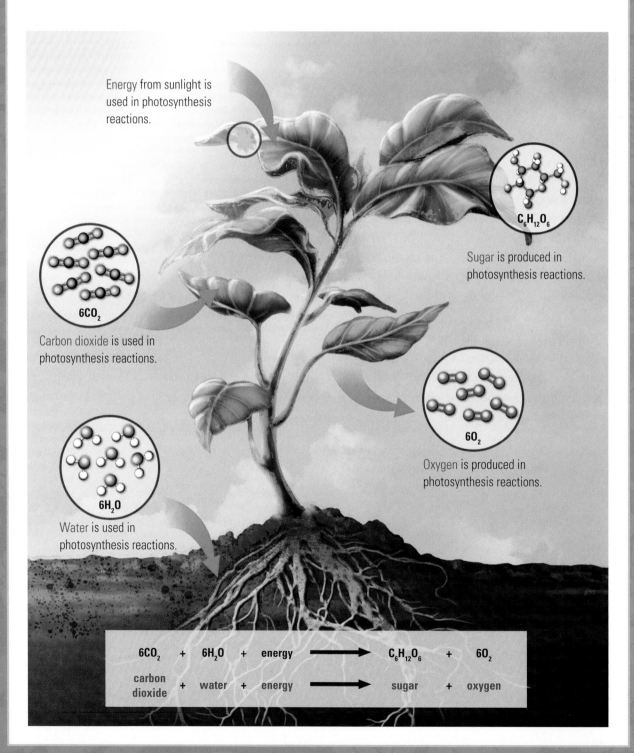

Energy from sunlight is used in photosynthesis reactions.

$6CO_2$

Carbon dioxide is used in photosynthesis reactions.

$6H_2O$

Water is used in photosynthesis reactions.

$C_6H_{12}O_6$

Sugar is produced in photosynthesis reactions.

$6O_2$

Oxygen is produced in photosynthesis reactions.

$$6CO_2 + 6H_2O + energy \longrightarrow C_6H_{12}O_6 + 6O_2$$

carbon dioxide + water + energy $\longrightarrow$ sugar + oxygen

3. Discovering Photosynthesis

A giant sequoia tree makes you wonder, where did it get the matter to grow so big? Scientists have conducted experiments to answer similar questions since the 1600s.

Scientists use evidence from experiments to explain how producers obtain matter through photosynthesis. These experiments are designed to test a question and to gather evidence to answer that question. In the late 1700s, a Dutch scientist named Jan Ingenhousz asked the question: how do plants use or produce gases? At that time, scientists knew that plants produced something in air that was important for the survival of animals—a gas later discovered to be oxygen. Ingenhousz placed plants under light and dark conditions, as shown in Figure 4.3. He also collected and analyzed the bubbles of gases they produced under light conditions. Ingenhousz observed that the green parts of plants produce oxygen only when exposed to light. In the dark, the plants do not produce oxygen. The evidence showed that when plants are exposed to light, they produce oxygen.

In the early 1800s, a Swiss scientist named Nicolas-Théodore de Saussure asked where plants get the majority of their mass. He sealed plants in jars so that he could keep track of the mass of carbon dioxide gas used by the plant. The evidence he collected showed that plants get about 70 percent of their matter from carbon dioxide. Most of the rest of a plant's matter comes from water.

Ingenhousz and Saussure made these discoveries based on evidence from experiments they performed years ago, but their work remains relevant today. Other scientists have since built on these basic explanations about where producers get matter. The result is that scientists now know many of the details of how photosynthesis works and how plants get matter.

Figure 4.3

In the 1770s, Ingenhousz became curious about how plants create and use different gases. He conducted experiments in his home with little more than glass jars and potted plants to use. Ingenhousz placed plants under glass jars in light and dark conditions and studied the resulting gases they produced.

Ingenhousz's Photosynthesis Experiment

In sunlight, plants produce oxygen bubbles and reduce carbon dioxide.

In the dark, plants produce carbon dioxide and no oxygen bubbles are formed.

4. Storing Energy and Matter

It would be inconvenient to have to go to the store every time you are hungry. One solution is to buy more food than you need right away and store the extra food in the refrigerator or cupboard. How do producers solve this problem?

Some of the matter and energy a producer captures during photosynthesis gets stored. Carrot and beet plants produce sugars through photosynthesis in their leaves and then store some in their roots for later use.

Stored Energy and Matter in Organisms Producers use some of the matter and energy they capture during photosynthesis right away to support life processes. Cells carry out chemical reactions that release the energy stored in the bonds of sugar molecules and use that energy to survive, grow, and reproduce. For cells, these sugar molecules are like gasoline for a car. Cells need them in order to work.

The sugars that producers make during photosynthesis are more than just a source of energy. They are also the building blocks of the producer's body. Producers combine sugar molecules into more complex molecules, such as starch or cellulose. **Cellulose** is the material that forms the rigid walls and support for plant cells. If you compare the molecular models of the sugar and cellulose in Figure 4.4, you can see that cellulose looks like many sugar molecules bound together. That is because producers use sugar molecules as the building blocks for producing cellulose.

Producers store some of the matter and energy they capture for use later. Some matter and energy is stored in the matter and chemical bonds of sugars and some is stored in the form of more complex molecules. Sometimes a producer needs to grow or work even when there is not enough light to carry out photosynthesis. Stored food can support that growth. Root vegetables, such as beets and carrots, taste sweet because their thick roots store sugars and starches, which are more complex sugar molecules, for the plant to use later. Fruits, nuts, and seeds store sugars that support the growth of a sprouting plant before it has developed leaves that can carry out photosynthesis.

Figure 4.4

Sugars are the building blocks of more complex molecules that producers use to build their body parts. Simple sugar molecules are combined through chemical reactions to produce more complex molecules, such as starch or cellulose. Cellulose makes up the bulk of plant bodies.

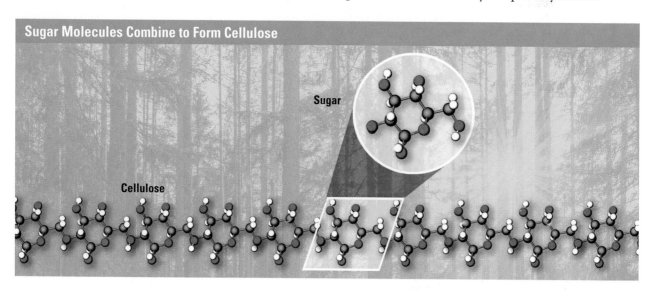

Sugar Molecules Combine to Form Cellulose

Sugar

Cellulose

When you eat plants, whether it is a carrot or a piece of bread made with wheat seeds, you are using the energy stored by the producer as your source of energy. Although producers form sugar through photosynthesis, they often store energy in different forms, such as more complex starch molecules. Healthy plant foods are usually a combination of sugars and more complex storage molecules.

Stored Energy and Matter in Ecosystems In addition to producers, other kinds of organisms benefit from photosynthesis. All other organisms get their energy ultimately from the energy stored by producers through photosynthesis, either by eating producers or by eating other organisms that eat producers. That is how photosynthesis provides the energy to make all of the living matter in ecosystems on Earth. How has this changed Earth's ecosystems?

Most biomass on the planet is that of producers. You can see evidence of photosynthesis on Earth from space. The green parts of land get their color from the chlorophyll in the cells of producers.

When scientists talk about living matter, they use the term *biomass*. **Biomass** is the combined mass of the bodies of organisms, which collectively represents stored energy. Producers create biomass through photosynthesis. They capture matter and energy from nonliving sources and transform it into sugar molecules and more complex molecules based on sugar, such as starch and cellulose. When an organism eats a producer, it uses the matter and energy stored in the producers and turns it into the matter and energy of that organism.

Earth has been transformed by photosynthesis. The planet's terrestrial surfaces are green because of chlorophyll in land plants, and the surfaces of its oceans are rich in phytoplankton. Without photosynthesis, Earth's land would likely be rocky, brown, and gray. There would not be oxygen in the atmosphere at the concentrations seen today without producers releasing oxygen as a product of photosynthesis over billions of years. Ultimately, photosynthesis is the origin of the vast majority of biomass on the planet. Without photosynthesis, the living parts of Earth's ecosystems would have no way of accessing matter or energy. Without photosynthesis, there would not be life on Earth as we know it!

5. Biomass Is a Source of Energy for Humans

If you want to travel someplace far away quickly, your best bet is to take a jet airplane. Jet engines get energy by burning fuel. But not all fuels generate the same amount of energy or have the same impact on Earth's ecosystems. How can engineers choose a jet fuel that has enough energy but also has the lowest possible impact on Earth?

Choosing a Fuel for Jets When engineers evaluate jet fuel, they must consider the criteria and constraints of getting a massive jet off the ground. Flight requires a lot of energy, so jet fuel must store lots of energy in its chemical bonds. But fuel has mass, too, and jets that are higher in mass will require more energy to fuel them. The best jet fuel must store as much energy as possible in the lowest possible mass. Jet fuels that meet these criteria are said to be efficient.

Fossil Fuels as Jet Fuel For decades, engineers have used fossil-fuel products as jet fuel. These fuels met the original criterion of being efficient. In the 2000s, some airline engineers redefined the problem. They added the constraint that jet fuels should be from renewable resources. But fossil fuels are not renewable resources. Renewable resources are ones that will not be used up if they are used at a low enough rate. Airlines are collaborating to look for alternative renewable sources of jet fuels.

Biomass as Jet Fuel Engineers are developing biofuels as an alternative to jet fuels. A **biofuel** is a material that is made from biomass and releases energy when it is burned. Manufacturers make biofuels by taking plant biomass, such as cellulose, and using chemical reactions to break it down into sugars again. They use those sugars to create alcohol that is used as fuel. Biofuels meet the criteria of the engineering solution because they store enough energy to fuel flight. But do biofuels satisfy the constraint as well? Can biofuels supply enough renewable energy to the jet industry?

Biofuels, which are produced from biomass, are renewable alternatives to jet fuels and other fossil-fueled products. Large production facilities like this one use biomass, such as urban wastes and crops, to generate biofuels that can be used as a source of fuel in many kinds of engines.

Constraints Help Identify the Best Source of Biomass To evaluate whether biomass supplies enough renewable energy to manufacture biofuels for jets, engineers look at the cost and environmental impact of biomass sources. The resource used to produce jet fuel has to be renewable within a reasonable time frame. It would not make sense to make biofuel from trees, unless trees could be planted and grown fast enough to replace them. The source of biomass must also be affordable. Energy crops that displace food crops can compete with other industries and drive up prices.

Engineers used these criteria and constraints to decide on a strategy for supplying jet fuel to the airplane industry. Engineers discovered that a high energy, renewable source of biofuel is derived from urban wastes. Grass cuttings, food scraps, cardboard, and wood scraps all come from producers and are a ready source of cellulose. There is a constant supply of this valuable trash in large cities. Like fossil fuels, biofuels made from urban wastes generate carbon dioxide when they are burned. However, they come from a renewable resource and they recycle materials that might otherwise enter a landfill. Biofuels address the needs of the airline industry by providing a low-cost and renewable source of fuel that also stores enough energy to power flight when it is burned in a jet engine.

Jets are not the only vehicles that can use biofuels produced from sustainable resources. It is not uncommon for gas stations to offer biofuels as an alternative to gasoline for cars.

LESSON SUMMARY

Capturing the Sun's Energy

Producers Capture Energy and Matter Producers, such as plants and single-celled organisms, make their own food.

Producers Use Photosynthesis Producers use the energy from sunlight, along with the matter in carbon dioxide and water, to create sugar molecules that store energy in chemical bonds.

Discovering Photosynthesis Scientists use experiments to discover how producers obtain matter through photosynthesis.

Storing Energy and Matter Producers store some of the matter and energy they capture in the form of sugars, starches, and cellulose. Biomass is the energy and matter stored in living things on Earth.

Biomass is a Source of Energy for Humans Engineers have discovered that a renewable source of fuels for jet engines is biofuel derived from urban wastes and crops, a source of biomass.

Ancient Energy from the Sun

POP! A piece of warm toast springs from your toaster. Toasting bread requires energy. Where does the energy come from? Would you believe that it came from sunlight that struck Earth more than 300 million years ago?

Most fossil fuels originated from the Carboniferous Period, a unique period in Earth's history when giant swamp forests dominated the land.

What happens when the battery in your mobile device needs charging? A warning appears on the screen—Battery Low. Your phone needs energy! As you plug it into a nearby electrical outlet, the screen glows. Without energy, your phone would not run.

It is not just phones that run on energy. Your family relies on energy to heat your home, power the vehicles you ride in, and cook your dinner. But do you know where this energy comes from? Sure, it comes from electrical outlets, a fuel pump, or the burners of the stove! But where did it come from . . . *originally?*

Like nearly all energy on Earth, it came from sunlight. But not the sunlight shining today. Instead, most of the energy we use today came from sunlight that shined during the Carboniferous Period, millions of years ago in Earth's history. That energy was trapped by producers and stored in the bodies of plants and animals. Over time, these organisms became the fossil fuels we use today for energy.

What is a fossil fuel? A fossil is the ancient remains of dead plants or animals. And fuel is a source of energy. So, fossil fuels are energy sources that come from the remains of plants and animals that lived and died long ago.

How Fossil Fuels Formed

The story of how fossil fuels formed begins more than 300 million years ago, during the Carboniferous Period. During this time, most places on Earth were hot, humid, and swampy. In this moist environment, plants and other producers thrived. Giant tree ferns, horsetail plants, primitive conifers, and other plants formed dense forests. Microorganisms, such as single-celled phytoplankton, were also abundant, especially in the oceans. These ancient producers converted the energy in sunlight into sugar, which they stored in their tissues. In this way, large quantities of the energy in sunlight that struck Earth during this period was converted to biomass.

Many animal species also flourished during this time. Giant flying insects, including dragonflies with foot-long wings, roamed the skies. Spiders and scorpions hunted for prey in the vegetation. Amphibians the size of crocodiles and primitive reptiles pursued prey in the swamps. When these animals ate plants, energy in the plant's tissues was transferred to them. This energy was stored in their bodies as biomass.

When these organisms died, many of them ended up at the bottom of swamps, lakes, or oceans, where they slowly decomposed. Over millions of years, thick layers of biomass formed. As the layers grew, so did their collective weight. Upper layers pressed down on the lower layers, concentrating the remains. At the same time, heat from within Earth's core "cooked" these layers of biomass. Over hundreds of millions of years, pressure and heat changed the biomass into the fossil fuels we use today, including oil, coal, and natural gas.

The energy contained in fossil fuels came from ancient producers. Ancient trees, related to these modern-day horsetail plants, lived during the Carboniferous Period and formed large quantities of plant biomass that ultimately became fossil fuels.

The formation of coal takes millions of years. Ancient biomass becomes trapped, and then changes form from pressure, heat, and lack of oxygen. Coal is eventually removed, via mining, so that people can use the ancient energy stored in it.

Carboniferous swamp with plants and animals, 300 milion years ago

Swamp plants decay under layers of sediment, 10 million years ago

Coal, the remnants of ancient plants and animals, is mined for fuel today

A layer of coal, or coal seam, is exposed between layers of rock.

Large machinery is used to excavate coal in strip mining.

Coal is crushed into powder and burned in coal-burning power plants.

The energy generated in a power plant travels to your home through electrical power lines.

How We Use Fossil Fuels

Fossil fuels are made up of molecules that contain lots of the element carbon. Let us trace the path of a carbon-rich molecule as it moves from the body of an ancient organism to a modern-day power plant, where it will be used to generate electricity.

Energy in sunlight is captured by an ancient horsetail plant and converted into sugar, which is a carbon-based molecule. The horsetail plant dies, falling to the bottom of a swamp. Soil and other dead horsetail plants fall on top of it. Over millions of years, the carbon-based molecules from horse-tail plants become buried deep in Earth's crust. These molecules are then surrounded by countless numbers of other carbon-based molecules that form a visible seam—or line—of coal underground.

Geologists use maps, along with aerial and satellite images, to create computer models that show where coal seams are located. Once a seam is found, mining begins. In strip-mining, excavators are used to remove layers of soil and rock from Earth's surface. The carbon-rich molecules in coal are scooped up and loaded into a train car that will transport it to an electrical power plant.

Once at the power plant, a machine grinds each chunk of coal into coal powder. The coal powder is sent to the furnace. As this carbon-rich molecule is burned, it releases energy, which is used to boil water. Steam from the boiling water spins a turbine, and a generator converts energy from the spinning turbine into an electric current.

Power lines carry the electric current from the power plant to our homes, where it is used to run devices and even charge batteries!

We use coal to provide electricity for our homes. Coal is located in layers of sediment, removed from the earth, and burned to generate electricity at some power plants. The electricity created is transported to the outlets in your home through a network of power lines.

Skipping the Fossils

As a society, we rely heavily on fossil fuels for our energy needs. But the burning of fossil fuels creates environmental problems and scientists find that fossil fuels are causing changes in Earth's climate. In addition, fossil fuels are a nonrenewable resource. That means they cannot be replaced once they are used up. Unfortunately, human demand for energy continues to grow.

You might ask, why not just go straight to the source and make use of sunlight directly? Can we skip the fossils and harness the sun?

To some extent, we already do. You may have seen solar panels on some of the roofs in your neighborhood. Much like plants, solar panels harvest the energy in sunlight and convert it to a different form of energy—in this case, electricity. Unlike fossil fuels, solar energy is both renewable and clean. Some challenges to using solar energy today are the cost of solar panels and the fact that technologies used to store solar-generated electricity for later use are not yet advanced enough to keep up with human demand for energy.

Humans have relied on fossil fuels for hundreds of years. But the future of energy production may involve leaving fossil fuels in the ground and using more solar energy and other renewable sources. ◆

Solar power allows people to harvest energy directly from the sun instead of relying on fossil fuels. These solar panels on the roof of a building collect the sun's energy and convert it into electricity.

Using Stored Energy

How do organisms use energy and matter?

Introduction

The acorn this squirrel has found to eat is the seed of an oak tree. The tree stored matter and energy in the acorn so that it could produce an offspring: a new tree. But instead of becoming a new tree, the acorn became food for the squirrel. The squirrel will use the matter and energy stored in this food to survive, grow, and reproduce. How does the squirrel get energy from the acorn? How does it build body structures out of the matter found in its food?

You learned in the last lesson that, through photosynthesis, producers capture the sun's energy to transform carbon dioxide and water into sugars and oxygen. The matter and energy that is stored as sugars and other molecules in the bodies of producers is then used by the organisms that eat them as their source of matter and energy. The matter and energy that was captured by a producer, such as an oak tree, does not just disappear when a predator, such as a squirrel, eats an acorn. That matter and energy stored in the acorn is conserved. Some of it becomes the matter and energy of the squirrel.

In this lesson, you will use models to explore how all organisms—producers like the oak tree and predators like squirrels—carry out a chemical reaction called cellular respiration. This reaction allows living things to use the energy stored in the chemical bonds of sugars. You will then learn how your body breaks down food to get sugars for energy and other molecules that are used as building blocks required for the growth and repair of your body. Finally, you will compare photosynthesis and cellular respiration—two processes that form the basis for how matter and energy flow through ecosystems.

Vocabulary

consumer an organism that gets energy and matter by eating or absorbing other organisms as food

cellular respiration the process that cells use to release the energy stored in sugars

mitochondria structures in cells that convert energy in sugar molecules into usable energy

carbohydrate a molecule used to store energy

fat a molecule that is used to store energy in the form of oils and is important in forming cells

protein a type of molecule that makes up much of an organism's structure and helps it function

---

Next Generation Science Standards

Performance Expectations

MS.LS1-7. Develop a model to describe how food is rearranged through chemical reactions forming new molecules that support growth and/or release energy as this matter moves through an organism.

Science and Engineering Practices

Developing and Using Models Develop a model to describe unobservable mechanisms.

Crosscutting Concepts

Energy and Matter Matter is conserved because atoms are conserved in physical and chemical processes.

Disciplinary Core Ideas

LS1.C. Within individual organisms, food moves through a series of chemical reactions in which it is broken down and rearranged to form new molecules, to support growth, or to release energy.

PS3.D. Cellular respiration in plants and animals involves chemical reactions with oxygen that release stored energy. In these processes, complex molecules containing carbon react with oxygen to produce carbon dioxide and other materials.

Consumers cannot produce their own food. Instead they get their food by eating other organisms. These dolphins are consumers that live in aquatic ecosystems and eat mostly fish.

1. Consumers

What if you could take a nap in the sun to get energy instead of shopping for and preparing three meals a day? While many kinds of organisms can use photosynthesis to produce their own food, you cannot, and neither can a dolphin. However, all organisms, including humans and dolphins, need matter and energy to live, grow, and reproduce. How do organisms that cannot use sunlight to capture energy get the energy needed for life?

Organisms that cannot produce their own food using photosynthesis are consumers. A **consumer** is an organism that gets matter and energy by eating or absorbing other organisms as food. All predators—whether they are herbivores, carnivores, or omnivores—are consumers. Some consumers eat producers, while others eat other consumers. A dolphin, for example, is a consumer, and so is a single-celled amoeba, like the one shown in the photograph. Dolphins consume fish and other aquatic animals. Amoebas consume smaller unicellular organisms.

Whether they are producers or consumers, all organisms use the energy stored in food as fuel to support everyday activities as well as growth and reproduction. Producers use the sugars they produce to get energy right away, or they store them for later use. After consuming food, consumers can use the energy they get from the sugars in the food right away, or they can store it.

The same is true of the matter that both producers and consumers get from food. Producers use the matter in the food molecules that they produce during photosynthesis to build and maintain their bodies, to grow, and to reproduce. When consumers eat producers, they take in the matter that makes up the bodies of those producers. Matter that made up the bodies of producers is then used to form the cells and body structures of the consumers that eat them. Any time a predator eats a prey organism, it is using that matter as a source of matter for its own body.

This amoeba is a consumer. Amoebas are unicellular organisms that eat other unicellular organisms. They extend a part of the cell around another cell and completely engulf it. They then use the matter and energy of that cell.

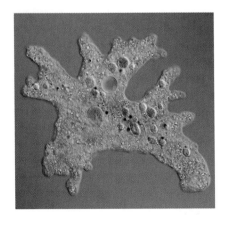

2. Sources of Matter and Energy

A tree produces its own food. A squirrel consumes food produced by the tree. Both kinds of organisms—producers and consumers—use food as a source of matter and energy. But do they use food in the same way? And how are other sources of matter and energy involved?

Once an organism has obtained food, it can use it for different purposes. It can use food for energy, for growth (adding matter to the organism's body), or for reproduction (making another organism). Each process happens through chemical reactions that involve matter and energy.

The table in Figure 5.2 is one way to model and compare the sources of matter and energy that are required to carry out those reactions. Notice that the exact source of matter and energy is different for producers and consumers.

Sources of Energy Producers and consumers get energy their cells need from sugar molecules. While producers capture energy from sunlight, they cannot use that energy directly to carry out cell processes. For the captured energy to be useful to the cells of a producer, it must first be stored in the chemical bonds of sugar molecules. The stored energy in sugars can then be used by both plants and animals. Consumers must eat other organisms to get this useful energy.

Sources of Matter Producers and consumers get matter from their surroundings, but they differ in the source of the matter they use to grow and build cells. Producers get matter from carbon dioxide and water in their surroundings. They use these molecules to make sugars and build their bodies. Consumers breathe in air and take in water, but they do not use this matter to produce sugars or build cells, as producers do. To get matter to build their cells, consumers must eat other organisms and use the matter in those other organisms to build their cells.

Where Consumers and Producers Get Energy and Matter	Producers	Consumers
Capture energy from the sun to make sugars	✔	
Use sugars for energy	✔	✔
Obtain matter from the air, water, and soil	✔	
Obtain matter from eating other organisms		✔

Figure 5.2

Use the table to compare how producers and consumers get the matter and energy they need. Both types of organisms use sugars for energy and as a source of matter. Producers are able to make those sugars through photosynthesis. Consumers must get sugars by eating other organisms.

3. Cellular Respiration

Lunch is served! If you are a producer, you get your sugar molecule "lunch" by carrying out photosynthesis. As a consumer, you get sugar molecules by eating a producer or another consumer. The squirrel at the beginning of this lesson is getting sugar molecules from the acorn that it is eating. Once you consume this energy, your cells can use the energy stored in sugars to carry out all of your cellular activities. How do the cells of a producer get energy from the sugars it makes? And, how do the cells of a consumer get energy from the sugars it eats?

Both producers and consumers carry out a process called cellular respiration. **Cellular respiration** is the process that cells use to release energy stored in sugars. This process gives cells the energy they need to carry out chemical reactions important for life.

Figure 5.3A

Cellular respiration happens in the mitochondria of every cell in an organism's body, including both consumers and producers. The function of mitochondria is to provide energy that cells can use to carry out life processes.

The Site of Cellular Respiration Cellular respiration takes place in structures inside cells. **Mitochondria,** illustrated in Figure 5.3A, are structures in cells that convert energy in sugar molecules into energy that the cell can use. In multicellular organisms, every cell in the body has mitochondria to carry out cellular respiration. Most unicellular organisms, such as amoebas and diatoms, also have mitochondria that carry out cellular respiration.

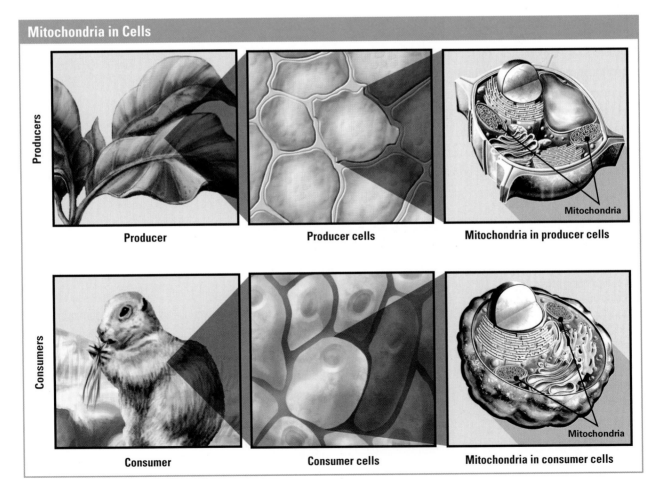

Mitochondria in Cells

Producers

Producer

Producer cells

Mitochondria in producer cells

Mitochondria

Consumers

Consumer

Consumer cells

Mitochondria in consumer cells

Mitochondria

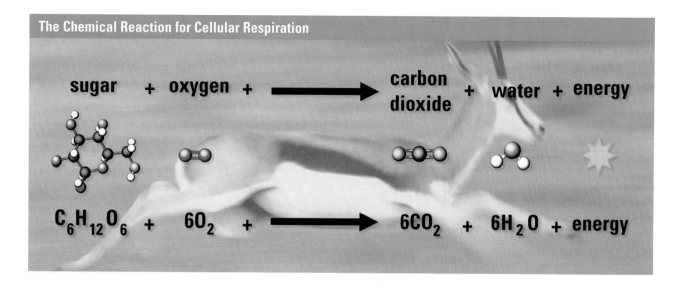

The Chemical Reaction for Cellular Respiration

sugar + oxygen + ⟶ carbon dioxide + water + energy

$C_6H_{12}O_6 + 6O_2 + ⟶ 6CO_2 + 6H_2O + energy$

The Process of Cellular Respiration Cellular respiration generates energy when molecules of sugar are broken apart and react with oxygen to produce carbon dioxide and water. This process releases the energy that was stored in the bonds of sugar molecules during photosynthesis. You cannot directly observe the changes in the molecules and energy in this reaction, but you can use a chemical equation to model the process and keep track of the reactants and products. The equation representing cellular respiration is:

sugar + oxygen → carbon dioxide + water + energy

You see in Figure 5.3B that the reactants are sugar ($C_6H_{12}O_6$) and oxygen (O_2). The products are carbon dioxide (CO_2) and water (H_2O). Energy is listed on the right side of the arrow, as a product. That is because energy stored in the bonds of the six-carbon sugar molecule is released as that molecule is broken down into six carbon dioxide molecules and six water molecules. The energy that was stored in the sugar molecule can then be used by cells for life processes.

Notice that the amount of matter on the reactant and on the product sides of the equation is the same. This is because atoms of matter are always conserved in chemical processes. Matter is not lost; it just changes form.

The Gases of Cellular Respiration Notice that the term *cellular respiration* includes a word used to describe breathing: respiration. Oxygen and carbon dioxide are the reactants and products of cellular respiration. When you breathe, you take in oxygen needed for cellular respiration and breathe out carbon dioxide gas.

Producers do not need to breathe in oxygen for cellular respiration. Recall that oxygen gas is one of the products of photosynthesis. Producers don't need lungs or gills because they already have the oxygen they need in their cells from photosynthesis.

Figure 5.3B

Cellular respiration is a chemical reaction where sugars break down into carbon dioxide and water, releasing energy. Because each molecule of sugar has six carbon atoms in it, there are six molecules of carbon dioxide that are produced when one molecule of sugar is broken down.

Matter and Energy in Cellular Respiration

Cellular respiration is the process by which cells release the energy stored in sugars and use that energy for survival, growth, and reproduction. Cellular respiration also uses the matter in sugars and oxygen and transforms it into the same amount of matter in carbon dioxide and water. This diagram illustrates the process of cellular respiration in both producers and consumers. The chemical reaction is shown in black below the diagram and a word equation is shown in blue.

Oxygen is used in cellular respiration reactions by producers and consumers.

$6O_2$

$6CO_2$

Carbon dioxide is produced by cellular respiration reactions in producers and consumers.

Energy is released by cellular respiration reactions in producers and consumers.

$C_6H_{12}O_2$

Sugar is used as a source of energy for both producers and consumers.

$6H_2O$

Water is produced by cellular respiration reactions in producers and consumers.

$$C_6H_{12}O_6 \ + \ 6O_2 \ \longrightarrow \ 6CO_2 \ + \ 6H_2O \ + \ energy$$

sugar + oxygen ⟶ carbon dioxide + water + energy

4. How You Get Energy and Matter

Your cells need sugars for energy, but you cannot survive eating a diet of sugars alone. You need a variety of foods to make up the variety of structures in your body. Eating plant foods, like fruits and vegetables, and perhaps animal foods, like fish and chicken, gives you the matter and energy you need to live and grow. How does that food build the different parts of your body?

When you chew your food, it is broken down into smaller particles. In your stomach it is then digested into smaller molecules. Those molecules travel through your bloodstream so that each cell of your body gets the molecules it needs to survive and grow.

Each of your cells uses the molecules it gets from food to carry out the chemical reactions that give you energy and help you grow. Some of the molecules in food are the same sugars that are reactants in cellular respiration reactions. These sugars are a source of energy for cells. Other chemical reactions combine small molecules to build different structures that make up your cell parts. Through these reactions, the matter in food is conserved as it gets transformed into the matter that makes up your body. Both kinds of reactions are essential for survival and growth.

One reason you eat food is to get sugars used to generate energy through chemical reactions like cellular respiration. Everything you do takes energy, whether you are asleep, awake, sitting still, or being active.

Carbohydrates Sugars, including the ones involved in photosynthesis and cellular respiration, are a type of food molecule called a carbohydrate. A **carbohydrate** is a molecule used to store energy. Sugars are called simple carbohydrates because they are made up of small numbers of atoms. Simple carbohydrates can also form building blocks of larger molecules called complex carbohydrates.

Simple carbohydrates can be combined through chemical reactions to build complex carbohydrates. Plants and other organisms combine sugars to make the complex carbohydrate cellulose. Another complex carbohydrate commonly found in plant foods, such as potatoes and corn, is starch. Your body—and the bodies of other animals—cannot carry out the chemical reactions that make cellulose. But you and other animals do make a complex carbohydrate called glycogen. Glycogen acts as a source of stored energy in your liver and muscles. If your body needs energy from sugar molecules, it can get that energy by breaking down complex carbohydrates, such as starch and glycogen. Through chemical reactions, these larger molecules get broken down into the simpler sugars they were originally made of.

Besides providing your body with energy, food also provides your body with the matter it needs to grow and build important structures. Food gives you the molecular building blocks for chemical reactions that make proteins, which allow your muscles to function, and the fats, which make healthy cell membranes.

Fats Fats are a second kind of food molecule. A **fat** is a molecule that is used to store energy in the form of oils. You can get fats from eating oily foods, such as avocados, nuts, olives, and fatty fish or meat. Through chemical reactions, your body uses fat molecules from foods to build its own fats. Fats in your body provide long-term energy storage and become part of healthy cells and body structures. They also allow your body to build essential chemical messengers that relay signals from cell to cell.

Proteins A third kind of food molecule is proteins. **Proteins** are a type of molecule that makes up much of an organism's structure and helps it function. Foods that are high in proteins include beans, nuts, eggs, fish, and meats. Your body breaks down the proteins it gets from foods. Then it uses the resulting products to build its own proteins through reactions that build larger molecules from smaller molecules. In the body, proteins make up a wide variety of structures. They help build muscles, move molecules into and out of cells, and carry out reactions.

5. Comparing Photosynthesis and Cellular Respiration

Your body has used up energy just learning about photosynthesis and cellular respiration! Before eating a snack to refresh your energy supply, think about how the two processes are alike. Both processes involve storing or releasing energy and both can be modeled by chemical equations. How else do these two processes compare?

When you compare the equations for photosynthesis and cellular respiration, you notice a pattern.

Photosynthesis

carbon dioxide + water + energy → sugar + oxygen

Cellular respiration

sugar + oxygen → carbon dioxide + water + energy

The reactants of each chemical reaction are the products of the other. The amount and kind of matter that make up the molecules in each process is exactly the same. The carbon, oxygen, and hydrogen atoms on each side of the equations remain balanced, but they are rearranged to form different kinds of molecules. Only the energy has a different source for each equation. Photosynthesis captures energy from the sun to form sugars that store energy in chemical bonds. Cellular respiration releases the energy stored in the chemical bonds of sugars. Together, the equations for photosynthesis and cellular respiration show how energy and matter move through ecosystems.

LESSON SUMMARY

Using Stored Energy

Consumers Organisms that cannot produce their own food using photosynthesis are consumers. Consumers must eat or absorb other living things in order to obtain energy and matter.

Sources of Matter and Energy Both producers and consumers get energy that their cells need from the energy stored in sugar molecules. Producers and consumers get matter from different sources.

Cellular Respiration Producers and consumers carry out a process called cellular respiration. Cellular respiration is a chemical reaction that cells use to obtain energy stored in the chemical bonds of sugar.

How You Get Energy and Matter Each of your cells uses molecules from food to carry out the chemical reactions that give you energy.

Comparing Photosynthesis and Respiration Photosynthesis captures energy from the sun to form sugars that store energy in chemical bonds. Cellular respiration releases the energy stored in the chemical bonds of sugars.

Your Body in an Extreme Sport

It sounded like fun when you and a group of friends decided to try something new: a three-mile muddy obstacle race known as a mud run. You trained together for months. As you stand at the starting line with your friends, you begin to have second thoughts: "What have I gotten myself into? Can my body handle the challenge?"

An extreme sport, like this mud run, is one that takes physical endurance and confidence in yourself. These athletes rely on their careful training and on support from one another to make it through the grueling race.

A mud run is one example of an "extreme sport," one that pushes your body close to its physical limits. Extreme sports are lots of fun—but they also require careful preparation. Extreme athletes train for months and pay special attention to their nutrition and rest to make sure they are ready. They also rely on the support of their teammates throughout training and especially on race day.

Three months ago, your friends asked you to run with them in a muddy obstacle race. How did you prepare for this event?

To exercise and be fit, eating healthy and drinking plenty of water is important. Proper training allows your body to use the energy you get from food efficiently.

Preparing Your Body

Physical training and eating right have been your top two priorities for the past three months as you prepared for the mud run. But are you confident that your efforts will get you to the finish line?

Training Your Body Preparing to run an obstacle race over rugged terrain requires endurance training and high-intensity workouts. Endurance training helps you stay strong during the long race. For training, you have been running three easy runs a week with gradual distance increases every two weeks. These workouts increase your lung capacity so that your blood can deliver more oxygen to your muscles. These easy runs also mean your cells make more mitochondria, the structures inside cells that produce the energy your muscles need during the race.

High-intensity workouts allow you to test your physical limits for short periods of time. You might do push-ups or lift weights to increase the strength of your muscles, tendons, and bones. Like endurance training, high-intensity workouts increase lung capacity and strength so that you can conquer the mud run's obstacles.

Fueling Your Body Just as many cars need gasoline to run, people need food to fuel their bodies. During training, you and your friends have had a well-balanced diet that includes complex carbohydrates, fats, and proteins. Complex carbohydrates provide your tissues with energy. Proteins provide the molecules you need to build and maintain muscles and other tissues. Fats provide energy and help keep your cells and tissues healthy. When you exercise, you also must keep your body well hydrated by drinking plenty of water.

Your cells can use oxygen to get lots of energy from sugars through cellular respiration. Or they can use sugar without oxygen to get smaller amounts of energy quickly. Both provide energy to help you get to the finish line in your extreme sport!

Conquering the Obstacle Course

Waiting at the starting line, your team looks over the obstacles and discusses how to work through them together. Confident your training has prepared your body to face this challenge, you smile with excitement as you hear the countdown—*3, 2, 1, GO!*

As you start running toward the first obstacle, your cells use the process of cellular respiration to produce lots of energy from the foods you have eaten earlier and the oxygen you breathe. The race has just begun and your body is able to take in plenty of oxygen to keep up with the increase in energy demand.

As you tackle your next obstacle—an army crawl through mud under a log structure—your body begins to demand more energy. Your breathing becomes heavier as your body tries to deliver more oxygen to your cells, but your breathing cannot keep up with the need for oxygen. At this point, your cells cannot use cellular respiration to get energy because it requires oxygen as a reactant. How do your cells get energy from sugar without oxygen?

For short periods of time, your cells can use a different kind of reaction to get energy from sugar. This reaction does not require oxygen, but it also does not give your cells as much energy, so it is only a temporary solution. But this temporary solution can help get you through the remaining obstacles and across the finish line!

Crossing the Finish Line

At last! You cross the finish line and collapse in a heap with your friends. Your body has cuts from crawling through long tunnels and bruises from climbing over high walls. But you are happy. Now it is time to celebrate with your friends and plan your recovery.

For immediate recovery, you go to an aid table and grab a cup of water to replace fluids you lost through sweating. You help yourself to two slices of pizza and a banana to replenish the fuel your body has used during the race. You pick up a bag of ice to place on and soothe your sore, aching muscles. Finally, you can sit down with your friends to celebrate.

The remainder of your day will focus on refueling, tending sore muscles, and getting plenty of rest. You stand up, put your arms over your head and complete a full body stretch, which decreases tension and pain in your muscles. After refueling at a local restaurant, you head home for a nice long nap.

You did it! After months of training and eating well with your good friends, you completed a challenging obstacle mud run together. Now that you have pushed your body to its limits, you know you can accomplish anything! ◆

After you have pushed your body to the extreme, you need to recover with good nutrition, rest, and support for your sore muscles. In the meantime, you can celebrate with your friends!

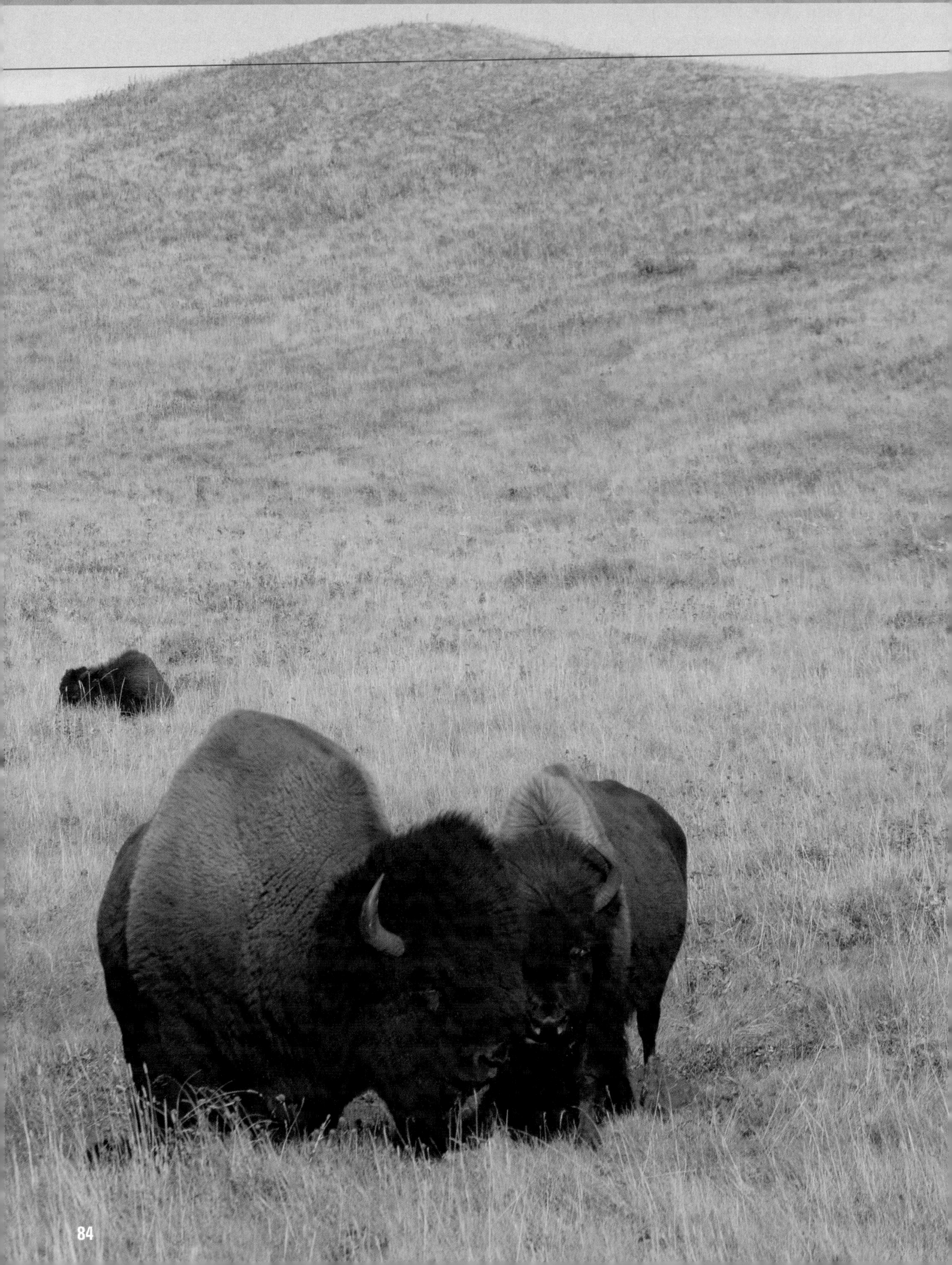

Food Webs and Trophic Pyramids

Vocabulary

food web a model that shows feeding relationships between organisms in an ecosystem

food chain an individual path in a food web

direct effect an interaction in a food web where one population directly affects the abundance of another

indirect effect an interaction in a food web where one population affects the abundance of another through its effect on a third population

decomposer a kind of consumer that uses the wastes or dead remains of other organisms as a source of energy and matter

trophic pyramid a model that shows how much energy is transferred from one stage to the next in a food chain

---

How do energy and matter move through ecosystems?

Introduction

Weighing 500 kilograms or more, American bison are among the largest land mammals in North America. Bison are herbivores and spend much of their time grazing on prairie grasses. An adult American bison can consume up to 8 kilograms of grass per day. That is roughly the size of 23 boxes of cereal! And yet the bison do not weigh 8 kilograms more at the end of each day. Why not? If bison eat 8 kilograms of food, why do they not gain 8 kilograms of mass? The answer lies in what happens to energy and matter as they are transferred from the grass to the bison.

In the last few lessons, you learned how producers use energy from the sun and raw materials from the environment to make sugars. You also looked at how organisms extract the energy and matter stored in sugars to fuel their metabolism and growth.

In this lesson, you will use models to track how energy and matter are transferred between organisms in an ecosystem. You will discover how energy and matter are recycled in ecosystems through organisms that consume the wastes or dead remains of other organisms. You will calculate how much phytoplankton energy goes into a tuna sandwich. Finally, you will see how scientists apply their understanding of feeding relationships to restore disrupted ecosystems.

Next Generation Science Standards

Performance Expectations

MS-LS2-3. Develop a model to describe the cycling of matter and flow of energy among living and nonliving parts of an ecosystem.

MS-ETS1-4. Develop a model to generate data for iterative testing and modification of a proposed object, tool, or process such that an optimal design can be achieved.

Science and Engineering Practices

Developing and Using Models • Develop a model to describe phenomena. • Develop a model to generate data to test ideas about designed systems, including those representing outputs and inputs.

Crosscutting Concepts

Energy and Matter The transfer of energy can be tracked as energy flows through a natural system.

Scientific Knowledge Assumes an Order and Consistency in Natural Systems

Disciplinary Core Ideas

LS2.B. Food webs are models that demonstrate how matter and energy is transferred between producers, consumers, and decomposers as the three groups interact within an ecosystem. Transfers of matter into and out of the physical environment occur at every level. Decomposers recycle nutrients from dead plant or animal matter back to the soil in terrestrial environments or to the water in aquatic environments. The atoms that make up the organisms in an ecosystem are cycled repeatedly between the living and nonliving parts of the ecosystem.

ETS1.B. • A solution needs to be tested, and then modified on the basis of the test results, in order to improve it. • Models of all kinds are important for testing solutions.

ETS1.C. The iterative process of testing the most promising solutions and modifying what is proposed on the basis of the test results leads to greater refinement and ultimately to an optimal solution.

1. Food Webs

When coaches strategize to win a game, they might use arrows that show how players should move. Could you use a diagram with arrows to show how energy and matter move in ecosystems?

Scientists use diagrams as models to study complex systems. A **food web** is a model that shows feeding relationships between populations in an ecosystem. Food webs, like Figure 6.1A, use arrows to represent the transfer of energy and matter from one organism to another. An arrow points away from prey and toward the predator because, when a predator eats prey, the energy and matter from the prey becomes energy and matter for the predator. Food web models help scientists understand how energy and matter move among populations in ecosystems.

Some organisms have many arrows pointing toward them because they prey on many species. Organisms with multiple arrows pointing away from them are prey to many kinds of predators. Matter and energy can take more than one path in a food web. Each path is a **food chain**. To find a food chain, start with a producer and follow the arrows until you reach a top predator. Can you find a food chain that traces the transfer of energy and matter between grass and red-tailed hawks? Matter and energy in grass eventually becomes matter and energy in the red-tailed hawk.

Figure 6.1A

Scientists use food webs as models to analyze the roles organisms play in an ecosystem. Many organisms are prey to more than one species of predator. Matter and energy transferred through a food web can follow different arrows and take more than one path.

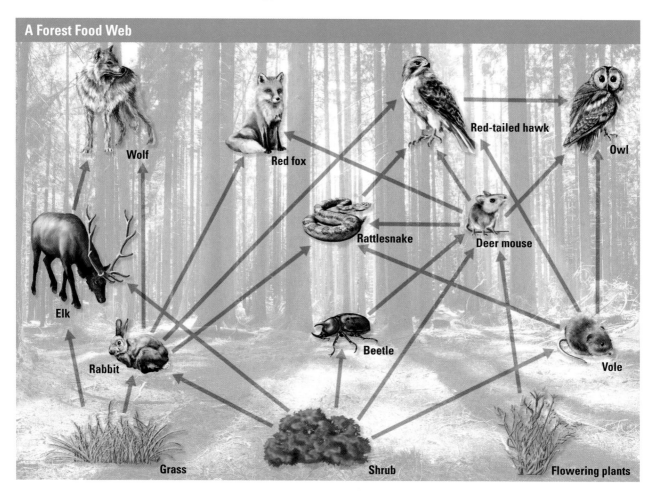

A Forest Food Web

Wolf · Red fox · Red-tailed hawk · Owl · Rattlesnake · Deer mouse · Elk · Rabbit · Beetle · Vole · Grass · Shrub · Flowering plants

A food chain tracks the transfer of matter and energy through a food web along a single path from prey to predators. An example food chain is shown in Figure 6.1B. Food chains always start with producers. No arrows point to producers because they get their energy and matter from their nonliving surroundings. Food chains end with top predators, such as the red-tailed hawk, because no other predators get matter and energy from hawks in this food web.

Food chains and food webs help scientists understand how populations affect one another. Rattlesnakes eat deer mice. When rattlesnakes eat deer mice, the deer mouse population decreases. This kind of interaction is a **direct effect,** an interaction in a food web where one population directly affects the abundance of another. The food web shows that a direct effect of an increase in rattlesnakes is a decrease in populations of their prey, deer mice.

Populations in a food web can also affect other populations in the food web, even if they don't interact directly. Rattlesnake populations can affect beetle populations even though rattlesnakes do not eat beetles. When rattlesnakes eat deer mice, there are fewer deer mice to eat beetles. This causes the population of beetles to increase. This kind of interaction is called an **indirect effect,** an interaction where one population affects the abundance of another through its effect on a third population.

Food webs illustrate that a change in one part of the ecosystem changes other parts through direct and indirect effects. What if the spread of a disease caused a decrease in the number of red-tailed hawks? The populations of mice, voles, and rabbits would increase as a direct effect. The populations of other predators of these prey, such as foxes, rattlesnakes, and owls, would increase as an indirect effect.

A Forest Food Chain

Red-tailed hawk

Energy and matter

Rattlesnake

Energy and matter

Deer mouse

Energy and matter

Beetle

Energy and matter

Trees

Figure 6.1B

A food chain shows the transfer of energy and matter from producers to consumers. In this food chain, the energy and matter from trees, the producers, are transferred to different consumers through feeding relationships. The matter and energy in trees find their way to red-tailed hawks.

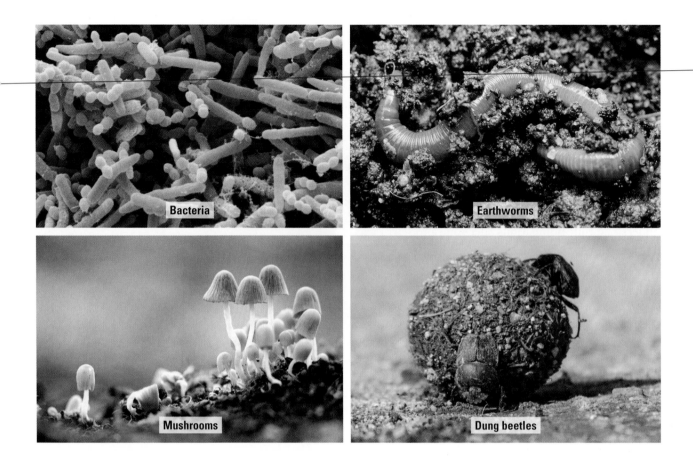

Bacteria

Earthworms

Mushrooms

Dung beetles

Decomposers consume once-living organisms or parts of organisms, including wastes. Bacteria, earthworms, mushrooms, and dung beetles all break down the remains of dead organisms or organism wastes.

2. Decomposers

Ewww, what is that smell? Something is rotting. Maybe it is an old peach covered in mold or a dead animal by the side of the road. Maybe it is a pile of wet leaves in the backyard. If you wait long enough, these decaying organisms or parts of organisms will eventually disappear. Where do they go? What happens to the bodies of organisms when they die?

Dead organisms are food for decomposers. A **decomposer** is a kind of consumer that uses the wastes or dead remains of other organisms as a source of energy and matter. Wastes include dung and parts of organisms that are shed naturally, such as skin cells, hair, or leaves. Decomposers get energy and matter from this food, just as other consumers do—through cellular respiration.

There are many different kinds of decomposers. Some decomposers are unicellular organisms, such as aquatic bacteria that break down dead organisms and release the molecules that made up the dead organisms back into the water. Other decomposers are multicellular, such as earthworms that feed on decaying matter in soil and dung beetles that collect and feed on the dung of herbivores. Other multicellular decomposers are fungi, such as mushrooms and molds. They consume the remains of other organisms by releasing molecules that break down the dead remains and then absorbing the resulting digested material.

How do decomposers fit into a food web? Because decomposers get their energy and matter from the wastes or dead remains of all kinds of organisms, decomposers get energy and matter from every part of a food web. Look at Figure 6.2. Arrows show how energy and matter is transferred from every organism in the food web to decomposers. For example, if the mouse avoids getting eaten by a predator, it instead dies of old age. Its matter and energy do not just disappear. They are transferred to decomposers that consume the remains of the dead mouse and use its matter and energy to fuel their life processes and build their cells and body parts.

What makes decomposers unique is that they can transform the matter they consume from the wastes and remains of organisms into the molecules that form the building blocks for other organisms. They are nature's recyclers. Decomposers make the molecules that were once part of the deer mouse's body available to a plant that is growing near where the deer mouse died. How does this happen?

When an organism dies, its body still stores matter and energy in the molecules that make up its cells. However, these materials are not useful to producers in the same way carbon dioxide and water are. Decomposers recycle these materials and release nutrients that are useful for producers and other organisms. Like all organisms, decomposers create waste products that include carbon dioxide and nitrogen-based molecules. Producers can use carbon dioxide for photosynthesis and the nitrogen-based molecules to build their body parts. Notice that in Figure 6.2 there are not arrows pointing from decomposers to producers. That is because producers do not get their matter and energy directly from decomposers by consuming them. Instead, they absorb the raw materials that decomposers produce from the environment.

Decomposers help complete cycles of matter in all ecosystems. Without decomposers to recycle remains and wastes, this matter would be locked away from other organisms forever. Only decomposers and non-biological processes, such as fire, release the useful nutrients in remains and wastes. And who recycles the matter stored in the remains of dead decomposers? Why, other decomposers, of course!

Figure 6.2

Arrows point from every organism in this food web to decomposers. This is because decomposers consume and break down the wastes and dead remains of all other organisms, releasing nutrients back into the ecosystem.

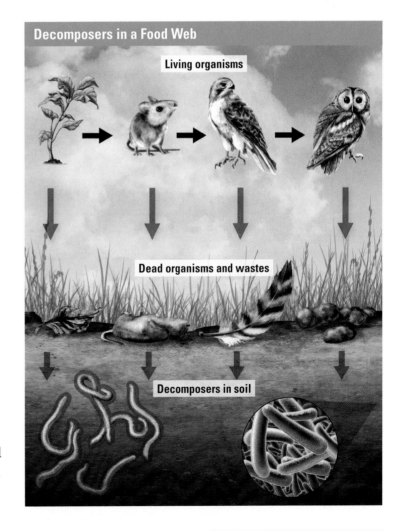

Decomposers in a Food Web

Living organisms

Dead organisms and wastes

Decomposers in soil

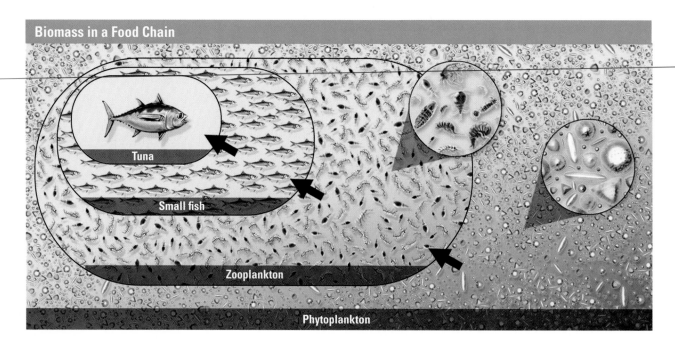

Biomass in a Food Chain

Tuna

Small fish

Zooplankton

Phytoplankton

Figure 6.3

Only a small fraction of the matter in phytoplankton producers eventually becomes matter that makes up a tuna, the top predator in this food chain. As organisms in the next level of the food chain consume the organisms below them, matter is lost. Arrows indicate matter moving between producer and consumer populations, as they do in food webs.

3. Biomass in Food Webs

When you make a tuna salad sandwich, you may use about 100 grams of tuna meat. Tuna are part of a food chain that starts with phytoplankton and goes through zooplankton and small fish. How many small fish did the tuna have to eat to make 100 grams of itself? How much zooplankton did the small fish have to eat?

To answer this question, scientists track the amount of matter transferred between populations in food webs. In doing so, they have observed a pattern. There is more matter, or biomass, in producers than in the first level of consumers. There is also more matter in each level of consumers than in the next level, and so on to the top of the food web. Where does matter go between levels of a food web?

To understand why matter is reduced at each level of a food chain, look at Figure 6.3. Each area represents the biomass of one level in a food chain. The biggest square, which contains the most biomass, is filled with phytoplankton, single-celled producers in aquatic ecosystems. Zooplankton are single-celled consumers that eat phytoplankton. Only a small portion of the phytoplankton biomass becomes zooplankton biomass. Large portions of the phytoplankton biomass is never eaten by zooplankton. Instead, it is consumed by decomposers, or it is not eaten by any other organism and stays in the ecosystem as biomass. Of the phytoplankton matter that is eaten by zooplankton, some is released as waste and some is transformed into carbon dioxide during cellular respiration.

This pattern of loss of biomass is repeated between every level of the food web. This is why the bison at the beginning of this lesson may eat 8 kilograms of grass in a day, but does not weigh 8 kilograms more at the end of the day!

4. Energy in Food Webs

Only a fraction of the matter in one level of a food web moves into the next level of a food web, but what happens to energy in food webs? How much of the energy in the phytoplankton population becomes energy in the zooplankton population or the tuna?

You could use a trophic pyramid to find out. A **trophic pyramid** is a model that shows how energy is transferred from one stage to the next in a food chain. Look at the trophic pyramid in Figure 6.4. Energy enters the food chain through phytoplankton, which store energy from the sun in the chemical bonds of sugar molecules. The phytoplankton use much of that energy to support their own metabolism. They lose some of that energy through wastes and as heat lost to the environment. As a result, only 10 percent of the energy in phytoplankton is available to zooplankton in the next trophic level. Zooplankton use this energy and also lose energy through wastes and heat.

Let us find out how much of the energy in phytoplankton makes it into a tuna. To find the amount of energy at each level in the trophic pyramid, calculate 10 percent of the energy in the level below it. You will find that 10,000 units of phytoplankton energy is needed to supply 10 units of tuna energy. That is a lot of energy lost as heat or lost to decomposers at every level of a trophic pyramid!

Figure 6.4

Each level in a trophic pyramid has only 10 percent of the energy of the level below it. At the producer level there are 10,000 energy units. Only 10 percent of that energy (or 1,000 energy units) is available to the next level, zooplankton. At the level of the top predator, the tuna, there is only 10 of the original 10,000 energy units.

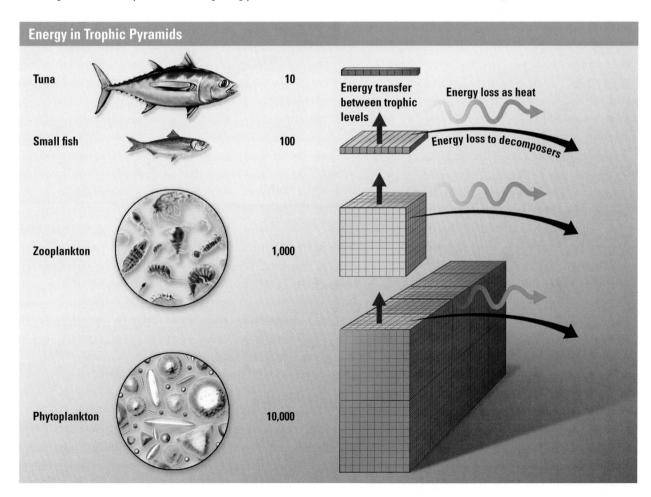

Energy in Trophic Pyramids

Tuna	10
Small fish	100
Zooplankton	1,000
Phytoplankton	10,000

Energy transfer between trophic levels

Energy loss as heat

Energy loss to decomposers

Biomass and Energy in Food Webs

Food webs are models of feeding relationships between populations of organisms in an ecosystem. In all food webs, energy and matter are transferred between living organisms through feeding relationships. Trophic pyramids show how energy cycles through an ecosystem by passing through producers, consumers, and decomposers. Energy and matter are lost as they move from producers through different stages of consumers. As a result, populations get smaller at each level. There are a lot more phytoplankton than hawks!

Producers capture energy from the sun and matter from molecules to form sugar. This forms the basis of all food webs.

Shrubs

Caterpillars

Energy is lost at every level of the trophic pyramid through loss to decomposers and heat.

Blue herons

Fish

Consumers get energy and matter by eating other organisms.

Matter is lost as it travels through food webs. As a result, there is less matter at higher trophic levels (red-tailed hawk) than lower trophic levels (deer mice).

Red-tailed hawk

Deer mice

Rattlesnake

Phytoplankton

Decomposers

Decomposers obtain energy and matter from every part of the food web.

Zooplankton

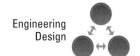

5. Using Trophic Pyramids to Restore an Ecosystem

For years, the city of Lahti in southern Finland dumped sewage waste directly into nearby Lake Vesijärvi. This sewage provided nutrients for algae, single-celled producers, that lived there. As a result, these producers grew out of control and began using up the oxygen in the water. Because the algae consumed it, the oxygen was not available for other aquatic organisms. Even after the dumping stopped in 1976, the algae still grew out of control. The water was cloudy from the algae, and locals could no longer find many fish in the lake. How did Finnish scientists use their understanding of how matter and energy flow through trophic pyramids to design a solution to this problem?

Removing a Predator To solve the problem of producers growing out of control, scientists designed and tested a possible solution. They knew that trophic pyramid models could be used to test the response of the ecosystem to changes in the food web. Zooplankton eat phytoplankton. If they could increase the number of zooplankton, it might decrease algae populations. To do this, they removed many of the second-stage consumers, the small fish, such as roach, that fed on zooplankton. They tested the results of this manipulation. While this solution did decrease populations of algae, it did not decrease it enough to return the lake to its previous, healthy condition. The solution would need to be modified further.

Patterns in the transfer of energy and matter through ecosystems can be used to manage ecosystems that are out of balance. This lake ecosystem provides an example of how scientists can use an understanding of trophic pyramids and food webs to solve problems associated with pollution in lake ecosystems.

Adding a Top Predator Scientists modified their solution. They increased populations of top predators in the ecosystem by stocking the lake with pike, a fish that eats other fish.

Scientists analyzed the effectiveness of the solution by collecting data. They performed tests to measure populations of algae and other species. In one test, they examined drops of lake water using a microscope. By counting the number of algae cells in a typical drop of lake water, they estimated the total population of algae in the lake.

The data showed that this modified solution was a success. The pike successfully reduced the population of second-stage consumers (smaller fish, such as roach), which then caused an increase in the population of first-stage consumers (zooplankton) and reduced the populations of producers (algae). Lake waters became clear again and fish populations grew plentiful enough for people to fish in the lake.

Assessing the Results With a trophic pyramid model of the Lake Vesijärvi ecosystem, scientists designed a solution to the problem of a large algae population. Scientists removed predators of zooplankton so that more zooplankton could eat the algae. They also added pike, a top predator, to increase zooplankton populations and reduce algae populations. Through testing and refining the solution, scientists restored balance to the lake ecosystem. Scientists continue to monitor populations to ensure that balance is maintained.

Scientists monitor the health of lake ecosystems by checking water quality and assessing the size of populations. This researcher is collecting data by weighing a fish.

LESSON SUMMARY

Food Webs and Trophic Pyramids

Food Webs A food web is a model of the many feeding relationships between populations in an ecosystem. Food webs are made up of many food chains.

Decomposers A decomposer is a special kind of consumer that get their energy and matter by consuming the wastes or remains of other organisms and recycles their nutrients.

Biomass in Food Webs Matter, or biomass, moves between consumers in a food web. Only a fraction of the biomass is available to each level of consumer in a food chain.

Energy in Food Webs Trophic pyramids show how the energy available to each organism decreases as it is transferred through different levels of a food web.

Using Trophic Pyramids to Restore an Ecosystem Scientists used understanding of trophic relationships to design a solution, and modified that solution after testing, to restore an ecosystem.

Dining in the Dark

You probably already know that parts of the ocean are extremely deep. But did you know that as much as **90 percent of Earth's oceans** are more than **200 meters deep**? That is almost as deep as two Statues of Liberty stacked on top of each other. Sunlight barely penetrates to this depth and, without enough sunlight, there are no producers. How do animals in deep ocean ecosystems get the energy they need to live?

As you go deeper into the dark water, you wonder how organisms find sources of energy to live here. Looking up from below the surface, you can see how light travels through shallower water but penetrates less and less as the water gets deeper.

Early in the morning, you embark on a journey to a spot above one of the deepest parts of the ocean, but you cannot just jump in. Your journey requires a special vessel that is capable of withstanding the immense pressures of the ocean's depths. The ship's captain shows you to the submersible you will use to descend. It is made of steel and nickel, and it has a glass dome for panoramic viewing. You climb inside and the captain lowers you into the water.

Splash! As you descend to 100 meters below sea level, you see phytoplankton floating in the water. Sunlight is able to reach to this depth. You see fish eating plankton and some fish eating other fish. You recognize some of the fish in this zone, such as tuna, because you have eaten them for dinner. Steering the submersible deeper into the ocean, you notice that it starts to get darker.

At 600 meters, light is scattered and dim. The ecosystem at this depth is different from the surface of the ocean. Phytoplankton were plentiful near the surface but are nonexistent here because there is not enough light to support photosynthesis. Squid, eels, and a swordfish catch your eye as they swim by the window. You steer the submersible deeper into the ocean to see what lives below.

At 1,100 meters, you are in total darkness! It is so dark. You cannot see anything through the window. You turn on the submersible's exterior lights. What could possibly survive here?

Marine Snow

As the lights turn on, you see small white flecks falling through the water from above. You radio your captain and tell her it looks like it is snowing. She informs you, "It is marine snow." As you watch the marine snow fall, a bizarre squid appears near the window. This deep red squid has strange "wings" protruding from its head, large eyes, and web-like skin between its tentacles. Clumps of marine snow stick to string-like filaments that extend from its body. It uses its tentacles to place the marine snow in its mouth. What a unique way to eat! You grab your deep ocean animal identification guide and see that this is a vampire squid. You ask the captain, "What is marine snow and why is a weird-looking squid eating it?"

The captain explains that marine snow is waste and decayed matter from organisms that live close to the ocean's surface. It slowly floats down and settles on the ocean floor. It may sound gross to eat flakes of waste and decayed matter, but this is the primary source of energy available to many creatures of the deep ocean.

YIKES! Out of the corner of your eye, you see a long fish swimming by with the most immense teeth you have ever seen!

Marine snow is a combination of tiny dead organisms, waste, and decayed matter that floats down from the upper levels of the ocean. It floats to the bottom of the ocean, where it forms the basis of a complex deep sea food web.

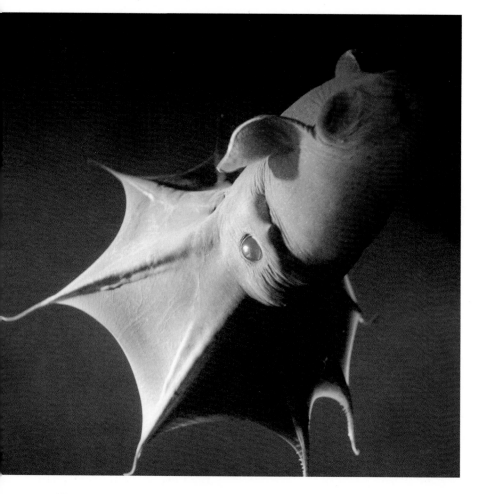

Survival in the deep, dark ocean requires features for catching food. Vampire squid use mucous on the suckers of their tentacles to gather bits of marine snow and transfer it to their mouth.

Like many predators in the deep ocean, viperfish and angler fish have special features that allow them to attract and hold on to prey. This is important because prey are hard to find in the deep ocean.

Catching Prey in the Dark

It is like something straight out of a horror movie—a small fish with a gaping mouth and massive teeth! Why does this fish need such big teeth? To frighten deep ocean explorers like you?

You use your guide to identify the fish as a viperfish. You observe as it notices a nearby squid. Suddenly, the viperfish opens its huge mouth wide and snaps it shut, trapping the squid with those massive teeth. The squid is larger than the fish, but it cannot wrestle itself from the fish's large teeth. The squid struggles to escape, but the viperfish's teeth curve inward and hold the squid securely. This viperfish has captured a meal! Prey are rare in this deep ocean ecosystem, so being able to hang on tight to keep your meal from escaping is critical to survival.

Peering through the window again, you are amazed to see points of light in the darkness, like the light from fireflies. You recall that some organisms are bioluminescent—they use chemical reactions to produce light in different parts of their bodies. What is the light used for? Could it be used to attract the attention of a meal?

Moving the submersible slowly closer to one of the lights, you catch sight of an angler fish. This bizarre creature has a moveable, spiny projection on its back with a glowing bulb on the end. As you watch, a small fish seems to be drawn to the light. The angler fish's dark body stays hidden, but the glowing bulb is held at the end of a stalk. The small fish swims closer to the light. Once the fish is close enough, the angler fish opens its jaws wide to engulf the smaller fish. The angler fish used the light to lure the fish to its mouth!

Amazed at the incredible features of deep ocean fish, you eagerly await your next stop—the ocean floor.

Whale Fall Ecosystems

You descend to the ocean floor and see a mass of organisms crawling over a mountain of decaying flesh. Moving closer, you notice that it is a dead humpback whale. This huge carcass has brought a nutrient-rich energy source to this nutrient-poor deep ocean ecosystem. The dead whale creates a food web that will persist for years to come.

You navigate around the whale to watch the feeding frenzy. Sleeper sharks tear away large hunks of flesh. Hagfish seize smaller bites. Strange crabs scuttle around to eat smaller pieces from the skin and bones. Soon, the captain says it is time to return to the surface.

Back on the ship, you describe what you saw. The captain says that you observed the first phases of a unique whale carcass ecosystem, called whale fall. First, large scavengers, like sleeper sharks and hagfish, eat large pieces of the carcass for up to two years. Then, smaller scavengers—such as crabs and shrimp—move in to feed. These organisms feed on the carcass for another few years, until only bones remain. At this point, special bone-eating worms eat through the bones. Bacteria cover the bones and decompose them further. Organisms like clams and tube-worms arrive and eat the bacteria. Scavengers and decomposers ensure that nothing goes to waste! Once the bones are consumed, 50 years later, this whale carcass ecosystem is gone, until the next whale fall.

Your amazing journey into deep ocean ecosystems has demonstrated that life can survive in extreme environments, as long as there is something to eat—even if it is just leftovers from above! ◆

When a large animal, like a humpback whale, dies and floats to the bottom of the ocean, it forms an island of abundant resources that supports a complex food web.

Tuna

Phytoplankton

Live humpback whale

Dead humpback whale

Hatchetfish

Fangtooth fish

Amphipods

Hagfish

Sleeper shark

Crabs

Carcass of the humpback whale

Global Cycles of Matter

How does matter move through ecosystems on Earth?

Introduction

The colorful leaves of these aspen trees quake and flutter in the autumn breeze. Rays of sunlight pierce through the branches, striking the fallen leaves that carpet the forest floor. Perched in a tree, a squirrel is eating seeds. What roles do the aspen trees play in recycling matter on Earth? What roles does the squirrel play? What about the decomposers that feed on the leaves that fall from the trees?

Atoms of carbon move through the living and nonliving parts of an ecosystem as components of different molecules, such as the carbon dioxide that the aspen trees use to make glucose, the glucose in the seeds that the squirrel eats, and the carbon dioxide that the squirrel exhales. Atoms of other kinds of matter also cycle through the living and nonliving parts of ecosystems. Did you know that nearly all of the atoms that make up matter on Earth have been on the planet since its beginning? Earth is like a spaceship that began its journey through space with everything its occupants needed to live. The same matter moves continuously in a global cycle throughout Earth's ecosystems, taking on different forms as it moves.

In this lesson, you will explore three global cycles of matter and consider how matter moves through ecosystems on Earth in different forms. You will learn that the total amount of matter on Earth stays constant, as none of it leaves or enters the biosphere. Finally, you will consider how humans change global cycles of carbon on Earth by burning fossil fuels and how people can re-plant forests to address problems caused by burning fossil fuels.

Vocabulary

law of conservation of matter a scientific law that states the amount of matter in a closed system stays the same, although the forms of that matter may change

water cycle a model that describes how water molecules move among Earth's ecosystems and atmosphere

carbon cycle a model that describes how carbon-based molecules move among Earth's ecosystems and atmosphere

nitrogen cycle a model that describes how nitrogen-based molecules move among Earth's ecosystems and atmosphere

reforestation the re-planting of forests that have been cut down

---

Next Generation Science Standards

Performance Expectations

MS-LS2-3. Develop a model to describe the cycling of matter and flow of energy among living and nonliving parts of an ecosystem.

MS-ETS1-2. Evaluate competing design solutions using a systematic process to determine how well they meet the criteria and constraints of the problem.

Science and Engineering Practices

Developing and Using Models Develop a model to describe phenomena.

Engaging in Argument from Evidence Evaluate competing design solutions based on jointly developed and agreed-upon design criteria.

Crosscutting Concepts

Energy and Matter Matter is conserved because atoms are conserved in physical and chemical processes.

Disciplinary Core Ideas

LS2.B. Food webs are models that demonstrate how matter and energy are transferred between producers, consumers, and decomposers as the

three groups interact within an ecosystem. Transfers of matter into and out of the physical environment occur at every level. Decomposers recycle nutrients from dead plant or animal matter back to the soil in terrestrial environments or to the water in aquatic environments. The atoms that make up the organisms in an ecosystem are cycled repeatedly between the living and nonliving parts of the ecosystem.

ETS1.B. There are systematic processes for evaluating solutions with respect to how well they meet the criteria and constraints of a problem.

Earth is like a spaceship, a closed system in the vast emptiness of space. Matter on Earth can change form as it cycles through ecosystems, but matter is neither created nor destroyed when it goes through these changes.

1. Earth is a Closed System

Planet Earth floats like a spaceship through the nothingness of outer space. There is no oxygen or water in outer space, and life cannot survive there. But Spaceship Earth contains everything that living things, like you, need. Where does the matter in your food, the water that you drink, and the air that you breathe come from?

All of the matter that makes up food, water, air, and your body became part of Earth when it formed 4.6 billion years ago. And it will continue to be part of Earth long after you are gone. The number of atoms, or amount of matter, on Earth never changes. This makes Earth a closed system. Scientists call this the "conservation of matter." The **law of conservation of matter** is a scientific law stating that the amount of matter in a closed system always stays the same, although matter may change form. A scientific law is a statement, based on evidence from repeated observations, that describes an aspect of the universe that is consistent and predictable. This law describes how matter on Earth behaves today, how it behaved in the past, and how it will continue to behave far into the future.

Although the total amount of matter on Earth remains the same, matter can change form by changing state or by combining with other substances. These global changes in matter can be modeled as diagrams. Matter changes form in global cycles through processes such as photosynthesis, feeding relationships between organisms, decomposition, and other natural processes. Global cycles of matter are important to maintaining healthy ecosystems on Earth because they make different forms of matter available to living things.

There are small exceptions to the model of Earth as a closed system. Some matter does leave Earth when humans send spacecraft into space. And space objects, like meteors, can bring small amounts of matter into the system. Even with these exceptions, scientists find the model of a closed system useful for understanding Earth's ecosystems.

2. The Water Cycle

Did you know that every glass of water you drink has molecules of water in it that a dinosaur once drank? Every molecule of water on Earth has been cycling through ecosystems since early in our planet's history. The first global cycle we will explore is the water cycle.

The **water cycle** is a model that describes how water molecules move among Earth's ecosystems and the atmosphere. Figure 7.2 is a diagram that illustrates the water cycle.

To follow the journey of a water molecule, start at the atmosphere in Figure 7.2. The water molecule is a part of a tiny droplet in a cloud. It combines with other water molecules to form rain. These molecules then fall to Earth and soak into the soil.

The water molecule in the soil is absorbed by producers, such as aquatic plants, where it becomes part of an aquatic plant cell. Other water molecules might be used in photosynthesis to make oxygen gas and sugar molecules. A grazing manatee eats the grass, taking in the water molecule. The manatee releases the water molecule in its wastes. Other water molecules in the manatee might be released as moisture when it exhales. Decomposers consume the manatee's wastes and return the water molecule to the soil. When sunlight warms the water molecule in the soil, it enters the atmosphere as water vapor, starting the cycle again.

Figure 7.2

If you start with water vapor in the atmosphere, at the top of the diagram, you can follow the path of a water molecule through different parts of Earth's ecosystems. Water changes states through different processes in the water cycle, including precipitation and evaporation.

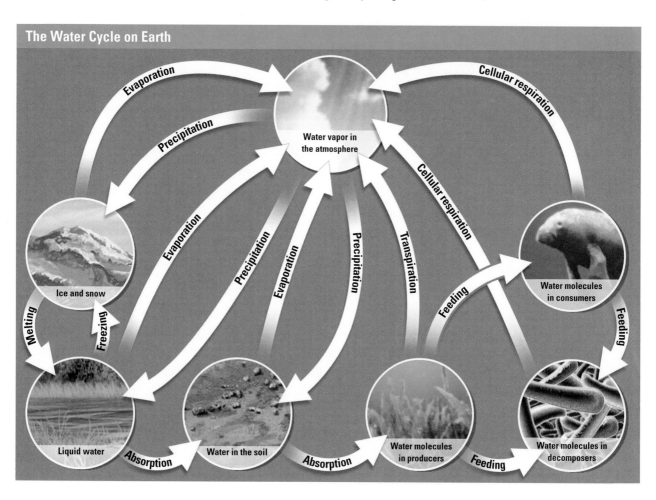

The Water Cycle on Earth

3. The Carbon Cycle

Take in a deep breath, then exhale. When you exhale, a carbon-based molecule called carbon dioxide is released. How can the journey of a carbon atom in the carbon dioxide you just exhaled be modeled on a global scale? What can the carbon cycle show?

Like water molecules, atoms of carbon move among the living and nonliving parts of ecosystems. You can follow the path of a carbon atom as it travels through an ecosystem. Follow the path of a carbon atom in Figure 7.3. Start on the left side of the diagram, in carbon atoms in producers. The carbon atom is part of a sugar molecule in an aquatic plant, which looks like an appetizing snack to a passing manatee.

Carbon is incorporated into living things in the ecosystem through photosynthesis. Producers, such as aquatic plant life, capture the carbon dioxide molecule from water and use it to produce oxygen gas and sugars. The carbon atom becomes part of a sugar molecule, but not for long. The aquatic plant uses the sugar molecule as a

This manatee eats aquatic plants and uses some of their carbon-based molecules to build its body structures. It uses other carbon-based molecules for energy and exhales carbon dioxide into the atmosphere. Some carbon dioxide remains dissolved in the water and is used by the aquatic plants that are food for the manatee.

source of energy for its cellular needs. Through the process of cellular respiration, the plant releases carbon dioxide, just like the manatee does. Consumers, like the manatee, get carbon from eating other living things. When the manatee eats the aquatic plant, the carbon atom gets incorporated into the consumer's body. It becomes part of a carbon-based molecule such as a protein or DNA molecule.

Carbon in living things is released into nonliving parts of an ecosystem through cellular respiration. When the manatee consumes the aquatic plant, or a squirrel consumes a seed, it uses the sugar molecule in the cell as a source of energy. A carbon atom that was part of the sugar molecule in the manatee's snack combines with oxygen and becomes part of a carbon dioxide molecule. When the manatee exhales the carbon dioxide molecule, it travels to the surface of the water and into to the atmosphere above. The carbon atom is now part of the carbon dioxide in the atmosphere. Other carbon dioxide molecules exhaled by the manatee remain dissolved in the water, which can be used by aquatic plants.

When the manatee dies, a decomposer consumes its remains. The carbon atom becomes part of the bacteria. When the bacterial cell dies, it is broken down by other decomposers. The carbon atom from the body of the bacterial cell might remain stored in the soil for years. Where the soil and atmosphere meet, carbon atoms are transferred between the two. When carbon atoms are stored under layers of soil for millions of years, they may form fossil fuels, which humans use as a source of energy.

Carbon atoms also move through ecosystems when carbon-based molecules are burned. Burning, or combustion, is a chemical reaction involving oxygen and a fuel. Wood is a fuel that comes from trees and stores energy from photosynthesis. Fossil fuels contain the energy stored in the remains of ancient organisms. When carbon in fuels is burned with oxygen, carbon dioxide is released. If this carbon dioxide molecule were dissolved in the Florida river where the manatee lives, it could be used by an aquatic plant in photosynthesis. Then, the carbon atom would be back where it started—part of an aquatic plant that might become another lunch for the manatee!

The **carbon cycle** is a model that describes how carbon-based molecules move among Earth's ecosystems and atmosphere. Figure 7.3 shows how carbon atoms move in ecosystems. Carbon atoms are never created or destroyed, but they change form throughout the cycle.

Figure 7.3

Start with carbon dioxide molecules in producers at the left of the diagram. Follow the path of a carbon atom through different parts of Earth's ecosystems. Carbon atoms become part of different carbon-based molecules through photosynthesis, cellular respiration, and other processes.

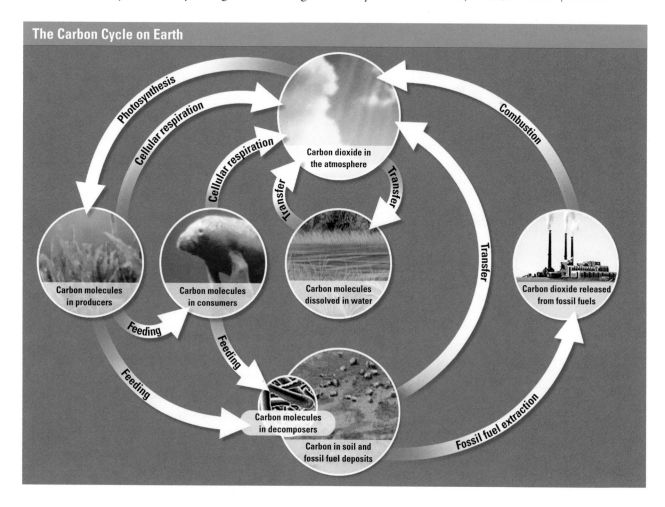

The Carbon Cycle on Earth

Photosynthesis

Cellular respiration

Cellular respiration

Cellular respiration

Transfer

Transfer

Combustion

Transfer

Carbon dioxide in the atmosphere

Carbon molecules in producers

Carbon molecules in consumers

Carbon molecules dissolved in water

Carbon dioxide released from fossil fuels

Feeding

Feeding

Feeding

Carbon molecules in decomposers

Carbon in soil and fossil fuel deposits

Fossil fuel extraction

4. The Nitrogen Cycle

Need a snack? A handful of peanuts can give you more than just energy. High-protein foods, like legumes and nuts, help your body build muscle. All living things use proteins, which are molecules that contain the element nitrogen. How do peanut plants get nitrogen?

As with carbon atoms, nitrogen atoms cycle among the living and nonliving parts of ecosystems. Earth's atmosphere contains large amounts of nitrogen gas. A whopping 78 percent of Earth's atmosphere is nitrogen gas! You can use Figure 7.4 to follow the path of a nitrogen atom and the different molecules that it becomes part of. The **nitrogen cycle** is a model that describes how nitrogen-based molecules move among Earth's ecosystems and atmosphere.

Start with an atom of nitrogen gas in the atmosphere in Figure 7.4. Although all organisms need nitrogen, few can use nitrogen as it is found in the atmosphere. There is only one process on Earth that can convert nitrogen in the atmosphere into more complex nitrogen-based molecules. This process is called nitrogen fixation and it can happen in two different ways. The first type of nitrogen fixation occurs when lightning passes through the atmosphere. The electrical energy causes nitrogen gas to react with oxygen gas. The resulting molecules mix with water and fall to Earth as ammonia.

Bacteria are an important part of the nitrogen cycle because they can convert nitrogen gas into different kinds of nitrogen-based molecules that are useful to producers. Farmers often plant crops like peanuts to improve nitrogen concentration in soils because these plants house those bacteria in their roots.

Nitrogen-fixing bacteria also convert nitrogen gas to ammonia. Most nitrogen fixation on Earth happens through the action of nitrogen-fixing bacteria. These bacteria are found in soil and in roots of certain plants, like peanuts. A bacterial cell living in the root of a peanut plant takes up the atom of nitrogen gas from the atmosphere. The bacterial cell carries out a chemical reaction that uses the nitrogen atom and other atoms to produce the nitrogen-based molecule ammonia. Some plants use this ammonia created by nitrogen-fixing bacteria to build the proteins and other molecules they need.

Another kind of bacteria, nitrifying bacteria, can convert ammonia into nitrates. Most producers need nitrates to grow and form important nitrogen-based molecules in their bodies. This means that, in nearly all ecosystems, the amount of available nitrates limits how well producers can grow. This is why farmers add fertilizers, which include nitrates, to soil when they grow crops.

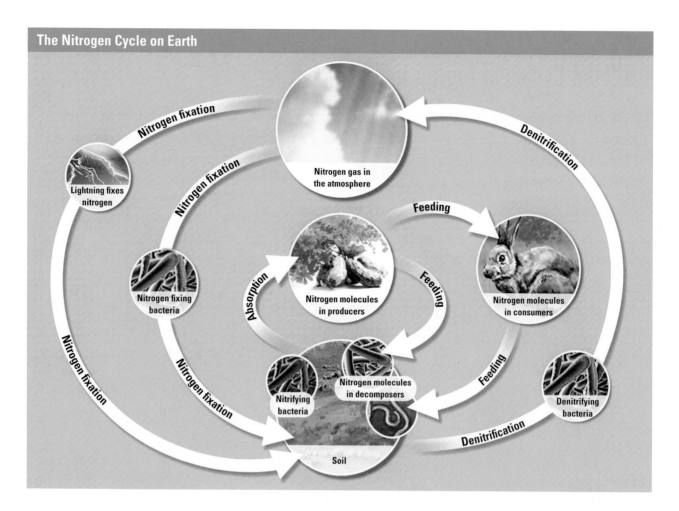

Consumers get the nitrogen-based molecules they need by eating producers or other consumers. When you eat a peanut, you use the nitrates in the peanut to help form proteins, complex molecules that contain nitrogen, in your own body. Rabbits eat leaves and flowers. They get the nitrogen-based molecules they need from producers.

Decomposers break down wastes and remains of dead organisms, recycling their nutrients and returning nitrogen atoms to the soil. When the peanut plant dies, decomposers, such as bacteria, break down the proteins in their bodies, leaving nitrogen-based molecules like nitrates and ammonia. Other bacteria, called denitrifying bacteria, convert those nitrogen-based molecules into nitrogen gas. The atom of nitrogen is again part of a molecule of nitrogen gas. It has returned to the atmosphere and completed the cycle.

Notice that a nitrogen atom can take different paths through the nitrogen cycle. Nitrogen fixing bacteria convert nitrogen into nitrogen-based molecules in the soil. There it may become part of a plant cell or be converted back into nitrogen gas in the atmosphere. This illustrates how matter on Earth constantly cycles through different forms, whether it is nitrogen, carbon, water, or other kinds of matter. Matter is never lost; it just changes form. Where did the matter in your body come from? Where will it go?

Figure 7.4

If you start with nitrogen gas in the atmosphere, at the top of the diagram, you can follow the path of a nitrogen atom through living and nonliving parts of Earth's ecosystems. Nitrogen atoms become part of different nitrogen-based molecules and the body structures of living things through the nitrogen cycle.

Global Cycles of Matter and You

The atoms and molecules of all matter on Earth cycle through the living and nonliving parts of its ecosystems. All of these atoms and molecules take on different forms, but the total amount of those atoms and molecules on Earth never changes. As you travel through the solar system on Spaceship Earth, you rely on the vital processes that make different kinds of matter available to you. Where do you fit in the water, carbon, and nitrogen cycles?

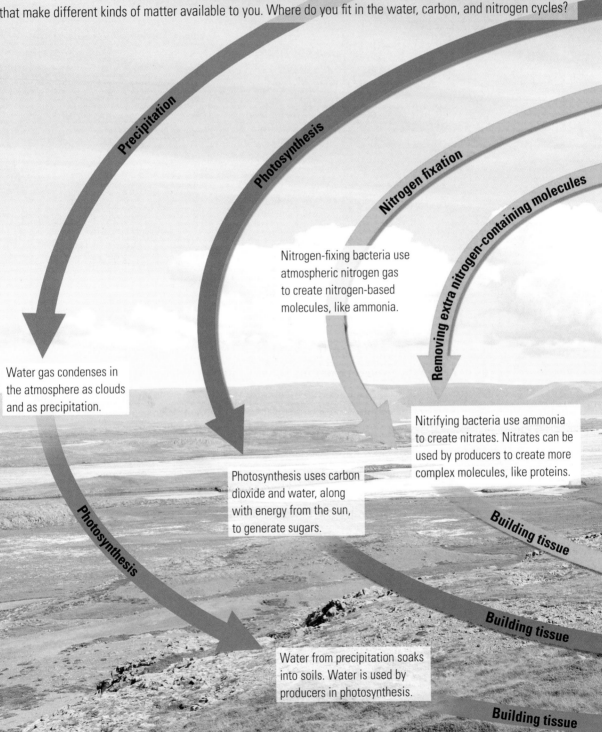

Precipitation

Photosynthesis

Nitrogen fixation

Removing extra nitrogen-containing molecules

Nitrogen-fixing bacteria use atmospheric nitrogen gas to create nitrogen-based molecules, like ammonia.

Water gas condenses in the atmosphere as clouds and as precipitation.

Nitrifying bacteria use ammonia to create nitrates. Nitrates can be used by producers to create more complex molecules, like proteins.

Photosynthesis

Building tissue

Photosynthesis uses carbon dioxide and water, along with energy from the sun, to generate sugars.

Building tissue

Water from precipitation soaks into soils. Water is used by producers in photosynthesis.

Building tissue

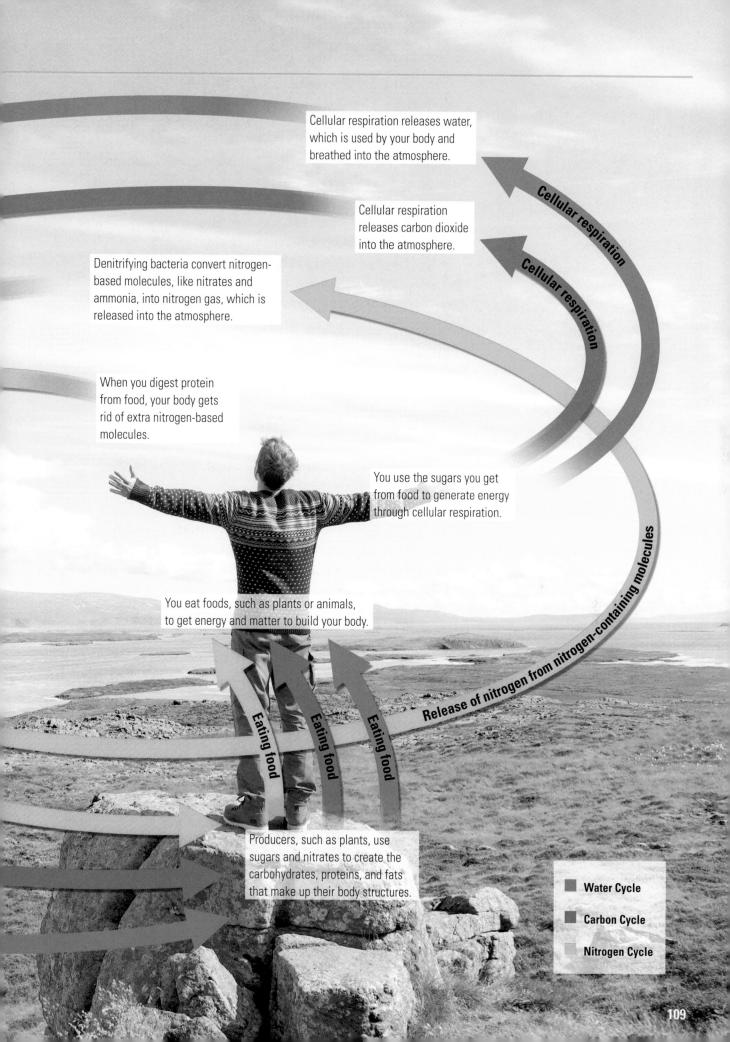

Cellular respiration releases water, which is used by your body and breathed into the atmosphere.

Cellular respiration releases carbon dioxide into the atmosphere.

Cellular respiration

Cellular respiration

Denitrifying bacteria convert nitrogen-based molecules, like nitrates and ammonia, into nitrogen gas, which is released into the atmosphere.

When you digest protein from food, your body gets rid of extra nitrogen-based molecules.

You use the sugars you get from food to generate energy through cellular respiration.

Release of nitrogen from nitrogen-containing molecules

You eat foods, such as plants or animals, to get energy and matter to build your body.

Eating food

Eating food

Eating food

Producers, such as plants, use sugars and nitrates to create the carbohydrates, proteins, and fats that make up their body structures.

■ Water Cycle

■ Carbon Cycle

■ Nitrogen Cycle

5. Designing Carbon Capture Solutions

Carbon atoms move among different parts of Earth's biosphere through the global carbon cycle. When carbon is captured through photosynthesis, it becomes biomass. Biomass that has been stored for millions of years deep in Earth is transformed into fossil fuels. Humans use fossil fuels for energy, which releases carbon atoms into the atmosphere. As people use fossil fuels, carbon dioxide enters the atmosphere, causing global climate change. How can humans address the problem of removing excess carbon dioxide in Earth's atmosphere?

Suppose you are an engineer designing a solution to this problem. First, you consider the criteria and constraints. Then, you evaluate different solutions to see if they satisfy those criteria and constraints.

Defining Criteria Criteria describe what must be done to meet the goals of the project. In this case, removing carbon dioxide from the atmosphere and storing carbon in a different part of the carbon cycle are the criteria. A solution that meets these criteria is to capture carbon atoms as biomass through reforestation projects. **Reforestation** is the re-planting of forests. When trees carry out photosynthesis, they capture carbon dioxide from the atmosphere and store the carbon atoms in their body structures as biomass.

Determining Constraints Once you have decided on reforestation as the solution, you must consider the constraints. Constraints are limitations on an engineering solution. First, you must decide on the best place for reforestation. Where in the world will trees store the most carbon? Do people already live in the place where you will plant new trees? Is there infrastructure already in place, such as roads, that make reforestation affordable?

Figure 7.5
Reforestation efforts can be used to capture carbon and manage carbon dioxide in Earth's atmosphere. This map shows which areas of the world support the fastest growing forests. Analyzing this kind of data helps scientists and engineers choose the best sites for reforestation efforts.

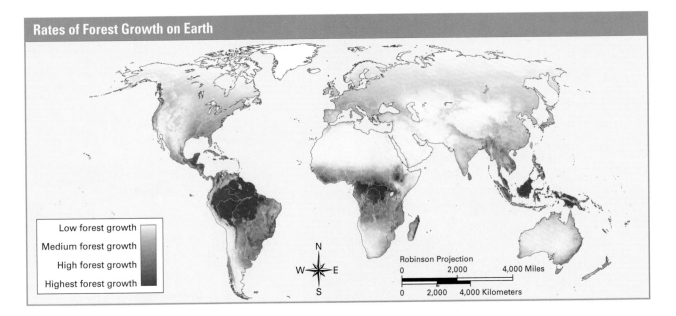

Rates of Forest Growth on Earth

Low forest growth
Medium forest growth
High forest growth
Highest forest growth

N
W　E
S

Robinson Projection
0　　　　2,000　　　　4,000 Miles

0　　2,000　　4,000 Kilometers

In the case of planting trees to capture carbon, an important constraint is the cost. To plant the most trees for the lowest cost that will capture the most carbon atoms, you must take into account how quickly the trees carry out photosynthesis. Trees grow faster in some ecosystems. They grow especially quickly in terrestrial biomes that have an abundance of light and water and long growing seasons. The faster the trees grow, the greater their rate of photosynthesis and the faster they can remove carbon dioxide from the atmosphere.

Evaluating Competing Solutions After considering all the criteria and constraints, you can choose the best location for reforestation. To figure out where trees grow fastest, scientists use maps like the one in Figure 7.5. Areas on the map that are dark green have the most sunlight and water available to plants. They also have the longest growing seasons. Forests in those places capture carbon dioxide and store its biomass at the fastest rate. Forests in other areas also remove carbon dioxide from the atmosphere, but at a slower rate.

You have narrowed it down to six places that make sense given what infrastructure is available and the social and environmental constraints of the area. How do you decide among them? You can address the final constraint by using the map to see where trees grow the fastest. Which area did you choose? Your reforestation project will help extract carbon from the atmosphere and store it in biomass.

Photosynthesis stores carbon in the cells of plants, so planting trees and other kinds of producers that live for many years can help remove excess carbon dioxide from the atmosphere.

LESSON SUMMARY

Global Cycles of Matter

Earth is a Closed System Matter cycles continuously among living and nonliving parts of Earth's ecosystems. Matter is never lost from Earth's ecosystems, but it does change form.

The Water Cycle Water molecules change form as they move through the living and nonliving parts of Earth in a global cycle.

The Carbon Cycle Carbon atoms move among the living and nonliving parts of Earth's ecosystems in different forms through photosynthesis, food web interactions, and decomposition.

The Nitrogen Cycle The nitrogen cycle describes how nitrogen atoms are transferred among organisms and their environments.

Designing Carbon Capture Solutions Engineers consider criteria and constraints in order to design and test solutions. Reforestation can be used to capture carbon dioxide from Earth's atmosphere and help to slow global climate change.

Could Humans Live on Another Planet?

Could humans live on Mars? Popular movies have sparked many people's curiosity about living on a distant planet. And it may not be science fiction. Some scientists think that colonies on Mars are a real possibility. In 1991, a group of scientists started a two-year long experiment to find out what the challenges of life on a planet like Mars might be. What did they discover?

A group of eight scientists set out to see if humans could survive in a closed model of Earth for two years. Before entering Biosphere 2, the team waved goodbye to the press and other people who had gathered to support the experiment.

On a warm fall day in 1991, eight people clothed in dark blue jumpsuits stood in front of a large complex of interconnected buildings in the Arizona desert. As news cameras snapped pictures, they smiled and waved to the crowd that had gathered. This team of scientists was beginning an experiment inside a closed model of Earth known as Biosphere 2. Their mission was to determine if humans could survive with no outside resources for two full years.

The Biosphere 2 mission was an interesting scientific experiment in itself, but the research conducted there could help us understand how humans can survive on other planets. If the team succeeded in living in the closed complex, scientists might be able to use a similar model of Earth's ecosystems to colonize other planets. Planets like Mars lack the water, food, and oxygen needed to support life. If people colonize a distant planet like Mars, they will need ecosystems to support them. They must produce their own water, food, and oxygen so that supplies will never run out. Basically, they will have to create a small, self-supporting version of Earth that could be replicated on a distant planet. What did these scientists discover about building a self-supporting ecosystem?

Building a Mini Earth

Earth is a complex system. Yet scientists who designed Biosphere 2 were charged with creating a fully-functioning miniaturized Earth within a relatively small area. How did they do it?

They assembled a team of experts from different areas— biologists, geologists, botanists, and hydrologists—to plan the design. The team members worked together to come up with solutions for how to replicate Earth's ecosystems in a way that would mimic how the ecosystems interacted naturally. The work required years of collaboration and study, but together, they built Biosphere 2.

Biosphere 2 is a sealed glass-covered building that covers 12,707 square meters in Arizona's Sonoran Desert. In order to be self-supporting, the structure needed to be airtight and large enough to allow matter to cycle throughout the artificial ecosystems. The glass walls kept air from escaping but allowed light energy in. The Biosphere 2 complex contained 2.6 million liters of water that constantly moved through the ecosystems as part of the water cycle.

To mimic large parts of Earth, engineers replicated five ecosystems: a rainforest, a savanna, a desert, wetlands, and an ocean with a coral reef. Land was set aside for raising crops and animals for food. Plants and animals were selected for their roles in cycling matter and energy in ecosystems. For example, some rainforest plants were selected because they undergo photosynthesis rapidly, using carbon dioxide and producing lots of oxygen. Bees and moths were selected to pollinate plants. Cockroaches and soil bacteria recycled dead material and wastes.

After four years of planning and building, Biosphere 2 was ready for testing. Within several months, problems began to appear.

Biosphere 2 was designed to be a fully-functioning miniature Earth that covers 12,707 square meters (or 3.14 acres) in the Arizona desert. This area was considered large enough to support the global cycles of matter needed to maintain ecosystems inside the structure.

Biosphere 2 encountered many challenges. Exposed concrete in the ocean ecosystem was a problem, as it trapped carbon dioxide that plants needed to produce oxygen. As a result, oxygen levels inside Biosphere 2 dropped to levels that were affecting the health of the team.

Systems Failure!

The crew strived to build a functioning closed system to model Earth. Just a few months into the project, systems were failing.

Oxygen levels inside Biosphere 2 dropped, from 21 to 14 percent. This made something as simple as walking up stairs very tiring. Fearing for their health, the crew planted more plants. When that did not work, oxygen was pumped into the complex. Later they discovered that bacteria in the soil were growing rapidly and consuming more oxygen than the scientists had first estimated. Also, exposed concrete in the ocean ecosystem was trapping carbon dioxide, preventing plants from cycling it into oxygen.

The ecosystems in Biosphere 2 were unable to support healthy populations of important animals, like pollinators. Bee populations disappeared, making it difficult to grow fruit and other food for the scientists.

The team also suffered from lack of food as their crops were not producing enough to meet their nutritional needs. In desperation, the team ate the grains and beans they had planned to use to grow crops. They also ate animals that were competing with them for food.

Insect populations that were introduced to Biosphere 2 either increased rapidly or went extinct. Bee pollinators died off, making it difficult for important food plants to reproduce. Cockroach and ant populations thrived and began to cause problems.

Clearly, the experiment did not go as intended. But was Biosphere 2 a failure? Certainly not! Scientists gathered important data that can be used to design closed ecosystems that support life.

Learning About Our Planetary Home

The biosphere we call home—Earth—is dynamic and complex, and trying to replicate it is difficult. Although the crew worked long hours removing weeds, cleaning water, hand pollinating plants, and monitoring conditions, maintaining healthy ecosystems proved to be a losing battle. What did the scientists of Biosphere 2 learn from the failures of the experiment?

Every problem the residents encountered was reported as a failure by the press. But enthusiasts looked at the failures as lessons to be learned. For example, avoiding the use of concrete would have kept oxygen levels from falling. Supporting pollinators through the various stages of their life cycles could have helped to prevent their extinction. Better agricultural practices, including more effective pest control, would have improved the food supply.

That is not to say that none of the team's efforts was successful. The team was able to recycle water using low-tech processes, such as filtering through plants and soil. This information was later used to help develop better waste-water recycling processes on the International Space Station and in developing countries. The Biosphere 2 scientists also did restoration work on the damaged coral reef and proved that these fragile ecosystems can be rehabilitated with human intervention.

Could we take what we learned from Biosphere 2 and use it to make Mars hospitable for humans? Some believe that the essentials for survival are already present on Mars, they just need to be changed to support human life. This transformation is known as terraforming. Mars already has a thin atmosphere and frozen water. So, terraforming Mars would involve warming the planet, altering the atmosphere, and introducing organisms. However, the cost of such an effort would surely be daunting.

Are you ready to live on Mars? It may be a while before you can pack your bags and head to the fourth rock from the sun. But while Mars may not yet be ready to support human life, lessons learned from continuing research at Biosphere 2 have helped us to understand what it might take to support life on another planet. ◆

Scientists use ongoing research at Biosphere 2 to understand how people might live in artificial ecosystems, such as the International Space Station or on planets like Mars. These experiments may one day allow humans to live permanently away from Earth.

Humans and Changing Ecosystems

OVERVIEW

As you stroll along a peaceful ocean coastline, you pause to pick up a colorful shell. It's an abalone shell, a marine animal that is also used by humans as a source of food. How is the population of abalones in this ecosystem impacted by human communities? How does the health of this coastal ecosystem impact the abalone population? In this unit you will explore the ways that humans rely on and impact ecosystems. You will prepare an investigative report that describes interactions between a human community and populations in a local ecosystem.

Phenomenon Based Storyline California abalone populations are in decline. As a television reporter, you research stories like this about the impacts of humans on ecosystems.

Investigations Use evidence of biodiversity in ecosystems and how biodiversity changes over time to create a presentation and make an argument about how biodiversity impacts ecosystems.

Investigations Work in groups to model the value of wetlands to human communities and prepare an argument to support a different community perspective on water use in the Great Lakes.

Investigations Examine evidence related to human resource use and its impact on ecosystems. Present an argument that describes a solution for protecting ecosystems and providing resources to human communities.

Engineering Challenge Students design and test a fishing net that protects marine biodiversity by catching only one type of sustainably harvested fish.

Performance Assessment Use a news report on abalone populations as a model for your investigation of a local interaction between humans and an ecosystem. After doing research and conducting interviews, you will put together your own news report.

UNIT 3

Performance Expectations

MS-LS2-5. Evaluate competing design solutions for maintaining biodiversity and ecosystem services.

MS-ESS3-4. Construct an argument supported by evidence for how increases in human population and per capita consumption of natural resources impact Earth's systems.

MS-ETS1-1. Define the criteria and constraints of a design solution with sufficient precision to ensure a successful solution, taking into account relevant scientific principles and potential impacts on people and the natural environment that may limit possible solutions.

MS-ETS1-3. Analyze data from tests to determine similarities and differences among several design solutions to identify the best characteristics of each that can be combined into a new solution to better meet the criteria for success.

MS-ETS1-4. Develop a model to generate data for iterative testing and modification of a proposed object, tool, or process such that an optimal design can be achieved.

Science and Engineering Practices

Asking Questions and Defining Problems
Define a design problem that can be solved through the development of an object, tool, process or system and includes multiple criteria and constraints, including scientific knowledge that may limit possible solutions.

Developing and Using Models
Develop a model to generate data to test ideas about designed systems, including those representing inputs and outputs.

Analyzing and Interpreting Data
Analyze and interpret data to provide evidence for phenomena.

Engaging in Argument from Evidence
• Evaluate competing design solutions based on jointly developed and agreed-upon design criteria. • Construct an oral and written argument supported by empirical evidence and scientific reasoning to support or refute an explanation or a model for a phenomenon or a solution to a problem.

Crosscutting Concepts

Stability and Change
Small changes in one part of a system might cause large changes in another part.

Cause and Effect
Cause and effect relationships may be used to predict phenomena in natural or designed systems.

Connections to Engineering, Technology, and Applications of Science: Influence of Science, Engineering, and Technology on Society and the Natural World
• All human activity draws on natural resources and has both short and long-term consequences, positive as well as negative, for the health of people and the natural environment. • The use of technologies and any limitations on their use are driven by individual or societal needs, desires, and values; by the findings of scientific research; and by differences in such factors as climate, natural resources, and economic conditions. Thus technology use varies from region to region and over time.

Connections to Nature of Science: Science Addresses Questions About the Natural and Material World
Scientific knowledge can describe the consequences of actions but does not necessarily prescribe the decisions that society takes.

Disciplinary Core Ideas

LS2.C. Ecosystem Dynamics, Functioning, and Resilience
Biodiversity describes the variety of species found in Earth's terrestrial and oceanic ecosystems. The completeness or integrity of an ecosystem's biodiversity is often used as a measure of its health.

LS4.D: Biodiversity and Humans
• Changes in biodiversity can influence humans' natural resources, such as food, energy, and medicines, as well as ecosystem services that humans rely on—for example, water purification and recycling.

ESS3.C: Human Impacts on Earth Systems
Typically, as human populations and per-capita consumption of natural resources increase, so do the negative impacts on Earth unless the activities and technologies involved are engineered otherwise.

ETS1.A: Defining and Delimiting Engineering Problems
The more precisely a design task's criteria and constraints can be defined, the more likely it is that the designed solution will be successful. Specification of constraints includes consideration of scientific principles and other relevant knowledge that are likely to limit possible solutions.

ETS1.B: Developing Possible Solutions
• There are systematic processes for evaluating solutions with respect to how well they meet the criteria and constraints of a problem. • Sometimes parts of different solutions can be combined to create a solution that is better than any of its predecessors. • A solution needs to be tested, and then modified on the basis of the test results, in order to improve it. • Models of all kinds are important for testing solutions.

ETS1.C: Optimizing the Design Solution
• Although one design may not perform the best across all tests, identifying the characteristics of the design that performed the best in each test can provide useful information for the redesign process—that is, some of those characteristics may be incorporated into the new design. • The iterative process of testing the most promising solutions and modifying what is proposed on the basis of the test results leads to greater refinement and ultimately to an optimal solution.

Connect Your Learning

You rely on many things that come from Earth's ecosystems, including your food, medicines, and home. As human populations grow, can Earth's ecosystems continue to provide these resources? By understanding the scientific ideas behind how healthy living systems work, you can explain many phenomena related to humans and their impact on ecosystems. You can use this expertise to solve problems in your community.

Humans and Changing Ecosystems

These scientists are exploring the many kinds of living things in a part of Africa. What are some of the living things you find near you? How do they benefit you and others in your community?

Human communities depend on ecosystems for resources. But humans often damage ecosystems. Volunteers help build artificial reefs to replace damaged ones. What are some threats to habitats in your area?

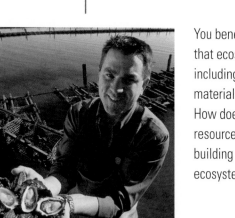

You benefit from resources that ecosystems provide, including food to eat and materials to build your home! How does the human use of resources, such as food and building materials, change ecosystems?

Biodiversity

Why is biodiversity important in ecosystems?

Introduction

Slimy or furry, feathered or leafy, microscopic or towering, a huge variety of species call Earth's ecosystems home. When you go to a local park, think of the organisms you see there—the trees, plants, birds, and insects. If you use a microscope to examine the soil under a rock or leaf, you might find tiny worms, single-celled organisms, and bacteria. Every place in the world is full of many kinds of living things! How does this variety of living things influence how ecosystems work? How do threats to species impact humans?

You have learned that the availability of resources influences populations of organisms. You have also learned that species interact with each other and with their environment in a number of ways. These interactions have developed over long periods of time and resulted in ecosystems that have unique sets of species adapted to the particular resources and interactions in that ecosystem.

In this lesson, you will first learn what biodiversity is and how it relates to ecosystem health. You will then look at the unique biodiversity found in ecosystems in three different biomes—tundra, kelp forest, and tropical rainforest. Then, you will think about why biodiversity is important and how it affects humans. Biodiversity reflects the amazing ways that nature has solved the challenges of survival and reproduction on Earth. You will explore how engineers and designers use the solutions that nature has devised as a source of inspiration to solve problems.

Vocabulary

biodiversity the variety of organisms on Earth or in a particular habitat or ecosystem

proportion the relationship between a part and a whole

niche the ecological role that a species plays in an ecosystem

extirpation when all of the members of a population die and the species no longer exists in that place

keystone species a species that affects the diversity of an entire ecosystem

extinction when all of the members of a species die and the species no longer exists

---

Next Generation Science Standards

Performance Expectations

MS-LS2-5. Evaluate competing design solutions for maintaining biodiversity and ecosystem services.

MS-ETS1-3. Analyze data from tests to determine similarities and differences among several design solutions to identify the best characteristics of each that can be combined into a new solution to better meet the criteria for success.

Science and Engineering Practices

Engaging in Argument from Evidence Evaluate competing design solutions based on jointly developed and agreed-upon design criteria.

Analyzing and Interpreting Data Analyze and interpret data to determine similarities and differences in findings.

Crosscutting Concepts

Stability and Change Small changes in one part of a system might cause large changes in another part.

Influence of Science, Engineering, and Technology on Society and the Natural World

Science Addresses Questions About the Natural and Material World

Disciplinary Core Ideas

LS2.C. Biodiversity describes the variety of species found in Earth's terrestrial and oceanic ecosystems. The completeness or integrity of an ecosystem's biodiversity is often used as a measure of its health.

ETS1.B. • There are systematic processes for evaluating solutions with respect to how well they

meet the criteria and constraints of a problem.
• Sometimes parts of different solutions can be combined to create a solution that is better than any of its predecessors.

ETS1.C. Although one design may not perform the best across all tests, identifying the characteristics of the design that performed the best in each test can provide useful information for the redesign process—that is, some of those characteristics may be incorporated into the new design.

Different ecosystems have different natural levels of biodiversity. Coral reef ecosystems have many species, including many kinds of fish, corals, sponges, and turtles.

1. The Importance of Biodiversity

You slide the diving mask over your eyes and slide into the clear, blue water. What you see is amazing! A sea turtle glides past and you spot brilliantly colored corals and anemones, each a different species. Small orange fish flit about like confetti in the breeze. A dizzying array of other fish species, of all colors and sizes, also feeds and hides in the coral. If you counted all the different types of living things in this place, you would find thousands, or even tens of thousands, of unique species. How do these species interact to form healthy and stable ecosystems?

Every ecosystem on Earth has a set of species that is found there naturally. That set of species differs from one ecosystem to another. Some places naturally have more species than others. In other words, every ecosystem has its own biodiversity. **Biodiversity** is the variety of organisms on Earth or in a particular habitat or ecosystem. How do scientists learn about natural levels of biodiversity on Earth?

Scientists for centuries have been exploring Earth's ecosystems and systematically describing the species they find there. This information is compiled and stored so that scientists of the future have access to it. This information includes the numbers of species in different ecosystems and the number of species of different kinds of organisms. What have scientists discovered about patterns of biodiversity on Earth from this information?

Scientists have identified and described about 1.9 million different species on Earth. But this is estimated to be only a fraction of the total species on Earth. Scientists discover new species every day. How do scientists organize this data about different species?

Scientists seek to understand biodiversity by classifying different species. They organize related species into larger categories, such as plants, fungi, and animals. There are also single-celled organisms and algae. What patterns do scientists see in the biodiversity on Earth?

Some categories of species are more numerous than others. Figure 8.1 organizes all of Earth's known species into groups of related organisms. Each wedge in the circle chart represents a group of species, such as plants or fungi. Notice that some wedges are larger than others. The wedges are different sizes because some groups have more species than others. Producers such as plants, algae, and many unicellular organisms may make up most of the biomass on Earth, but together these groups represent less than a quarter of the world's total species, 23 percent. Insects, on the other hand, make up the largest wedge in the circle chart, 52 percent. That means that more than half of all of Earth's known species are some kind of insect!

A circle graph like the one in Figure 8.1 lets you explore proportions. A **proportion** is the relationship between a part and a whole. For example, a slice of pizza compared to the whole pizza can be described as a proportion. The proportion of Earth's known species that are insects is estimated to be 52 percent. If there are 1.9 million identified species on Earth, how many are insects? You can use the estimated proportion to find the answer. If you multiply 1.9 million by 52 percent, you get nearly 990,000. That is a lot of insect species!

Let us explore how biodiversity in different ecosystems on Earth influences those ecosystems.

Most animal species on Earth are insects, like this strange giraffe weevil. There are over 86,000 species of weevils on Earth and almost a million (1,000,000) species of insects.

Figure 8.1

A circle graph representing Earth's biodiversity shows that some groups of related species are more numerous than others. Insects and other animals make up 72 percent of the total species on Earth.

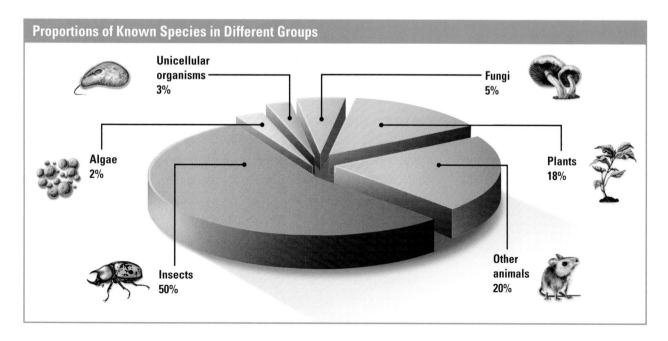

Proportions of Known Species in Different Groups

Unicellular organisms 3%

Fungi 5%

Algae 2%

Plants 18%

Insects 50%

Other animals 20%

Tundra ecosystems naturally have fewer species than other ecosystems because of harsh conditions and limited resources. Some species, including the caribou shown here, survive these harsh conditions by migrating away from the tundra during colder months and returning when there are plants available to eat in the warm season.

2. Fragile Tundra Ecosystems

If you have a steady hand, you can build a house of cards by leaning playing cards on one another for support. What happens if you remove a card? The others that depend on it for support may fall. Ecosystems are the same way. The loss of one species can change interactions in an entire ecosystem. How does this work in a tundra ecosystem, in which biodiversity is relatively low?

Arctic tundra ecosystems, like the one pictured here, are an example of an ecosystem where the total number of species is low compared to other types of ecosystems. Tundra ecosystems are found near Earth's poles or near the tops of tall mountains. They have long, harsh winters and short summers. Species in tundra ecosystems must be able to survive extreme cold conditions and long periods where there is little food. Few species can survive these conditions, so tundra ecosystems have relatively low levels of natural biodiversity. For much of the year, the ground is frozen. Trees cannot grow, but smaller plants, like shrubs, grasses, or mosses survive. Caribou graze on the grasses, mosses, and small plants in the tundra. Caribou can withstand cold conditions, but they also escape harsh tundra winters by migrating. Caribou migrate to warmer places during the winter and return to the tundra during summer. Other animal species hibernate to escape the harsh winters, including polar bears.

Polar bears are the largest predators in Arctic tundra ecosystems. Their main prey are seals, which swim in the sea beneath thick layers of ice. Seals cannot breathe underwater and eventually have to come up for air. Polar bears wait at places where there are holes in the sea ice. When a seal comes up to one of these places to take a breath, a waiting polar bear can grab it. Polar bears are the main hunters of seals from sea ice. This is the polar bear's niche. A **niche** is the ecological role that a species plays in an ecosystem. No other species fills this niche in Arctic tundra ecosystems.

When polar bears hunt seals, other species benefit as well. After a polar bear has captured a seal and eaten its fill, it leaves behind large parts of the seal's carcass. These leftovers provide food for Arctic foxes, gulls, and other birds in tundra ecosystems, especially during the cold winter months when there is little to eat. Polar bear populations have a positive effect on populations of other species that eat seals but are unable to hunt and capture seals themselves.

Because tundra ecosystems have low biodiversity, a threat to one species can have a large impact on many other species. A small change in one part of the ecosystem can cause large changes throughout other parts of the ecosystem. For example, Earth's climate is changing, and coastal sea ice in the Arctic is breaking up as a result. With less sea ice to hunt on, it is harder for polar bears to capture seals. They cannot catch seals in the water if they have to swim after them. The result is that polar bear populations are decreasing. When polar bear populations decline, many other species are impacted. Disruptions to many populations in tundra ecosystems can result in permanent changes to both the populations of species there and the ecosystem.

Having relatively low biodiversity means that tundra ecosystems are fragile. That is, their stability is more easily threatened by changes than ecosystems that have more biodiversity. For any ecosystem, a change in the population of one species can affect the populations of many other species due to their interactions. But with a tundra ecosystem, a small change is likely to have widespread effects. As Earth's climate changes and polar bear populations decline, the populations of other Arctic species will also decline and the Arctic tundra ecosystem may never be the same.

Arctic ecosystems have low biodiversity and small changes can have a large impact on the ecosystem. Healthy polar bear populations can have a positive impact on the populations of other species, such as Arctic foxes or birds. When polar bear populations decline, many other species are impacted.

Kelp forests are ecosystems with intermediate levels of biodiversity. The tall stalks of kelp provide food and shelter for many organisms, including fish and other marine organisms. Sea otters live, play, and raise young in kelp forests and prey on many kinds of animals that also live in these ecosystems.

3. Keystone Species in the Kelp Forest

Rays of sunlight pierce the dense curtain of kelp shading the forest below. The greenish brown blades provide both shelter and food for the forest creatures that live here. And right now, these creatures need shelter because a predator is nearby! This predator darts in and out of the leaves looking for prey. Without this predator, the forest will die. What is this unique predator?

The predator is a sea otter, a unique species found only in kelp forest ecosystems. Kelp forests are not like other forests. Kelp are not trees; they are large seaweeds that float in the ocean. They have root-like structures that anchor them to the sea floor and grow long stalks that float and reach to the surface. These large seaweeds grow in dense clusters, as trees do, giving the impression of an undersea forest.

Kelp forests are marine ecosystems that are intermediate in biodiversity. Biodiversity in kelp forests is not as low as the tundra, or other low biodiversity ecosystems, but not as high as the highest biodiversity ecosystems, such as coral reefs or tropical rainforests. Kelp forests are found in areas where cold ocean water rises to the surface, bringing with it many nutrients. These nutrients are important resources that support large populations of many marine species. These organisms use kelp forests to reproduce, find shelter, and hunt for food. Sea otters are one important species that live in kelp forests. They are marine mammals that eat crabs, clams, mussels, and sea urchins.

Sea otters are one of many species that make up the biodiversity of kelp forest ecosystems. However, at one time, their numbers were decreasing rapidly. For years, humans hunted and killed sea otters in great numbers for their thick, soft fur. As a result, sea otter populations decreased so quickly that many kelp forests along the Pacific Coast of North America had lost all of their sea otters, a situation called extirpation. **Extirpation** is when all of the members of a population in an ecosystem die and the species no longer exists in that place. Extirpation of a population only applies to a population in a particular place, not to the entire planet.

After the extirpation of sea otters, scientists discovered that kelp forests started to die. They also observed declines in other species that relied on kelp. But sea otters do not eat kelp, they eat animal prey such as sea urchins. Why were kelp forests disappearing along with the sea otters?

After careful study, scientists realized that sea urchin populations increased when sea otters were absent. This is because sea otters eat sea urchins and control their populations. Sea urchins eat kelp, starting at their root-like bases and grazing along their length. Increased sea urchin populations meant that new kelp "trees" could not grow because sea urchins ate them. As kelp forests died, many of the species that live in and depend on kelp forests also declined or disappeared. Efforts to protect sea otters, including bans on hunting and protection of marine ecosystems, have increased their numbers. In areas where sea otters have returned, kelp forest biodiversity has recovered—mainly because sea otters again control sea urchin populations.

Certain species can impact the biodiversity of an entire ecosystem. A change in the population of a species can affect many other populations in the ecosystem. For example, when the population of sea otters affects populations of a large number of other species, it is called a keystone species. A **keystone species** is a species that affects the biodiversity of an entire ecosystem. You have already learned about two other keystone species in Lesson 3: prairie dogs and beavers. Each of these species acts like a keystone, the angled stone at the top center of an arch, such as the arch of a stone bridge. An arch's keystone supports the weight of the other stones in the arch and holds up the entire structure. Similarly, keystone species support large groups of other species through the special role they play in their ecosystems.

The biodiversity of ecosystems is enhanced through the presence of keystone species. Sea otters eat sea urchins, which gives sea urchin prey—kelp—a chance to grow into a healthy kelp forest and support many other species.

4. Many Niches in Tropical Rainforests

A hike through a tropical rainforest ecosystem is never quiet. During the day, you hear dozens of different bird songs and monkeys calling out from among the branches and vines. At night the rhythmic chirping of frogs and the high-pitched buzzing of insects takes over. Each voice is a different species and the different sounds hint at the variety of animals that live in rainforest ecosystems. And those are just the species that you can hear! What explains this abundance of life in rainforest ecosystems?

Tropical rainforest ecosystems have very high levels of biodiversity. An individual rainforest tree can be home to nearly 1,000 different species of beetle—not to mention all the other different kinds of insects, amphibians, fungi, and other organisms that also live on that single tree! There are so many species in rainforests that scientists are still discovering over 100 new species there each year. How can so many different species survive in one place?

Rainforests are found in areas of Earth that have warm temperatures and plenty of rainfall throughout the year. Recall from Lesson 1 that temperature and precipitation are the two nonliving aspects of the environment that influence what kind of terrestrial biome is found in an area. Warm, wet conditions provide an abundance of resources to support the growth of producers. There can be 650 tree species in one small area of some tropical rainforests, about the same as the number of tree species in the entire United States. Each of the trees in a tropical rainforest supports other producers that make it home, including ferns, vines, and mosses. Scientists use climbing equipment to reach the tops of tall rainforest trees and study the abundant ferns, vines, and mosses that grow on their branches. They may also discover new species as part of their research!

With so many producers, there are plenty of resources for consumers of all kinds. In tropical rainforests, scientists estimate there are millions of species of insects that make those trees, ferns, vines, and mosses their home. Those insects may be preyed on by thousands more species of other insects, lizards, birds, and mammals. And there could be even more species of parasites on them all.

The biodiversity of rainforest ecosystems is high due to their warm and wet conditions. This scientist is conducting research in the treetops of a rainforest. There are so many species in rainforests that most newly discovered species are found in rainforests.

With access to abundant resources throughout the year, rainforest species have evolved specialized niches. A lesser anteater has large claws that can easily break apart termite mounds and ant nests. This characteristic helps anteaters access their main source of prey.

Stability of resources in rainforests means that many species can become specialized for very particular niches. Some species may eat only one kind of prey. Others may live their whole lives in only a particular part of the forest, such as high in the trees or on the forest floor. These are specialized niches because few other species fill exactly the same ecological role in that ecosystem. A tundra species would not survive if it ate just one type of plant because there would not be enough of that plant throughout the year. In rainforests, many species eat one type of plant because it is available throughout the year.

Lesser anteaters are found in rainforests and have the specialized niche of eating mainly ants and termites! Both insects are available year round in rainforests. Anteaters have special features that help them find and eat ants and termites. They have large claws so that they can climb trees and break open the nests of ants and termites found there. They have long, sticky tongues to quickly gather large numbers of ants and termites before they scurry away. There are few consumers that specialize in eating ants and termites, so lesser anteaters don't have much competition for this abundant source of prey.

Rainforest producers also have specialized niches. Some tropical orchid species, for example, live only on rainforest trees. The growth of many, tall trees is typical of tropical rainforests. Under the dense cover of rainforest trees, some producers have difficulty getting the sunlight they need. Some tropical orchids are specialized to live on the trunks and high branches of rainforest trees so that they can reach the sunlight. They do this by having specialized roots that let them cling to the bark or branches of tall trees.

Niche specialization contributes to high biodiversity. Organisms with specialized niches are less likely to compete with each other. A mammal that eats only ants does not compete for food with a mammal that eats only fruit. A plant that has roots that cling to bark does not compete with a plant rooted in soil. Two populations that do not compete with one another can thus live side by side. When many specialized populations are able to survive together in a small area, then many species can live together. The result is high biodiversity.

An orchid's specialized niche is living on trees high up in the canopy. Their specialized roots help them cling to tree bark and soak up water from the rain that falls on the tree and flows down its branches.

Biodiversity in Earth's Ecosystems

Terrestrial Ecosystems In terrestrial ecosystems, there is more biodiversity in tropical areas near the equator, where there is lots of sunshine, warmth, and rainfall. Biodiversity decreases as you approach the poles.

Arctic tundra

Deciduous forest

Boreal forest

Arctic tundra ecosystems are cold places with low levels of biodiversity. These harsh conditions mean that few species can survive in these ecosystems.

Deciduous forest ecosystems are found in areas where climate changes seasonally. Biodiversity is higher than in the Arctic or boreal forest ecosystems because the conditions are not as extreme.

Boreal forest ecosystems are found in places that are cold for longer periods during the year. Biodiversity is low in these ecosystems, but higher than in Arctic tundra ecosystems.

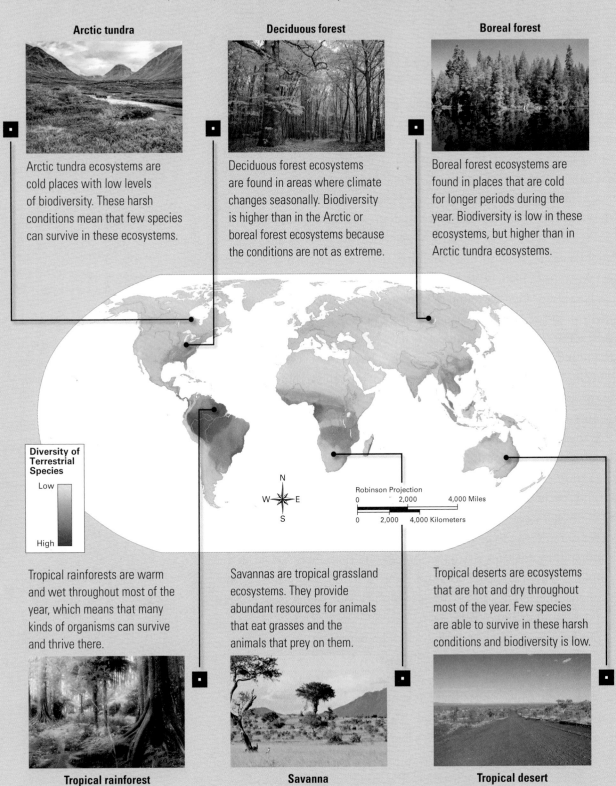

Diversity of Terrestrial Species

Low

High

Robinson Projection

0   2,000   4,000 Miles

0   2,000   4,000 Kilometers

N W E S

Tropical rainforests are warm and wet throughout most of the year, which means that many kinds of organisms can survive and thrive there.

Savannas are tropical grassland ecosystems. They provide abundant resources for animals that eat grasses and the animals that prey on them.

Tropical deserts are ecosystems that are hot and dry throughout most of the year. Few species are able to survive in these harsh conditions and biodiversity is low.

Tropical rainforest

Savanna

Tropical desert

Aquatic Ecosystems In aquatic ecosystems, biodiversity is highest where there are abundant nutrients and light, including shallow coastal areas where coral reefs and marshes are found and near the equator.

Arctic ocean

The Arctic Ocean surrounds the North Pole and is covered by ice during large parts of the year. Organisms have to be able to endure harsh conditions.

Coastal marsh

Coastal marshes represent combinations of terrestrial and aquatic ecosystems and provide abundant resources for many kinds of organisms.

Coastal eelgrass beds

Shallow, quiet coastal areas support the growth of aquatic plants like eelgrass. These ecosystems provide abundant resources for many kinds of marine organisms.

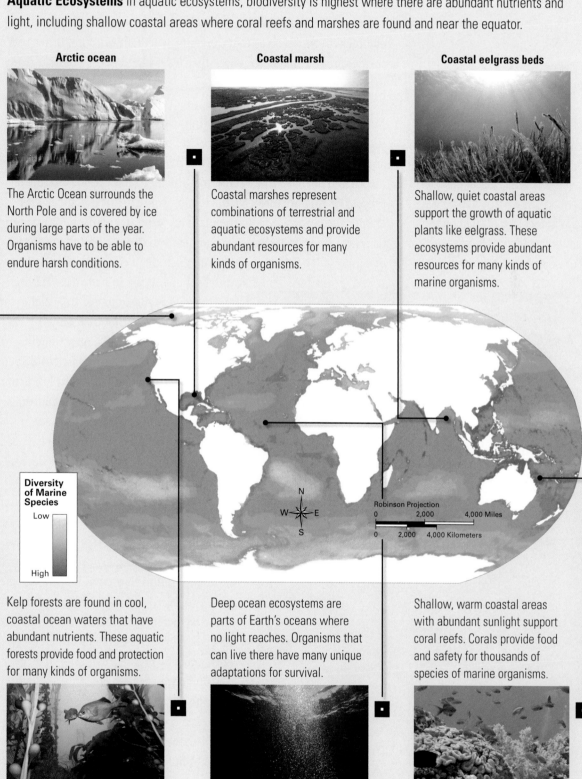

Diversity of Marine Species
Low
High

N W E S

Robinson Projection
0   2,000   4,000 Miles
0   2,000   4,000 Kilometers

Kelp forests are found in cool, coastal ocean waters that have abundant nutrients. These aquatic forests provide food and protection for many kinds of organisms.

Deep ocean ecosystems are parts of Earth's oceans where no light reaches. Organisms that can live there have many unique adaptations for survival.

Shallow, warm coastal areas with abundant sunlight support coral reefs. Corals provide food and safety for thousands of species of marine organisms.

Kelp forest

Deep ocean

Coral reef

5. Humans Benefit from Biodiversity

Many plants, including plants found in tropical rainforests and plants near you, have special molecules that can be used to treat human ailments. The bark of willow trees contains a chemical that people once used to reduce fever and cure a headache. This chemical is the active ingredient in aspirin. Purple foxglove plants produce a chemical in their leaves that prevents heart failure. What other useful species are out there? In what other ways could people benefit from exploring biodiversity?

Many important medicines come from plants. One example is Madagascar periwinkle, a flowering plant native to rainforests on the island of Madagascar. Gardeners love periwinkle for their pink flowers and glossy, green leaves. But periwinkle also has an important medical use. Scientists have discovered that the plant has unique chemical properties that are effective in treating some forms of cancer. Two chemicals harvested from the plant are used in chemotherapy, a type of cancer treatment that uses chemicals to slow or halt the growth of cancer cells. Scientists continue to study periwinkle and the many different chemicals in its leaves. Further study could result in better treatments for cancer and many other diseases.

Medicines are not the only benefits humans have gotten from particular species. Humans rely on many different kinds of living things for resources and materials and thus rely on biodiversity. Many of the foods you eat and the materials you use come from natural resources derived from particular species. For example, silk fabrics are woven from natural fibers that the silkworm moth caterpillar produces to make its cocoon. This farmed species was originally bred from a species of silkworm moth still found in the wild. Other species have provided valuable uses for solving some of society's problems. Scientists have discovered species of bacteria that consume and naturally break down oil, potentially offering a way to help clean up accidental oil spills that can devastate coastal areas. As scientists continue to explore ecosystems and discover new species and new information about known species, more and more opportunities arise for developing new technologies and products.

Many species have unique properties that scientists can apply towards new technologies, materials, and medicines. The Madagascar periwinkle is more than just a pretty flower. The plant contains chemicals that research has shown can effectively treat some forms of cancer.

When a species goes extinct, Earth loses biodiversity and humans lose important information about that species. Gastric brooding frogs offered knowledge about how to protect living tissues from corrosive stomach acids. With this frog's extinction, scientists could no longer use this information to improve human health.

Each new species that people discover is a mystery worth exploring because it could have unique characteristics that provide us with potentially important and useful knowledge. In the 1970s, for example, scientists discovered a new frog species in the forest streams of Queensland, Australia. These frogs, called gastric brooding frogs, were unusual because females raised their young inside their stomachs. They swallowed the fertilized eggs but somehow managed to not digest them! The presence of chemicals in the eggs caused females to stop producing stomach acids. Once the frog eggs had developed into tadpoles and then froglets, the mother spit them out of her mouth. After that, she could return to eating and digesting food normally. Scientists were very excited to study such a unique animal.

Unfortunately, soon after this frog species was discovered, it became extinct. **Extinction** is when all of the members of a species die and the species no longer exists. When a species goes extinct, it cannot be replaced. Extinction also means that biodiversity is decreased.

The loss of biodiversity, even the loss of just one species, is a loss of potential knowledge. Scientists had hoped that by studying the gastric brooding frogs, they could learn more about how the frogs turned on and off their ability to produce stomach acids. If scientists could have discovered how gastric brooding frogs do this, it could have meant potential treatments for many human illnesses associated with stomach acids, for example, stomach ulcers or acid reflux disease. It also could have meant potential treatments for helping people recover quickly from stomach surgery. With the loss of the gastric brooding frog, humans lost the important knowledge it could have revealed.

Scientists are still discovering new species, some of which could help humans. Each new species offers a new opportunity for research and understanding. There is so much out there yet to be explored. What more could scientists learn from studying new and unusual species? Could the next new species offer benefits as promising as that of the Madagascar periwinkle? Will you be the scientist who discovers it?

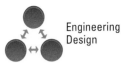

Engineering
Design

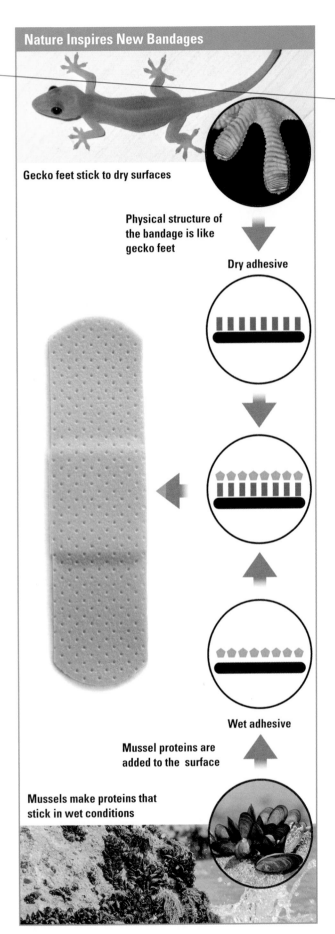

Nature Inspires New Bandages

Gecko feet stick to dry surfaces

Physical structure of
the bandage is like
gecko feet

Dry adhesive

Wet adhesive

Mussel proteins are
added to the surface

Mussels make proteins that
stick in wet conditions

6. Engineering a Super Bandage

Yeeouch! It can hurt to tear an adhesive bandage from your skin. You can loosen its sticky grip by getting it wet. This makes it less painful to remove, but it is a problem when you want it to stick during water sports. What would it take to design easy-to-remove bandages that stick under dry and wet conditions?

Biodiversity offers more than just raw materials for making new products. Engineers also look to biodiversity for ideas on how to solve engineering problems. To create removable bandages that can hold skin together in wet or dry environments, you would need a material that will stick under both conditions. Engineers working on the design of a bandage that meets all of these criteria used biomimicry, drawing inspiration from two species famous for their sticking abilities: geckos and mussels.

Adhesive Inspired by Gecko Toes Geckos easily climb walls and ceilings with textured toe pads that allow them to cling to slippery surfaces, even glass! But geckos do not stick permanently. Their toe pads can stick and un-stick themselves to a surface easily. Engineers realized that this ability could be applied to produce bandages that are easy to remove. They designed an adhesive pad with a texture similar to gecko toe pads like the one shown in Figure 8.6. They found that the gecko-inspired pad would stick and un-stick repeatedly to a dry surface. However, it did not function well on wet surfaces. They concluded that a bandage inspired by gecko feet alone would not meet the criterion of sticking effectively under wet conditions.

Figure 8.6

Biodiversity represents nature's innovations to solve problems in the world. Engineers combined two of nature's innovations, gecko feet and mussel glue, to design bandages for people that can stick under wet and dry conditions while still being easy to remove.

Adhesive Inspired by Mussel Glue To find inspiration for a wet adhesive, scientists turned to an animal that lives in water: mussels. Mussels have a soft body protected by two hard shells. They produce a protein-based glue that allows them to bind tightly to wet rocks. The researchers tested how well a mussel-inspired glue would stick to different surfaces. They realized it would be perfect for applications in wet environments, such as closing layers of tissue after surgery. But mussel glue wouldn't make the best removable bandage, because it doesn't meet all the criteria for success. It doesn't stick and un-stick easily like gecko toe pads do.

New Combined Solution Using the results of their research, engineers combined the solutions inspired by both species to come up with a design for a bandage that meets all of the criteria for success. The improved bandage design, shown in Figure 8.6, has the physical structure of a gecko's textured toe pad and its surface is covered in a gluey material similar to the proteins that mussels create. The result is an easy-to-remove adhesive pad that works in both wet and dry conditions. The bandage design promises more than an all-weather remedy for everyday cuts. It could be used to help people whose sensitive skin is moist and delicate, such as premature babies.

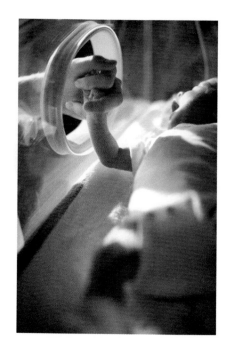

Premature babies would benefit from a bandage that sticks under wet and dry conditions but can be removed without damaging delicate skin.

LESSON SUMMARY

Biodiversity

The Importance of Biodiversity Every ecosystem on Earth is characterized by a natural level of biodiversity. Scientists have described patterns of biodiversity in ecosystems.

Fragile Tundra Ecosystems Tundra ecosystems have low levels of biodiversity. Small changes to populations in tundra ecosystems can have large impacts on populations of other organisms.

Keystone Species in the Kelp Forest The presence of keystone species in an ecosystem affects the biodiversity of the entire ecosystem.

Many Niches in Tropical Rainforests Tropical rainforest ecosystems support many species with specialized niches.

Humans Benefit from Biodiversity Scientists are still discovering new species, some of which could help humans.

Engineering a Super Bandage Using the results of tests as a guide, engineers combined the solutions inspired by two species to come up with a design for a bandage that meets all of their criteria for success.

Nature Detectives: Biodiversity Scientists

Earth is filled with amazing creatures that do incredible things. Scientists estimate that there could be 8 million to 100 million species. But only about 2 million species have been discovered. Discovering new species is the job of biodiversity scientists, and they do much more. What does a biodiversity scientist do?

Welcome to the Jungle

Rain falls as two scientists quietly track animals in a secluded Madagascar rainforest. They are biodiversity scientists, and their job is to observe, describe, and classify the species we share Earth with.

Madagascar is an island that has been separated from other land masses for over 88 million years. This long separation from the rest of the world means that nearly all species found there are unique to the island. They are not found anywhere else in the world! The job of these scientists is to describe and understand that impressive biodiversity.

Biodiversity scientists explore ecosystems to discover new things about our dynamic planet. These two biodiversity scientists are documenting undiscovered species on the island of Madagascar.

How to Become a Biodiversity Scientist

Do you love exploring? If so, you may want to become a biodiversity scientist. You will need two important things. First and most importantly, you need a curiosity about nature's unknown. This career may have you climbing trees, overturning rocks, and devising ways to understand and protect ecosystem biodiversity.

Second, to pursue your goals, you will need a college education in some area of life science. In college, you should study biology, including a specialization in a particular group of organisms, like plants or amphibians. Your science classes will include field experiences, lab work, and research. Some classes will focus on identifying species and the roles they play in an ecosystem. For example, you may team up with a group of classmates to identify different species of frogs in an area near your college and the roles they play in that ecosystem. Through your data collection, your team may notice that one species of frog has an unusually small population. Upon further research, your team might discover that their breeding area overlaps with an area recently harvested for trees. Your team would use their knowledge of conservation policy to advocate for protecting the breeding grounds.

Biodiversity scientists learn to identify and understand different species of organisms. For example, they learn how to distinguish between the different species of frogs pictured here and understand how they survive in their habitats.

These scientists spend long hours studying birds that they collected in the foothills of Mount Gorongosa. They discovered and described the biodiversity of this little studied area. Documenting biodiversity requires a lot of research and traveling to different locations.

Exploring the World

After graduating from college, you are ready to explore Earth's living wonders. Maybe you will join a team working in Gorongosa National Park, in Mozambique. This area is virtually unexplored, but has some of the highest levels of biodiversity in the world. What will you and other scientists learn about this fascinating area?

Exploring biodiversity requires teamwork. You and several other scientists travel to a field site. There, you set up camp, including living quarters and a field laboratory. Each of the team members has a different specialization—you may study birds, but other members of the team will study insects, mammals, or even roundworms!

From camp, you venture out to observe and collect the species that you encounter. Some days you hike for many miles in rocky terrain or dense undergrowth. Often, you use nets or traps to capture organisms for more detailed study in the field laboratory. When you return to camp, you spend your time making careful observations on the organisms that you collected and recording data on each. These data can be used to help identify areas that are especially important to protect. At the end of your expedition, you can identify how many species are found in the different habitats of Gorongosa National Park. You may even have discovered new species!

Discovering New Species

Discovering a new species is about the most exciting thing that can happen to a biodiversity scientist. As a biodiversity scientist, where might you go to discover a new species?

You might travel to far away places that have not been thoroughly explored, such as Gorongosa National Park. Another remote area that is relatively unexplored is the island of Borneo in Southeast Asia. In recent years, scientists have discovered many new species in this forested, tropical area, including one of the smallest frogs in the world. The Matang narrow-mouthed frog was discovered on the island in 2010. These miniscule frogs are so small that scientists initially thought the adult frogs—which only measure about 12 mm in length—were juveniles of a different species!

You can also discover new species in areas closer to home. Would you believe another new species of frog was discovered in a heavily populated area of New York City in 2012? A frog researcher recorded an unusual croak from a city pond. After locating the frogs and taking samples of their DNA, the researcher discovered he had found a new species of leopard frog. It was given a scientific name that honored a local scientist, *Rana kauffeldi*. New technologies, like digital audio recording and DNA sequencing are helping scientists discover more about the biodiversity we share the world with.

You don't have to be a scientist to help discover a new species. Residents of Los Angeles are participating in a citizen science project that involves placing insect traps in backyards and school gardens. So far, 30 new species of flies have been discovered through the efforts of dedicated citizen scientists. Try your hand at finding a new species. It might be as close as your backyard! ◆

A bioblitz is an event where scientists and members of local communities gather to survey the biodiversity of an area. This Alaskan girl is showing off a snow scorpionfly that she found that was not previously known from this area.

New species are discovered every day. In 2010, one of the smallest species of frog, the Matang narrow-mouthed frog, was discovered in the forests of the Southeast Asian island of Borneo.

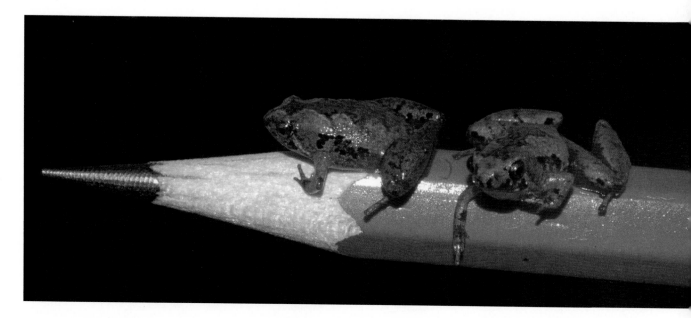

The Importance of Healthy Ecosystems

How do humans rely on healthy ecosystems?

Introduction

Whether you are splashing, floating, soaking, or just cooling off on a hot day, it is fun to play in water—clean water, that is. We all need clean water to drink and bathe in. It is not safe to drink water from a puddle in a parking lot or take a bath in a ditch. Where does the clean water you use come from? How did it get clean?

You know from your exploration of the water cycle that water is constantly moving through ecosystems. As water moves through soil, clouds, wetlands, and the other parts of the water cycle, it is naturally filtered of impurities and disease-causing organisms. Humans usually also treat water with additional filters and chemicals before considering it truly safe to drink. But healthy ecosystems do most of the work of making water clean. And humans rely on this service to get the clean water we need for drinking, washing, and watering crops.

In this lesson you will explore what makes an ecosystem healthy. You will then learn about ways that healthy ecosystems benefit humans. Next you will look at several examples of how even small changes to ecosystems cause disruptions that affect humans. You will end this lesson by thinking about how engineers use ecosystem functions to design economical solutions to environmental problems.

Vocabulary

ecosystem service a natural process humans rely on that healthy ecosystems provide, such as cleaning water and conserving soil

natural resource a material or source of energy found in nature that benefits humans

disease resistance a characteristic of organisms that makes it unlikely for them to be infected with or die from diseases

scavenger an organism that eats other organisms that are already dead

---

Next Generation Science Standards

Performance Expectations

MS-LS2-5. Evaluate competing design solutions for maintaining biodiversity and ecosystem services.

MS-ETS1-1. Define the criteria and constraints of a design problem with sufficient precision to ensure a successful solution, taking into account relevant scientific principles and potential impacts on people and the natural environment that may limit possible solutions.

Science and Engineering Practices

Engaging in Argument from Evidence Evaluate competing design solutions based on jointly developed and agreed-upon design criteria.

Asking Questions and Defining Problems
Define a design problem that can be solved through the development of an object, tool, process, or system and includes multiple criteria and constraints, including scientific knowledge that may limit possible solutions.

Crosscutting Concepts

Stability and Change Small changes in one part of a system might cause large changes in another part.

Influence of Science, Engineering, and Technology on Society and the Natural World

Science Addresses Questions About the Natural and Material World

Disciplinary Core Ideas

LS2.C. Biodiversity describes the variety of species found in Earth's terrestrial and oceanic ecosystems. The completeness or integrity of an ecosystem's biodiversity is often used as a measure of its health.

LS4.D. Changes in biodiversity can influence humans' resources, such as food, energy, and medicines, as well as ecosystem services that humans rely on—for example, water purification and recycling.

ETS1.A. The more precisely a design task's criteria and constraints can be defined, the more likely it is that the designed solution will be successful. Specification of constraints includes consideration of scientific principles and other relevant knowledge that are likely to limit possible solutions.

An ecosystem that is functioning normally provides many ecosystem services for human communities. Ecosystem services include providing natural resources, such as clean water, materials, rich soil, and a wide variety of plants and animals.

1. Healthy Ecosystems Provide Services

This mountain meadow ecosystem is not as serenely still as it looks in the photograph. It is bustling with activity. Populations of organisms are competing with each other for valuable resources. Producers are carrying out photosynthesis, predators are hunting for and consuming prey, and decomposers are breaking down wastes. At the same time, organisms of many types and sizes are carrying out cellular respiration. In other words, it is a picture of a healthy ecosystem. It is also a nice place to take a hike. What else does a healthy ecosystem provide for humans?

Healthy ecosystems provide important services for humans and human communities. An **ecosystem service** is a natural process humans rely on that healthy ecosystems provide, such as water purification. Ecosystems naturally filter wastes and debris out of water as it travels through the different parts of the water cycle. In addition to water purification, ecosystems are important in cycling nutrients, creating and protecting soil, and maintaining healthy populations of species to protect biodiversity.

Ecosystems provide so many services that it would be difficult to name them all, but we will explore some examples in this lesson. How do human communities benefit from the ecosystem services and resources provided by healthy ecosystems?

An important ecosystem service is providing natural resources that humans use as raw materials. A **natural resource** is a material or source of energy provided by nature that benefits humans. Natural resources include minerals, water, wood, and other materials and substances. The building that you are in, whether it is your home or school or local library, is made from materials like wood, stone, minerals, and metals that come from Earth's ecosystems. Natural resources also include products harvested from plants and animals in ecosystems. The foods that you eat and the chemicals used to make medicines or health products come from ecosystems. Without healthy soil and pollinators, many of those foods and important chemicals would not be available to you.

In the meadow ecosystem in the photo, the activities of producers, consumers, and decomposers are constantly making and revitalizing a layer of soil. Producers, like meadow flowers, take nutrients from the soil as they grow and reproduce. At the same time, they shed dead leaves and other wastes. Consumers, like grasshoppers munching on leaves, also use nutrients and recycle matter as they grow before leaving behind their bodies when they die. Decomposers, like fungi, use the energy and matter stored in those organisms and break down nitrogen and carbon-based molecules, releasing them into the soil. A rich layer of soil develops as plants and animals in this meadow ecosystem die and are decomposed. Farmers cannot grow crops of corn or soybeans without thick, healthy layers of soil. This process of nutrient cycling must occur for crop plants to grow season after season and produce the ingredients you buy from the grocery store.

Pollination is an important ecosystem service that helps plants reproduce and create fruits, seeds, grains, and nuts. Pollinators, like bees, butterflies, and moths come to flowers to drink nectar the flower produces. In this process, their bodies become covered with pollen from the flower. When they fly to another flower, they transfer pollen to the new flower. Many plants rely on pollinators to transfer pollen, and they cannot reproduce without the help of pollinators.

Without pollinators, farmers near the meadow would not be able to produce the fruits, seeds, grains, and nuts that they grow and sell. For example, bee populations supported by the meadow also visit flowers of farm plants, like apples, oranges, green beans, and squash. Some of your favorite foods rely on pollinators!

Humans rely on ecosystem services. Farms rely on wild areas like this meadow for natural resources, such as soil and healthy populations of pollinators. The meadow builds and protects soil that farmers need to grow their crops. It also produces pollinators that visit the crops and help them reproduce.

Humans Rely on Ecosystem Services

Healthy, functioning ecosystems perform important services, such as cleaning water in aquatic ecosystems, cycling nutrients to make them available to other living organisms, and maintaining healthy soil communities. The chart below shows a wide variety of ecosystem services, more than can be explored in this lesson. Take some time to examine this diagram. Can you think of ways that ecosystems provide each of these services?

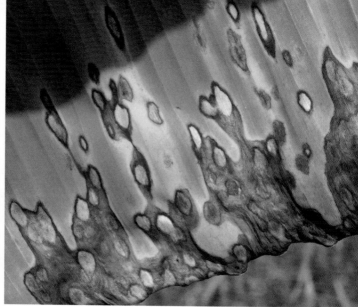

2. Ecosystem Change Impacts Human Food Supplies—Bananas

Suppose you are hankering for a banana but the familiar fruit has gone extinct! It may seem silly, but it is possible that the bananas you eat may die out soon. How can ecosystem services save bananas?

The natural biodiversity of healthy ecosystems provides an important ecosystem service. Recall that every ecosystem has a natural level of biodiversity, which means that each ecosystem has its own set of unique species. Each of those species has individuals that differ from one another in their traits. Having a variety of traits can benefit a population when conditions change. When disease strikes, some individuals may have traits that help them survive the disease. Others may have traits that help them survive a different disease.

Scientists use the natural biodiversity found in healthy ecosystems to develop new varieties of crops that have disease resistance. **Disease resistance** is a characteristic of organisms with natural traits that makes it less likely for them to be infected with diseases.

Humans grow the same kinds of crops over large areas, creating ecosystems that have low diversity and little variety. In places where people grow bananas, they usually only grow one variety of banana, called Cavendish bananas. These bananas have fruit that is sweet, tasty, and does not have seeds, and the trees produce lots of bananas. Cavendish bananas have traits that make them safe from a fungus called Panama Disease that has driven other varieties of bananas to extinction. However, a new fungal disease, called yellow sigatoka leaf spot, has arisen that affects Cavendish banana plants. When the spores of this fungus move to a new area, Cavendish banana trees there sicken and die.

Scientists are looking to ecosystems to find wild varieties of bananas that can withstand the new fungal disease. By finding and using the variety of traits found in the biodiversity of natural ecosystems, they can find banana varieties with resistance to this new disease. They may even be able to develop bananas that taste better than Cavendish bananas.

Biodiversity protects populations from disease. The banana variety that most people eat is susceptible to a new fungal disease, yellow sigatoka leaf spot disease. Scientists use wild varieties resistant to the disease to develop new, disease-resistant bananas.

Scientists use biodiversity in healthy ecosystems to improve food crops. Using traits of wild bananas, scientists can improve disease resistance in bananas you find in the grocery store, as well as improve flavor and size.

Scavengers consume dead animals, which can positively impact human health. Vultures are scavengers that feed off of the carcasses of dead animals. These dead animals can harbor disease or feed other animals that harbor disease.

3. Ecosystem Change Impacts Human Health— Vultures and Rabies

A flock of vultures gathers around a dead cow. They pick bits of flesh off of the bones and stick their heads into the body to find the best parts. This might sound gross to you, but a vulture would disagree. Vultures provide ecosystems with a much needed cleanup crew. Without vultures, dead animals might accumulate and rot. Populations of other organisms, including ones that cause or carry disease, would increase as they eat dead animals. What happens when vultures are not there to provide this ecosystem service?

Humans rely on animals like vultures to remove dead or dying organisms that are potential sources of disease or infection from ecosystems. Vultures are called scavengers. A **scavenger** is an organism that eats other organisms that are already dead. Vultures do not hunt and kill the food they eat. Instead, they eat the carcasses of animals that have already died from another cause. Eating carcasses not only provides vultures with a convenient source of food, it also benefits other organisms that live in the ecosystem. What happens to an ecosystem when vulture populations begin to disappear?

Scientists were puzzled when they noticed a dramatic decline in vulture populations in India. What was the cause of this decline? Scientists examined patterns in the vulture deaths and discovered that the increase in vulture deaths was associated with the use of a common veterinary drug in cattle. The drug is safe for cattle but, when vultures ate the remains of cattle that had been given the drug, the vultures died. Widespread use of the drug caused three common species of vultures to nearly become extinct in just a few years.

Using a drug on cattle seemed like a small change to the ecosystem, but it caused a series of indirect effects that created a big problem for humans. When vulture populations decreased, more carcasses were available to other scavengers, such as feral dogs. With a decrease in competition from vultures, feral dog populations began to rise. You might think that an increase in feral dogs would be beneficial because these scavengers could take over the dirty job left vacant by vultures. But feral dogs are a health problem for humans. Dogs can carry rabies, a fatal disease for humans. In India, most people get rabies from dog bites. More feral dogs meant that more people were getting rabies from dogs. Figure 9.3 shows how these trends are related. As populations of vultures decreased, populations of feral dogs increased. The number of humans who contracted rabies from dogs also increased, leading to a higher death rate in human communities.

The decline of vultures in India is a good example of the importance of services provided by healthy ecosystems. When populations of scavengers in ecosystems were disrupted, ecosystem services were also disrupted. Before the disruption in India, the ecosystem was providing an important, but unrecognized, service to humans: disease prevention.

Like vultures, feral dogs are scavengers. However, they can carry rabies and transmit the disease to humans through bites.

Figure 9.3

The line graph shows how feral dog populations increased (red line) as vulture populations decreased (blue line). As a result, the number of humans who were bitten by feral dogs and infected with rabies also increased.

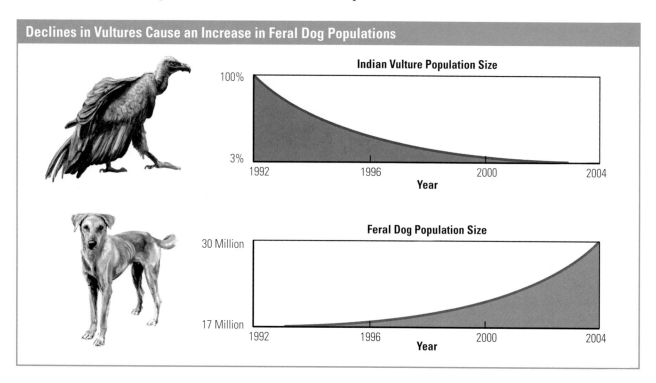

Declines in Vultures Cause an Increase in Feral Dog Populations

Indian Vulture Population Size

100%

3%

1992   1996   2000   2004
Year

Feral Dog Population Size

30 Million

17 Million

1992   1996   2000   2004
Year

When humans destroy or build on coastal dunes, those ecosystems can no longer protect coastal communities. These coastal ecosystems naturally provide a flood control service, which is lost when the ecosystem is destroyed.

4. Ecosystem Change Impacts Human Environments— Flooding

It has been raining and storming for days and the ocean waves are crashing against the shore. As the surging water rolls over the coastline, it eats away at the beach, removing sand and soil. It even begins to tear away pieces of the road that follows the shoreline. As the water creeps higher and higher, it approaches buildings situated nearby. Soon, the ocean flows into homes, causing people to flee and destroying property. How can ecosystems protect human communities from surging coastal waters?

Healthy ecosystems provide a service by reducing the risk of flooding. During storms, coastal ecosystems such as marshes, swamps, and sand dunes absorb water that would otherwise flood nearby ecosystems or human communities. You have learned how wetland ecosystems provide a buffer against flooding along the Gulf Coast. Other coastal ecosystems, such as dunes, also prevent flood damage to nearby ecosystems. Healthy dune ecosystems, with healthy populations of beach grasses, reduce the impact of storms and prevent soil erosion. People benefit from this ecosystem service when property and lives are protected from flooding.

When humans build towns, roads, and other structures in sensitive coastal areas, they often destroy coastal wetland and coastal ecosystems. Vegetation, like dune grasses, that help protect coastlines from erosion and flooding, are removed and replaced with artificial structures. The ecosystems that previously protected human property and nearby wildlife from floods and storm surges are not healthy enough or large enough to provide the service they have in the past. This, along with rising sea levels resulting from climate change, threatens coastal ecosystems and the human communities near coasts around the world.

Healthy coastal ecosystems reduce flooding. When coastal ecosystems, like dune ecosystems, are damaged by human development, then flooding becomes more frequent and threatens lives and property in coastal communities.

When ecosystem services are disrupted, humans suffer. One result of climate change and the destruction of coastal ecosystems is that flooding along coastlines has increased. Not only have floods become more common, they have become more devastating. In the United States, flooding is now the leading cause of property loss and fatalities due to natural disaster. What can be done about this problem?

Fortunately, scientific understanding of how coastal ecosystems work can be used to restore the services they provide. When human communities make efforts to apply scientific understanding to restore healthy coastal ecosystems, they can protect against flooding and reduce the risk of damage to property and loss of human life.

Communities of people that live near coasts are beginning to recognize the importance of services provided by ecosystems. They are adopting new ways of protecting their coastlines. River diversions, can reestablish natural buffers against flooding and storms. On sandy coastlines, people are restoring dunes and establishing natural populations of beach grasses. Beach grasses prevent erosion when their roots hold onto soil and slow the flow of water over land. Coastal communities can also work to prevent development in coastal areas so that ecosystems are not further damaged by building homes, hotels, or roads. By allowing coastal ecosystems to function naturally, ecosystems can once again help to protect human communities from the risk of flooding.

When human communities disrupt ecosystems, such as coastal dunes, they often disrupt ecosystem services. Fortunately, communities, scientists, and engineers can find ways to restore ecosystems so that they can enjoy the benefits of ecosystem services.

Coastal dune ecosystems help prevent damage from flooding by reducing erosion. People can help to restore a healthy coastal ecosystem by planting new beach grasses and encouraging the regrowth of existing populations of dune plants.

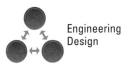
Engineering
Design

5. Clean Drinking Water for New York City

There are nearly 9 million people living in New York City. Every one of them needs fresh water to drink. Residents enjoy over 1 billion gallons of clean water every day. However, in the early 1990s, New York City faced a water crisis. The city's water treatment plants were stretched beyond their limits, and the number of residents needing water was increasing. How did engineers find a way to supply clean water to this huge population?

Defining the Criteria—Providing Clean Water for Millions of People Engineers attacked the problem of providing clean water to millions of people by precisely defining the criteria for a successful solution to New York City's drinking water problem. There were three criteria. First, drinking water needed to be clean: the water should be free of dirt particles and treated with chemicals to make it safe to drink. Second, there must be enough water for the large population of the city. Third, the solution needed to meet the needs of New York City's population as it continued to grow into the future.

Defining the Constraints—Protecting the Environment and Saving Money Next, engineers determined the design constraints. For example, how the solution will impact humans and the environment. One constraint was that the solution be economical. The solution should be something that the city could afford over time. Another was that the solution would help protect the environment.

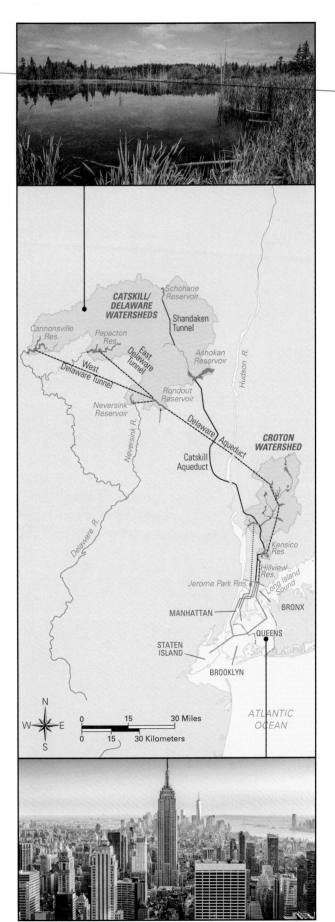

Engineers analyzed criteria and constraints to redesign a water supply system that relies on ecosystem services. Wetlands upstream from New York were protected to naturally filter the city's supply of clean water.

A possible solution was to build larger water treatment plants to serve the increasing population. Building large water treatment plants would be expensive and would likely not meet the city's needs in the long term as populations continued to grow.

In addition to being expensive, water treatment plants can damage the environment. Research shows that chemicals used to disinfect water can be dangerous in large amounts. Engineers wanted to find an affordable solution that provided an adequate water supply and protected ecosystems near the city. The solution of building larger water treatment plants did not meet the precisely defined criteria and constraints of the problem.

Use Ecosystems to Clean Water To find a successful solution, engineers used their scientific knowledge of ecosystem services to address the criteria and constraints. Instead of building expensive water treatment plants, engineers invested in protecting surrounding ecosystems that naturally purified drinking water for the city. Watersheds are large areas of land where rainwater naturally flows into rivers and wetlands. In this process, water is naturally cleaned and filtered. Water that flows through these areas needs little chemical treatment to drink. New York City's solution involved protecting nearby watersheds so that they could continue to provide this ecosystem service. This solution protects ecosystems, saves money, and provides some of the best drinking water in the world!

For an ecosystem to provide services that benefit humans, it must be healthy. Scientists monitor the water quality in the wetlands that supply New York City with water to ensure that the ecosystems are functioning as they should.

LESSON SUMMARY

The Importance of Healthy Ecosystems

Healthy Ecosystems Provide Services Healthy ecosystems provide important services for human communities. Ecosystems provide natural resources that humans use as raw materials.

Ecosystem Change Impacts Human Food Supplies—Bananas Scientists use the natural biodiversity of healthy ecosystems to develop new varieties of crops.

Ecosystem Change Impacts Human Health—Vultures and Rabies When populations of scavengers in ecosystems are disrupted, ecosystem services are also disrupted.

Ecosystem Change Impacts Human Environments—Flooding When humans make efforts to restore healthy coastal ecosystems, they can protect against flooding and reduce the risk of damage to property and loss of human life.

Clean Drinking Water for New York City Engineers used their scientific knowledge of ecosystem services to find a successful solution to provide clean water to millions of people.

The Ocean's Changing Menu

For thousands of years, humans have set out in fishing boats and hauled in nets full of fish, crabs, shrimp, and clams. Seafood has been on the menu at tables everywhere from fast food restaurants to Hollywood galas. But how might this important ecosystem service of oceans change in the future? How will this change what kind of seafood we eat?

Bounty of the Sea

The ocean is an important source of food for people. World-wide, 3 billion people get their primary source of protein from the ocean. According to the U.S. Department of Commerce, Americans consume over 4.8 billion pounds of seafood a year. Another source says Americans eat 15.5 pounds of fish or other seafood per person each year! Is there enough fish to ensure that the ocean will continue to feed the world at this rate? Not without putting new ideas to work!

Some experts have concluded that most commercial, or large-scale, fishing is an unsustainable way of getting food from the ocean. When a method is unsustainable, resources are being used up faster than they can be replaced. Scientists are trying to understand how to change unsustainable methods of harvesting food into methods that are sustainable. A sustainable practice is one that results in a resource, such as fish to eat, remaining available for long periods of time. Fishing for some species of fish can be sustainable. Small-scale fishing, such as when you might use a fishing pole in a nearby river or lake, is sustainable. Other methods of raising and capturing fish can be sustainable, such as some ways of growing fish in aquatic "farms."

In the United States, the most popular foods that people eat from the ocean are shrimp, salmon, and tuna. Are those ocean foods harvested in a sustainable way?

Many kinds of food come from the ocean. More than half of all seafood that Americans eat is shrimp, salmon, and tuna. Have you had a tuna sandwich lately?

The Cost of Overfishing

Is fishing for shrimp, salmon, and tuna sustainable? The answer can be complicated. Large-scale commercial fishing of most tuna species is not considered sustainable. Why not?

The high demand for tuna has led to overfishing by commercial fishing operations. Overfishing means the removal of more fish than the population can replace. The bluefin tuna population in the Atlantic Ocean decreased over 90 percent between 1950 and 2003. If overfishing continues, this fish species faces extinction.

Large-scale commercial fishing operations often use fishing methods that harm other species, such as using large nets to scoop up schools of fish. Large nets can also catch dolphins, sea turtles, and other fish. This is called "by catch." Species caught as by catch in nets are not eaten, but they do die. These fishing practices cause decreases in many populations of ocean organisms.

Not all commercial fishing practices are unsustainable. Some species of fish can be sustainably caught, such as flounder and mackerel. They have large populations and reproduce quickly, so populations can better withstand large-scale fishing. But scientists are also finding new sources of food that can be harvested sustainably from the oceans. What might be on your lunch plate in the future?

Tuna are top predators in the marine food chain. They help maintain balance in marine ecosystems through their impact on food webs. Populations of bluefin tuna in the Atlantic Ocean are threatened by unsustainable fishing.

A kelp "farmer" uses diving gear to check on her crop. Kelp farming is a sustainable way to use the ocean as a source of food for humans. Scientists calculate that if there were a global network of kelp farms roughly the size of Washington state, enough food could be provided for the entire world population.

Kelp Burgers Anyone?

If you are looking for sustainable food from the ocean, consider seaweed! Seaweed can be grown sustainably throughout the ocean and can supply large numbers of people with a healthy food source.

Even if you said, "yuck!" you have probably eaten seaweed before. Seaweed has been used for a long time in the manufacturing of ice cream, puddings, yogurt, and even chocolate milk. Red seaweeds have a substance called carrageenan that can be used to thicken and stabilize foods.

People all around the world eat seaweed. Seaweed-wrapped sushi and crunchy seaweed chips are found in supermarkets everywhere. But top chefs aren't stopping there. They add kelp, a type of seaweed, to ground meat to make kelp burgers. Or they fry up another kind of seaweed, called dulse, which tastes like bacon.

Seaweeds are some of the fastest growing producers in the world, which makes them highly sustainable. Kelp grows up to a foot long in just three months. Farmers grow seaweed along stacked rows of nylon ropes in coastal marine ecosystems. This allows ocean farmers to grow lots of seaweed in a small space. Farming seaweed can be combined with other kinds of ocean farming, such as sustainable farming of clams, oysters, or mussels.

Sustainable Choices for Your Menu

Seaweed farmers are helping make sustainable use of the ocean. Next time you're hungry for a crunchy snack, try some crispy and protein-rich seaweed chips! But there are other ways that we can all choose sustainable and nutritious foods from the oceans.

Another good source of food from the ocean that can be grown and harvested in sustainable ways is shellfish, like clams, mussels, and oysters. Ocean farmers can actually grow animals like these alongside seaweed farms. They can be grown in the same way, by placing young mussels or clams on ropes and allowing them to grow in the ocean. When they have grown to full size, they can be peeled off of the ropes and enjoyed in soups, cooked, or even raw!

Your family can use information on sustainability if you buy fish or other foods at the supermarket. There's even an app for that! The app compiles information on how different kinds of fish are harvested. When you search for the seafood, it gives you a color code that indicates how sustainable it is. Red means that the item is not sustainable; yellow means that it is somewhat sustainable; and green means that it is highly sustainable. Seafood restaurants and grocery stores use this color code on their menus.

Using tools like this can help you to make informed choices about what you or your family buys. When you buy something, even if it is a can of tuna to make a sandwich, you are impacting the decisions made by your grocery store or the commercial fishing company that harvests tuna. Choosing to buy tuna that was harvested in a sustainable way, from tuna populations that are stable or in ways that reduce by catch, is like a vote for a more sustainable approach to using the ocean's resources. Your everyday decisions, even about the food you eat, impacts ecosystem health all over the world. If humans make sustainable choices to reduce their impact on ocean species and ocean ecosystems, then healthy ocean ecosystems can continue to provide the important service of helping to feed the world. ◆

Other ways of harvesting sustainable foods from the ocean are to farm animals like clams, mussels, or oysters.

Engineering Solutions for Protecting Ecosystems

How do humans affect coral reefs and other ecosystems?

Introduction

What are these divers doing with this cage-like structure in the ocean? It may look like sea trash, but it is actually a new home for sea life. These divers have installed a support structure and are placing young corals and other reef animals onto it. What will happen to the coral reef ecosystem as these corals and reef animals grow on the cage?

This reef is an illustration of how humans can be the cause of both negative and positive effects on ecosystems. Human activities often change ecosystems. Can humans also protect and restore ecosystems?

In this lesson, you will explore the cause and effect relationships between growing human populations and changes in Earth's ecosystems. You will learn about six important ways that humans disrupt ecosystems and how humans can design solutions to solve the problems associated with those disruptions. You will examine how scientists and local communities use models to design ways to restore an aquatic ecosystem along the Atlantic Coast. Finally, you will reflect on how human societies make decisions that can impact ecosystems.

Vocabulary

per capita a measure of something per person; for example, per capita income is the ratio of total income to people

over-exploitation harvesting species from the wild faster than those populations can recover, resulting in population decline

emerging disease a disease that has recently appeared in human populations, often as a result of new interactions with species in ecosystems

habitat degradation changing or destroying natural ecosystems in ways that disrupt their healthy functioning

invasive species a species that has been introduced to a place where it is not naturally found and causes ecological or economic harm

climate change a long-term change in climate patterns on Earth, including changes in average global temperatures and the frequency of severe weather

---

Next Generation Science Standards

Performance Expectations

MS-ESS3-4. Construct an argument supported by evidence for how increases in human population and per-capita consumption of natural resources impact Earth's systems.

MS-LS2-5. Evaluate competing design solutions for maintaining biodiversity and ecosystem services.

MS-ETS1-4. Develop a model to generate data for iterative testing and modification of a proposed object, tool, or process such that an optimal design can be achieved.

Science and Engineering Practices

Engaging in Argument from Evidence
• Evaluate competing design solutions based on jointly developed and agreed-upon design criteria.
• Construct an oral and written argument supported by empirical evidence and scientific reasoning to support or refute an explanation or a model for a phenomenon or a solution to a problem.

Developing and Using Models Develop a model to generate data to test ideas about designed systems, including those representing inputs and outputs.

Crosscutting Concepts

Cause and Effect Cause and effect relationships may be used to predict phenomena in natural or designed systems.

Stability and Change Small changes in one part of a system might cause large changes in another part.

Influence of Science, Engineering, and Technology on Society and the Natural World

Science Addresses Questions about the Natural and Material World

Disciplinary Core Ideas

ESS3.C. Typically as human populations and per-capita consumption of natural resources increase, so do the negative impacts on Earth unless the activities and technologies involved are engineered otherwise.

LS2.C. Biodiversity describes the variety of species found in Earth's terrestrial and oceanic ecosystems. The completeness or integrity of an ecosystem's biodiversity is often used as a measure of its health.

LS4.D. Changes in biodiversity can influence humans' natural resources, such as food, energy, and medicines, as well as ecosystem services that humans rely on—for example, water purification and recycling.

ETS1.B. • There are systematic processes for evaluating solutions with respect to how well they meet the criteria and constraints of a problem.
• A solution needs to be tested, and then modified on the basis of the test results, in order to improve it.
• Models of all kinds are important for testing solutions.

ETS1.C. The iterative process of testing the most promising solutions and modifying what is proposed on the basis of the test results leads to greater refinement and ultimately to an optimal solution.

Each of these people must have access to clean water, food, and shelter. These necessities come from natural resources that are extracted from ecosystems. The result is that human populations have an impact on ecosystems.

Figure 10.1

In the past 200 years, the human population has grown to more than seven times what it was in 1800—and it is still growing! This growth results in a greater need for natural resources to support those people.

1. Predicting the Impact of Human Populations on Ecosystems

Each morning, you use water to brush your teeth and get yourself ready for the day. You might ride in a car or a bus to get to school or sports practice, using fuel along the way. Throughout the day, you may use electricity for light and to charge your phone. You eat food for snacks and meals. As the day goes by, you use water for drinking, bathing, and cleaning up. By the end of an active day, you have used a variety of resources. All of those resources come ultimately from Earth's ecosystems. Have you ever thought of what kinds of natural resources you, your family, or your neighbors use? How does this use of natural resources affect Earth and its ecosystems?

When there are large numbers of people, greater amounts of natural resources are needed to support them. No matter where they live on Earth, people need clean water, food, and shelter. It also takes energy to heat or cool their homes, refrigerate and cook their food, and transport their goods—and themselves—from place to place. Ecosystems provide the raw materials for meeting these needs in the form of natural resources like soil, wood, water, and fossil fuels.

The global human population has grown throughout history and is continuing to grow at an increasing rate. Figure 10.1 shows how Earth's human population has changed over the past 2,000 years. For most of the last 2,000 years the human population remained relatively stable. In the year 1800, there were about 1 billion people on the planet. By 1927, 130 years later, that had doubled to 2 billion people. It doubled again in only 47 years to 4 billion in 1974. Since 1800, Earth's human population has grown so rapidly that now there are well over 7 billion people and the population is predicted to reach 8 billion by around 2025. The steep line on the graph shows that the population has grown dramatically in a very short time and it is continuing to grow at a rapid rate.

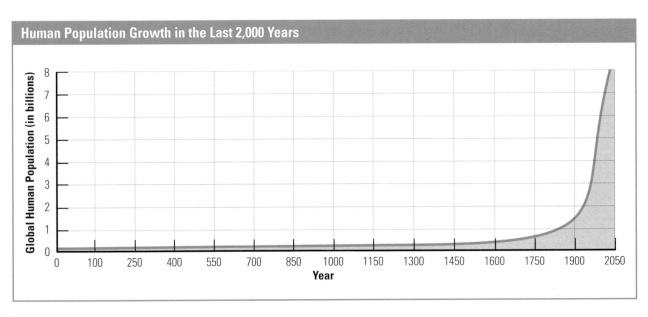

Human Population Growth in the Last 2,000 Years

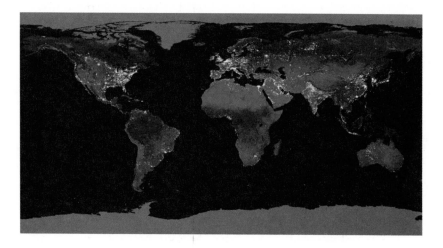

Satellite images of Earth at night show areas of dense human populations. Large human population, coupled with increased per capita natural resource use, means that humans are disrupting Earth's ecosystems at greater rates.

Not only are there more humans on Earth these days, but each person also uses more natural resources than a person typically did in the past. Another way of saying this is that the per capita use of natural resources has increased. **Per capita** is a measure of something per person. For example, per capita income is the ratio of total income to people, so average income per person. If you add together all the energy used by everyone in the world, then divide that by the number of people in the world, that number is the amount of energy used per person—the per capita energy use of the human population. A typical person today uses more than twice as much energy as someone who lived during the early 1900s did.

What has caused per capita energy use to increase? Many people in today's societies drive, eat foods that were shipped long distances using fossil fuels, or buy a new phone every few years—all activities that use energy. These activities did not exist in the past. What do you predict happens to ecosystems when you multiply a larger human population by a greater per capita use of natural resources?

Both human population size and the per capita use of natural resources have increased over the last few hundred years. This growth has caused increased impacts of humans on ecosystems. You can see evidence of human impact on Earth from space. This image is made from satellite photographs of Earth's surface. At night, areas with dense populations of humans show up as brightly lit spots. These are places where the activity of bustling cities lights up the night sky. This shows just how much human populations have changed Earth's ecosystems through their population size.

As the human population grows and uses natural resources at faster and faster rates, ecosystems cannot replace those natural resources as quickly as they disappear. When ecosystems are disrupted in this way, they lose the ability to provide ecosystem services. The rate of species extinction has increased globally because of disruptions to ecosystems. What can humans do to decrease their negative impacts on Earth's ecosystems?

Natural resources that humans rely on, such as wood, come from ecosystems. This forest ecosystem has been almost completely destroyed to supply wood for human communities. The ecosystem may not recover from this large disruption.

Human Populations Are Changing Natural Resources

As human populations increase, more natural resources are extracted from ecosystems for human use. The rate of human population growth and per capita consumption is directly related to the loss of critical natural resources, such as fresh water, minerals, energy resources, and land that is usable for growing food.

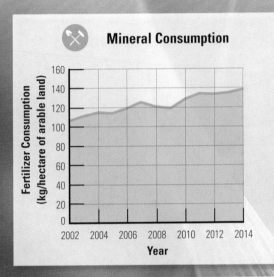

Mineral Consumption

As human population increases, consumption of resources also increases. The larger human population uses more mineral resources extracted from ecosystems.

Amount of Cultivated Land

Humans are changing ecosystems rapidly as population and resource use grows. For example, nearly 40% of Earth's terrestrial area is used for agriculture.

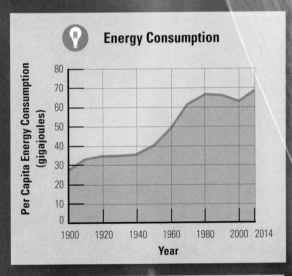

Energy Consumption

Per capita energy consumption is increasing as each person on Earth uses, on average, more energy resources for heating homes and fueling vehicles.

Available Fresh Water

As population and per capita consumption increases, humans use more natural resources. The amount of water available per person continues to decrease.

Efforts to reduce overfishing in Lake Malawi have reduced snail populations and decreased the spread of bilharzia. This makes the lake safer for local human communities.

2. Over-Exploitation: Overfishing Changes Ecosystems

On a hot day, a group of friends walks to a lake to cool off. At the lake, they see a sign, "Beware Bilharzia." What does it mean?

The human population near Lake Malawi, in southeastern Africa, doubled between the 1980s and 2010s. Around the same time, there were outbreaks of parasitic worm infections in humans living near the lake. This infection, called *bilharzia*, is devastating to humans, causing illness and fatigue for years. The parasitic worms live in snails for part of their lifetime, then migrate to people. The increase in parasitic infections was caused by an increase in snail populations, but what caused the increase in snail populations?

The human population boom around Lake Malawi resulted in over-fishing, which caused changes in other populations in the ecosystem. Overfishing is a form of over-exploitation. **Over-exploitation** is harvesting species from the wild faster than those populations can replace individuals that were harvested, resulting in population decline. As humans removed more fish from the lake, the prey populations of those fish increased. One important kind of prey for the fish is freshwater snails. These snails can be infected with parasitic worms, which can then be transmitted to humans as they wade in the water. As snail populations increased, so did populations of parasitic worms, and more people became infected with bilharzia.

To reduce bilharzia infections near Lake Malawi, scientists worked with local communities to find solutions that promote a healthy ecosystem but were not expensive or difficult to implement. These are important constraints in communities that do not have access to other sources of income or food. These communities rely on fish from Lake Malawi for their food and livelihoods. They arrived at solutions that allowed fishing, but also reduced snail populations. Local fishermen use nets with larger holes that catch only larger fish and protect the smaller fish species that mainly eat snails. This practice reduced overfishing in the lake. By reducing overfishing, snail populations decreased and bilharzia infections also declined.

A sign warns people that contact with local water can cause a devastating disease, bilharzia. This disease is spread by snail populations, which increased when local populations over-fished Lake Malawi.

Harmful materials become pollution when humans introduce them to ecosystems. Plastic wastes can harm living things in aquatic ecosystems, including sea turtles, when they become trapped by them or when they mistake plastic objects for food.

The choices you make, such as whether to buy a drink in a plastic bottle or use a reusable container, can impact ecosystems near you and around the world.

3. Pollution: Plastics in the Oceans

The impacts of natural resource use on ecosystems do not only happen half a world away. Your own resource use makes a difference too. Imagine you are buying a sports drink. How do you choose which brand to buy? You might choose based on taste or cost. But if those factors do not help you make your final decision, then perhaps you should think about what is best for sea turtles. What does your choice at the store have to do with sea turtles?

If your drink bottle is plastic or you have your purchases put into a plastic bag to carry home, then it can be a matter of life and death for sea turtles and other ocean creatures. Every year, millions of metric tons of plastics end up in Earth's aquatic ecosystems. Most plastics do not break down naturally. They build up over time, becoming a large source of pollution. Ocean creatures, such as fish, sea birds, and sea turtles mistake plastics for food and eat them. In 2014, one study of sea turtle populations in the Indian Ocean found that half of them had plastic in their stomachs and intestines. Almost all animals cannot digest plastic. When they accidentally eat it, they can be injured or killed. Aquatic organisms, like sea turtles, can also become trapped in plastic trash. Sea turtles around the world are threatened by eating and being trapped in plastics.

To protect ecosystems from plastic pollution, people can modify how they use and dispose of plastics. Families can avoid using plastics or recycle them in order to reduce plastic waste. When your family chooses to buy products that are not packaged in plastic, that could put pressure on companies to use less plastic in their packaging.

Engineers can find ways to reduce plastic use. Engineers are developing new materials that are similar to plastic, but are biodegradable, meaning they break down over time through natural processes. Scientists have even discovered bacteria and some worm species that consume plastic and may be used to break down plastic wastes. It is up to society—and people like you—to decide how to help protect aquatic ecosystems and sea turtles from plastic pollution.

4. Emerging Diseases: New Viral Infections

In the late 1990s, a deadly disease called Nipah virus infected workers on pig farms in Malaysia. Over 100 people died, more than one-third of those who were infected. People in that area had been raising pigs for generations, but the virus had never been reported in humans. What caused the virus to suddenly start infecting people?

Though pigs spread Nipah virus, they were not the original source of the virus. Fruit bats living in nearby forests had likely been carrying the virus for thousands of years. But these bats do not naturally interact with pigs or humans. The virus spread to humans because these human communities only recently moved into the forest where the fruit bats live. People began to raise their pigs under trees where the bats roost and eat fruit. As the bats eat, they drop leftover bits of fruit, some of which might be contaminated by the virus. Pigs that ate those leftovers became infected with the virus. Then, humans working on the pig farms caught the virus from the pigs.

As human populations expand further into ecosystems, they more frequently come into contact with wild animals and the diseases that they carry. The Nipah virus is only one example of these emerging diseases. An **emerging disease** is a disease that has recently appeared in human populations, often as a result of new interactions with wild species in ecosystems. In recent decades, scientists have identified many emerging diseases, including SARS, Ebola, Zika, and HIV.

Public health officials design ways to reduce how often new diseases infect human populations. Efforts involve educating people about contact with wild animal populations and how to avoid transferring disease. To prevent new infections by the Nipah virus, scientists recommend keeping farm animals away from the trees that bats use for roosting. This avoids spreading the virus between these animals. They also suggest that farmworkers wear protective gear when handling animals to prevent them from becoming infected when animals get the disease. By addressing the conditions that have led to outbreaks of emerging diseases, people can slow or stop their spread.

Emerging diseases often enter human populations as a result of new interactions between humans and wildlife. As human populations grow, they expand into previously uninhabited ecosystems, including wild fruit bat habitats.

Pig farms built in wild fruit bat habitats led to the emergence of the deadly Nipah virus infections. Scientists helped local communities avoid infections by moving pig farming away from areas where fruit bats roost.

5. Habitat Degradation: Coffee Agriculture

You grab your binoculars for a walk in the local park. There it is! The little black-and-white bird, just like the one that you saw last summer. But you never see these birds in the winter at your park. Where do they go each year?

Many birds, like this black-and-white warbler, migrate between different areas throughout the year. In summer, they are found in North America, including in your local park. In winter, these birds fly south to Central and South America. Birds that migrate need healthy ecosystems in both of the places they live—your local park and tropical forests. But some forest ecosystems these birds depend on in Central and South America are being destroyed to grow coffee.

As human populations grow and require more land for agricultural production, ecosystems suffer from habitat degradation. **Habitat degradation** is changing or destroying natural ecosystems in ways that disrupt their healthy functioning. Coffee farmers cut down tropical forests to plant coffee trees. In the process, they displace or destroy populations of forest organisms, like black-and-white warblers and other species. Is it possible to grow coffee trees and protect forest ecosystems at the same time?

Most coffee agriculture involves growing only coffee trees on the farm, such as in the photo on the left. Agricultural scientists know that coffee trees also grow well in the shade of taller trees, such as in the photo on the right. Farmers traditionally grow coffee that way because taller trees help conserve and fertilize soil, as well as provide homes for the pollinators of coffee trees. Mixed areas of forest and coffee farmland do not produce as many coffee beans as farms with only coffee trees, but shaded farms protect healthy forest ecosystems and their associated biodiversity. People who want to buy "forest friendly" coffee will often pay extra money for it. Agricultural systems can be modified in similar ways to reduce their negative impacts on ecosystems. These systems can still provide people with the food and products they want, while also protecting ecosystems.

Many species rely on healthy, tropical forests in Central America, including black-and-white warblers. When the forests they rely on are cut down for coffee agriculture, this displaces or destroys populations of the many species of animals that rely on those tropical forest ecosystems.

Left: Coffee trees grown in fields on their own often yield a lot of coffee beans. Right: Coffee trees grown under taller trees yield fewer beans but provide healthy forest habitat for the species that rely on it.

6. Invasive Species: Asian Carp and the Great Lakes

Aliens have invaded! They are not aliens from another planet, but aliens from another ecosystem. How do these aliens affect the ecosystems they invade?

Asian carp are an **invasive species,** a species that has been introduced to a place where it is not naturally found and causes ecological or economic harm. In the 1970s, people brought Asian carp from Eurasia to the United States and released them. They hoped that they would eat aquatic weeds and snail pests in lakes and fish farms.

Asian carp are doing too well in their new home. They eat large amounts of plankton, reducing the supply of prey that native fish species need. Asian carp have few predators, so their populations continue to grow. Wildlife managers worry that Asian carp will move into Great Lakes ecosystems and eliminate threatened native fish populations. How can scientists stop Asian carp from reaching the Great Lakes?

To control invasive species, scientists must find ways to control their populations and minimize their spread to new areas. Engineers have come up with one way to prevent the spread of Asian carp into the Great Lakes. In Chicago, they built electric barriers across canals and rivers. The barriers, shown in Figure 10.6, produce an electric current in the canal, which discourages fish from swimming past.

Scientists design strategies to reduce populations of invasive species and prevent them from moving into new areas. This aquatic scientist is part of an effort to remove Asian carp from lakes and rivers near the Great Lakes.

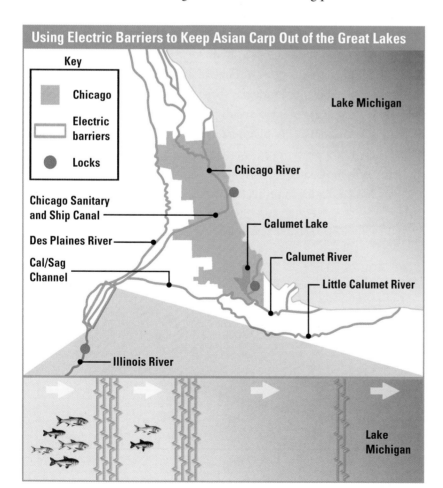

Figure 10.6
Engineers can design ways to minimize the impact of invasive species. It is hoped that electric barriers in canals that pass through Chicago will prevent the spread of Asian carp to Lake Michigan.

7. Climate Change: Sea Level and Temperature Changes Affect Coastal Communities

Suppose you were planning a vacation to Miami Beach, Florida, or San Diego, California, 20 years from now. Pack a swimsuit, flip-flops, and sunscreen. Also, bring your wading boots because roads and sidewalks may be flooded. What will coastal cities like Miami Beach or San Diego look like as sea levels rise?

Sea levels are rising globally as a result of climate change caused by human activities, such as burning fossil fuels. **Climate change** is a long-term change in climate patterns on Earth, including changes in average global temperatures and the frequency of severe weather. Increasing average global temperatures are causing rising sea levels. When sea levels rise, low-lying coastal cities like Miami Beach and San Diego flood more frequently during storms. Flooding damages infrastructure and poses a risk to human life. Flooding also threatens local ecosystems by destroying dune and marsh plants and disrupting populations of animals. You have read about how restoring coastal wetlands protects inland communities from flooding. What can scientists and engineers do to prevent damage caused by sea level rise?

One way to address the problem of sea level rise is to predict its impact and design solutions that reduce the impact. Scientists feed data on past and present climate into computer models. Models use the data to make predictions about how climate might change in the future. These models can be used to make predictions like those in Figure 10.7. This graph shows a range of estimates of sea level rise in the future based on those models. These predictions can help people living in coastal areas make plans to protect property and the health of coastal ecosystems. City planners use sea level predictions to decide where they might prevent or lessen damage caused by flooding. Models result in predictions that allow planners to predict sea level rise and develop strategies to protect coastal communities and ecosystems.

As sea levels rise, coastal communities like Miami face many challenges, including increased flooding that will endanger residents, destroy property, and damage local ecosystems.

Figure 10.7

Global average sea level has risen more than 6 cm in the last several decades and may rise another 15 to 65 cm by the year 2050. Scientists use computer models to predict how much climate change will cause sea levels to rise.

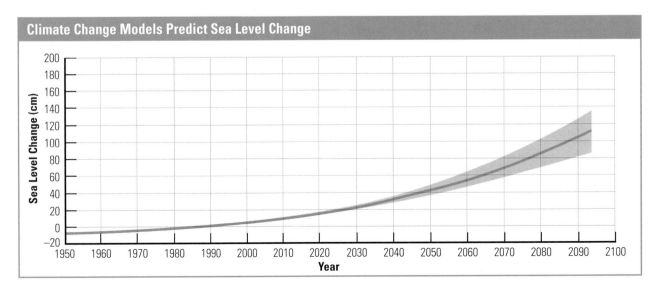

Climate Change Models Predict Sea Level Change

8. Restoring Long Island Sound's Ecosystem

Engineering
Design

Long Island Sound is an aquatic ecosystem that once supported many species of seafood, such as fish, lobster, and oysters. Decades of over-exploitation of these seafood populations have damaged the health of the ecosystem. The ecosystem has also been damaged by pollution from human communities. These changes disrupt populations of producers that form the basis of the sound's food web.

Members of the fishing industry want healthy seafood populations, and local communities would like to make sure that the sound has clean water and healthy populations of native species. How can scientists improve the health of the Long Island Sound ecosystem?

Developing a Model of Ecosystem Health When you gaze out across Long Island Sound from the shores of New York or Connecticut, it looks beautiful. But being beautiful does not necessarily indicate health. How can scientists and engineers determine the health of a large, complex ecosystem?

A useful way to measure the health of an ecosystem is to develop a model that describes normal populations of living things and normal levels of nonliving parts of the ecosystem. Scientists then take measurements of these parts of the ecosystem over time and compare them to the model. If the measurements are similar to the healthy model, then the ecosystem is considered healthy. If the measurements are different, then the ecosystem may not be healthy.

In Long Island Sound, scientists measured three parts of the ecosystem: dissolved nitrogen levels, dissolved oxygen levels, and populations of wildlife species. They used a research boat to collect water samples at different depths and tested the samples for nitrogen and oxygen. The scientists also dragged a large fishing net through the water. They then counted, weighed, and measured the different kinds of living things that were captured.

Long Island Sound is located between the Connecticut coast and Long Island, New York. It is a large, complex aquatic ecosystem. More than 23 million people live near the sound, and pollution from their activities has negatively impacted populations of wildlife species. Scientists created a model of a healthy sound ecosystem to compare to actual conditions at different points in time.

Comparing Ecosystem Conditions to the Model

A model of a healthy Long Island Sound ecosystem can help identify what parts of the ecosystem are disrupted. Water measurements taken in 1987 showed low levels of oxygen and high levels of nitrogen in large parts of Long Island Sound. Scientists know that high nitrogen levels are often the result of pollution. When nitrogen levels are high, the growth of producers, such as algae, increases. Producers extract oxygen from the water during photosynthesis. The decomposition of algae also extracts oxygen from the water. The result is low oxygen levels in the water. When aquatic ecosystems are low in oxygen, aquatic consumers cannot get the oxygen they need to survive. This reduces populations of wildlife, such as lobsters, fish, and oysters.

The biggest source of nitrogen pollution in the sound is sewage treatment plants that release wastes into the water. Because increased nitrogen levels cause decreased oxygen levels, scientists decided the best strategy was to reduce nitrogen levels in the sound.

By regularly testing oxygen levels and reducing pollution, people have successfully improved the health of the Long Island Sound ecosystem. As a result, wildlife populations, such as those of some fish species, increased. A growing fishing industry is becoming part of Long Island Sound communities once again.

Using the Model to Restore Ecosystem Health

Scientists can use the model of a healthy ecosystem to monitor solutions and make adjustments. In the 1990s, communities living near the sound limited nitrogen pollution released into the ecosystem from sewage treatment plants. They continued to monitor oxygen levels and measure populations of wildlife in the sound.

By 1997, scientists started seeing an impact of reduced nitrogen in the sound. Areas of low oxygen levels in the sound were greatly reduced, and wildlife populations had improved. Lobster populations had doubled as well as some populations of fish, including summer flounder. Many fish populations continued to recover into the 2000s. Scientists and communities continue to monitor different aspects of the Long Island Sound ecosystem, compare them to the model of a healthy ecosystem, and make modifications that improve its health.

By 2016, the health of Long Island Sound had improved, but it had not yet reached the levels outlined in the healthy ecosystem model. Although many fish populations have recovered, the health of lobster populations has not recovered as much as was hoped. Much remains to be done, but continued monitoring and modifications to the ecosystem allow scientists and local communities to have measurable, positive impacts on the health of Long Island Sound.

9. Science, Society, and You

In a just few years, young people like you will become voters. Science can help voters make choices related to Earth's ecosystems. What is the role of science in planning for the future? Science is a system of understanding the world through evidence and experiments.

Science cannot tell you what to do. But you can use scientific approaches to decide whether the evidence supports a decision, solution, or plan. Science can help predict the impact of human actions on ecosystems. It also predicts the impact of ecosystem change on humans. As an amateur scientist, how will you use evidence to understand the world around you and your place in it?

Society can use scientific knowledge to make decisions that can both provide for a growing human population and protect ecosystem health.

LESSON SUMMARY

Engineering Solutions for Protecting Ecosystems

Predicting the Impact of Human Populations on Ecosystems Human populations impact ecosystems through population growth and increased per capita use of natural resources.

Over-exploitation: Complex Interactions Changes in fishing practices help restore healthy ecosystems and prevent disease in human communities.

Pollution: Plastics in the Ocean To protect ecosystems from plastic pollution, people can modify how they use and dispose of plastics.

Emerging Diseases: New Viral Infections Human population increase means that humans come into contact more frequently with wild animals and the diseases that they carry. Public health officials find ways to prevent new diseases from infecting human populations.

Habitat Degradation: Coffee Agriculture Agriculture can be modified to reduce its negative impact on ecosystems while still providing people with the food they want.

Invasive Species: Asian Carp and the Great Lakes Scientists find ways to control invasive species and prevent their spread to new areas.

Climate Change: Sea Level Changes Sea levels are rising globally as a result of climate change. By modeling climate change, human communities can take action to reduce its impact.

Restoring Long Island Sound's Ecosystem By measuring an ecosystem's health over time, scientists and engineers can test how changes to the ecosystem might restore its health after a disruption.

Science, Society, and You Science can help you predict the impact of humans on ecosystems and of ecosystems on humans. This understanding can influence the decisions that society makes.

Northern Elephant Seals: Back from the Brink!

It is hard to imagine, but northern elephant seals were nearly hunted to extinction in the late 1800s. How did scientists use their understanding of elephant seals to save the species? What can understanding the unique abilities of elephant seals teach us about our own health?

In the 19th century, northern elephant seals like this young one, were hunted to near extinction. Northern elephant seals are found in the northern hemisphere in the Pacific Ocean, which is why they are called "northern" elephant seals.

Before electricity became widely used, some people relied on lamps that burned oil to light their homes. Much of this oil came from blubber, layers of fat under the skin of marine animals such as whales and seals. Because elephant seals are large—a male can weigh 2,000 kilograms—hunting them for their blubber was very profitable.

Northern elephant seals were also easy to hunt. Thousands gathered each year on sandy coasts of the Pacific Ocean. They are clumsy on land, which made them easy for hunters to kill. By the end of the 19th century, northern elephant seals were nearly extinct.

Saving the Species

Eight years had passed without a single sighting of a northern elephant seal along the Pacific Coast beaches where they were once found. Then, in 1892, a scientific expedition found a small group living off the coast of Mexico's Baja Peninsula on Guadalupe Island. This small population survived there for the next 20 years.

Finally realizing that the species would be lost forever if they did not protect it, the Mexican government took action. In 1922, it made Guadalupe Island a biological reserve, a protected area, for northern elephant seals. Signs posted on the island stated that it was against the law to capture or kill the seals. Troops were posted on the island to ensure that the rules against hunting were followed.

This action turned out to be just what the elephant seals needed to recover. Understanding their life cycle and behavior explains why. Elephant seals spend most of the year foraging in the ocean where they are safe. But they come onto land for several weeks twice a year, where they are vulnerable to hunters. In winter, males come ashore to battle for dominance with other males. Shortly after, females arrive to give birth to young pups and nurse them. Later, in the spring, all elephant seals come back onto the island in order to molt, or shed their old fur.

Mexico's conservation efforts paid off, and this small seal population began to recover. By 1961 northern elephant seals had colonized Pacific Coast beaches from Mexico to central California. Today, all marine mammals in U.S. coastal waters are protected from illegal hunting under the Marine Mammal Protection Act of 1972 and other international laws. Meanwhile, northern elephant seal populations continue to increase every year, and some estimates put the total population at 150,000.

What can we learn by studying how northern elephant seals live? Scientists hope to help humans by studying how the seals dive deeply for long periods.

Scientists study a male northern elephant seal as it spends a few weeks at Año Nuevo State Park along the mid-California coast. In the past, the seals on land were vulnerable to hunters. Today they are protected by the Marine Mammal Protection Act. Can you see why this animal is called an elephant seal?

Scientists glue GPS tracking devices to elephant seals, like this female, so that they can study their unique adaptations to a life spent diving in the ocean. When seals surface, data about their dives gets sent to the researchers via satellite. The device does not hurt the seals and falls off when the seal molts.

Dynamo Divers

Like you, elephant seals are mammals with lungs. Although they spend their lives diving in the ocean, they must breathe air at the water's surface. But don't challenge an elephant seal to a breath-holding contest—an adult seal can hold its breath for a long time!

How do scientists know this? They use tracking devices, like the one shown in the photo, to collect data on elephant seals when they dive. Data show that their dives regularly reach 600 meters and can last more than 90 minutes.

Elephant seals are uniquely adapted for diving deep underwater. First, they store large amounts of dissolved oxygen in their blood. At the surface, they breathe rapidly for several minutes to move oxygen into their blood. Then, before diving, they exhale completely, emptying their lungs of air. As they descend, pressure from the weight of the water above collapses their lungs. This decreases their buoyancy, or ability to float, and makes it easier for them to dive.

Elephant seals have other abilities as well. During a deep dive, elephant seals "shut off" blood flow to some organs and not others, only supplying those organs needed to stay alive. At the same time, the heart rate decreases to as little as three beats per minute. These changes help seals conserve oxygen during their long dives. Could this information be helpful to saving human lives?

Using Seal Science Secrets

Scientists are hoping that learning about northern elephant seal diving abilities can save human lives. Their ability to restrict blood flow to organs without damaging them is a physical feat that scientists hope can be used to help human victims of heart attacks or strokes.

During a northern elephant seal's dive, non-essential organs are "shut off" from a supply of blood. Yet when the seal surfaces and blood flow is restored, organs that went without oxygen for an hour or more are not damaged.

Humans are not as lucky. When a human suffers a heart attack or stroke, the heart and brain stop receiving oxygen-rich blood. Within minutes, tissues in those organs die. Understanding how elephant seal organs are able to survive for long periods without oxygen could help humans avoid brain damage, heart damage, or even death.

Research on elephant seals continues on the beaches they use for breeding and molting. Visitors are welcome to visit and observe these magnificent marine mammals in ways that don't disturb them. Some of the largest breeding locations are on the California coast. Here you can find thousands of elephant seals on the beach in winter. It's hard to believe that they were once so close to extinction! Sometimes a species just needs a helping hand. ◆

Elephant seals are back! As scientists continue to research northern elephant seals, we can look forward to benefitting from an understanding of how these amazing animals survive in their unique deep-water environments.

Learning Resources

The whole Earth and everything beyond it is the subject of science. This set of learning resources includes some essential thinking tools you need in order to explore, investigate, and explain how the world works.

Science and Engineering Safety

Science and Engineering Practices

Crosscutting Concepts

Literacy in Science

Mathematics in Science

Measurement Units

Laboratory Safety

To think like a scientist, you have to act like one. This means making observations, experimenting, and carrying out other types of investigations. The same goes for solving engineering problems. You have to propose, build, test, and improve your designed solutions. All of these things are fun and interesting, but there can be risks involved in handling equipment and materials. What do you have to be aware of to stay safe when practicing science and engineering?

Your teacher may ask you to sign a Science Safety Contract and discuss it with your parents. This is an important first step towards science safety. Before working in the science lab, review these rules.

☑ Understand the hazards and rules for a particular investigation before you begin.

☑ Make sure your personal clothing is safe for the lab. Do not wear loose clothing, especially long sleeves.

☑ Wear closed shoes to protect your feet.

☑ If you have long hair, tie it back.

☑ Wear safety goggles, protective aprons, and gloves when required by your teacher.

☑ Transport and handle all equipment and chemicals as directed by your teacher.

☑ Report breaks, spills, or other accidents to your teacher right away.

☑ Report injuries to your teacher right away, and follow your school's first aid procedures.

☑ Know where safety equipment is in the lab you use and when or how to use it.

☑ Dispose of materials in the designated containers at the end of the investigation.

☑ Clean up your work area and wash your hands at the conclusion of the investigation.

☑ Know what to do in case of a hazardous event such as a power failure, earthquake, or emergency evacuation.

☑ Be aware of safety for everyone in your group.

Planning Investigations

Designing your own investigations is a chance to act like a real scientist—and that includes keeping yourself and others safe.

- ☑ Choose equipment and materials that your teacher tells you are safe to use.

- ☑ Plan how you will handle the materials safely, including how you will dispose of materials that cannot be used again.

- ☑ Include safety steps when writing your procedure.

- ☑ Always obtain permission from your teacher before carrying out your investigation plan.

Field Trip Safety

Some of the most important thigs you can do to stay safe on a field trip is to be prepared in advance.

- ☑ Return a signed parental permission form to your teacher before a field trip.

- ☑ Check the weather forecast so that you can choose appropriate clothing. If there is any possibility of severe weather, make sure there is a plan for taking shelter.

- ☑ No matter the weather, wear footwear that encloses and protects your feet.

- ☑ Wear clothing, hats, or sunscreen to protect yourself from sunburn. Remember, you can get burned on a cloudy day as well as on a sunny one.

- ☑ Learn in advance the types of organisms you may encounter that are dangerous and should be avoided.

- ☑ During the field trip, don't touch plants unless instructed by your teacher or guide.

- ☑ Know how to get first aid for poisonous plants and animal stings and bites.

- ☑ Never eat or put in your mouth anything you find outdoors without permission.

- ☑ Wash up carefully after an outdoor science activity.

- ☑ If the area you visited has ticks, inspect your clothing and body for ticks at the end of the field trip.

Safety for Living Things in the Classroom

When you investigate living things, you can't just think about yourself. You have to think about the organisms in your care, too.

☑ Understand appropriate and humane treatment of animals. This includes selecting a suitable container to house the animals and making sure the temperature is within the proper range for that species.

☑ Help make sure that animals kept in the science classroom are provided with adequate water, food, and that their containers are kept clean.

☑ Keep handling of animals to a minimum and never disturb sleeping animals.

☑ Plan for appropriate care of living things over weekends, holidays, and vacations.

☑ Don't bring personal pets or unknown plants or animals into school, as they may be poisonous, venomous, or negatively affect the other living things in your science classroom.

☑ Never carry out investigations that will cause discomfort, pain, or disease to animals.

☑ Return native wild species to their natural environment.

☑ Never release non-native species into the natural environment.

☑ Wash your hands and surfaces after handling living things.

Asking Questions

Asking questions is central to science. Scientists learn about the natural world by asking questions and trying to answer them. As scientists learn about the natural world, they come up with more questions to answer. What kinds of questions do scientists ask, and how can you learn to ask them?

Questions drive the scientific process. Scientists ask testable questions to guide their research and gain scientific knowledge. This knowledge can lead to new questions to be answered.

Questions Scientists ask questions about the natural world and about current scientific ideas. The types of questions scientists might ask include: What causes a particular phenomenon? How do different factors affect observations? Why did an event occur?

Testability Science can only answer questions that are testable, which means that a scientist must be able to gather evidence to answer the question. To determine if a question is testable, ask yourself: How can the answer to this question be determined? Would the answer be a fact or an opinion? Can I design an investigation to answer this question?

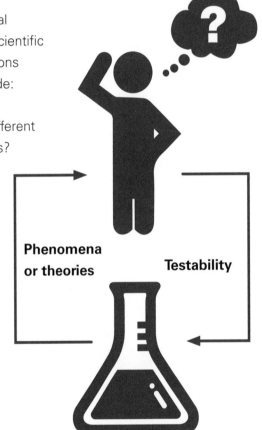

Phenomena or theories

Testability

Science Testable questions can lead to new scientific knowledge, which can lead to new questions. Ask yourself: How can I gather data to answer this question? How well does this data support the answer? Are there other possible answers that this data could support?

Phenomena and Theories Scientists ask questions based on observed phenomena and scientific theories. The questions may be asked to clarify ideas or to introduce new ideas. Ask yourself: What other questions does this new understanding raise? How does this explanation relate to other scientific ideas or theories?

If you go to cities around the world, you will probably see a couple of pigeons or maybe a couple of hundreds of pigeons. Unlike many other wild animals, pigeons do not seem to mind living around people. How might you research pigeons to find out why that is?

Asking Questions You can start your research by asking questions. These questions might include: Why are pigeons more common in cities than other species of birds? What birds lived in an area before an area was developed? How does the diet of a city pigeon compare with the diet of a pigeon living in the country?

You can ask testable questions to learn about the natural environment. For example, if you are studying pigeons, you might ask questions to compare the diet of city pigeons with the diet of country pigeons.

Determining Testability After scientists come up with questions, they pick at least one question to investigate further. Suppose that you wanted to find the answer to the question "How does the diet of a city pigeon compare with the diet of a pigeon living in the country?" The question you are trying to answer must be testable. To determine this, you might ask: What kind of investigation will help answer the question? What evidence do I have to gather to answer the question?

Conducting Science You may want to start your investigation on pigeon diets by reviewing research done by other scientists. Some questions you may consider are: What other research has been done on pigeon diets? What methods did other scientists use? How will my investigation differ or improve on previous investigations?

Coming Up with Phenomena and Theories While investigating pigeon diets, you may try to connect your observations with known phenomena and theories. Ask yourself: What do my observations say about pigeon nutrition? How does a pigeon's diet compare with that of other species of birds? How do my results relate to phenomena like the adaptation of pigeons to their environment?

The fact that asking questions in science often leads to new questions may seem frustrating, but it is actually a good thing. The cycle of questions leading to more questions means that science will always grow and improve.

Defining Problems

Before engineers can begin designing a solution, they have to define the problem they are trying to solve. By thoroughly defining the problem, engineers know exactly what qualities the solution must have and what obstacles they may need to work around to achieve the solution. What do engineers have to do to define a problem?

Defining problems involves clearly identifying the problem, the boundaries and components of the problem, and the criteria and constraints of the problem's solution.

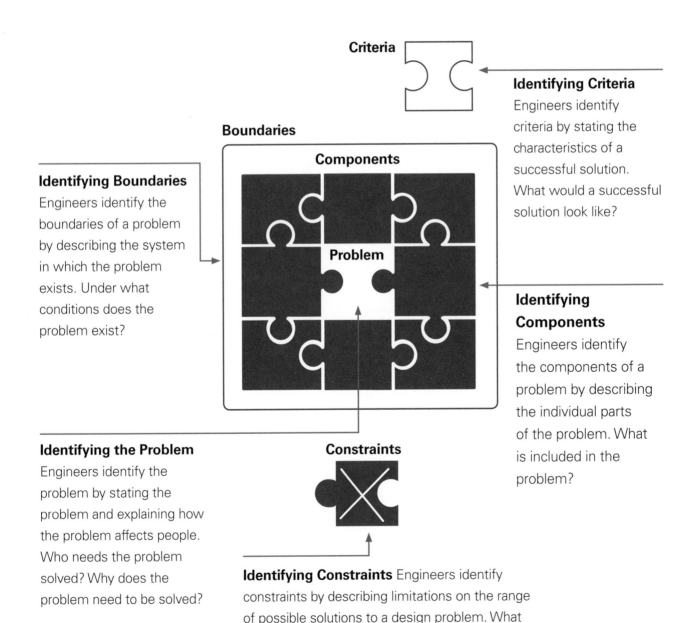

Criteria

Identifying Criteria
Engineers identify criteria by stating the characteristics of a successful solution. What would a successful solution look like?

Boundaries

Components

Identifying Boundaries
Engineers identify the boundaries of a problem by describing the system in which the problem exists. Under what conditions does the problem exist?

Problem

Identifying Components
Engineers identify the components of a problem by describing the individual parts of the problem. What is included in the problem?

Identifying the Problem
Engineers identify the problem by stating the problem and explaining how the problem affects people. Who needs the problem solved? Why does the problem need to be solved?

Constraints

Identifying Constraints Engineers identify constraints by describing limitations on the range of possible solutions to a design problem. What would make a solution impractical or unusable?

Defining a problem by identifying boundaries, components, criteria, and constraints is the first step in finding a good solution. Making healthy lunches that students will eat is a problem that many schools struggle with.

If you could buy anything to eat at your school cafeteria, what would you get? You probably want foods like pizza and cake. But pizza, cake, and other popular foods tend not to be healthy. What can school cafeterias do to encourage students to eat better foods?

Identifying the Problem Kids across the country eat most of their lunches at school. School cafeterias try to provide nutritious meals, but often the healthy parts of the meals end up in the trash. So, the problem is providing healthy foods that students will eat.

Identifying the Boundaries and Components The boundaries of this problem surround the school and the people in it. The components of the problem include the food, the students, school kitchen, kitchen staff, and administrators. The students eat the food that is prepared by the kitchen staff, while the administrators purchase the food and approve the meals. However, many things are not important to the problem, such as the color of the walls and whether lunch tables have chairs or benches to sit on.

Identifying Criteria and Constraints The criteria and constraints of a successful solution can be organized in a table.

Criteria	Constraints
• meals are nutritious	• budget (need to afford food)
• at least 85% of students eat the meal	• kitchen (need right equipment to prepare food)
• meal plan has variety	• time to prepare food

Solving the problem of serving healthy school lunches is not easy, but understanding the problem will help find a solution. If the solution is successful, it will be good and delicious.

Developing and Using Models

Scientists use models to explain and understand natural phenomena. Scientific models can be physical models such as a globe or a drawing of a cell. Scientific models can also be conceptual models, which means that they are collections of related ideas. For example, the big bang theory is a conceptual model to describe how the universe began. How can you learn to develop models the way a scientist would?

When scientists develop a model, they identify the components of the model, describe the relationship between the components, and explain the connections between the model and the real world.

Model **Real World**

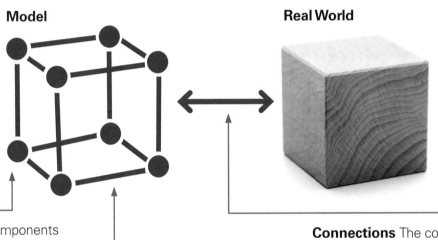

Components Components are the parts that make up the model. Each component represents something in the real world. When you develop a model, you have to decide which parts of the real word are important to represent and which are not.

Relationships The relationships in a model describe how the components interact. When you develop a model, the relationships you describe help you understand how the components of the model work together and make predictions about the model.

Connections The connections between a model and the natural phenomenon it represents make the model useful. Models simplify the phenomenon to make it easier to observe, understand, predict, or quantify.

Scientists develop some models by combining what they have learned about a particular phenomenon. However, sometimes scientists use a simple, common object as a model to help explain something in nature. For example, lasagna could be used as a model for sedimentary rock. The common object used as a model has some similar features to the phenomenon it is modeling, but it generally cannot explain everything about the phenomenon. How is lasagna a good model for sedimentary rock formation, and how does it fall short?

Components The layers of lasagna represent the layers of rock in sedimentary rock. The different layers in lasagna—noodle, cheese, and meat—can represent different kinds of rock.

Relationships Lasagna layers are distinct, so you can see each layer. One relationship in this model is the order of the layers. Using this relationship, you can see how the lasagna was built even if you did not see it being assembled. You know the lasagna was built up so that the first layer is at the bottom and the last layer is at the top.

Scientists develop models to explain or describe natural phenomena. Lasagna is a useful model for describing the structure and formation of sedimentary rock, but it cannot compare in terms of timescale.

Connections The structure of the lasagna and the way it was built are similar to the structure and the formation of sedimentary rock. The layers in sedimentary rock are distinct and easy to see. Sedimentary rock is also built up with the oldest rock layers at the bottom and the newest rock layers at the top.

However, lasagna and sedimentary rock have important differences. A person can build a lasagna in about 15 minutes, but sedimentary rock may take millions of years to build up. Studying the layers in sedimentary rock can tell you about the environments in which the layers formed. Studying lasagna layers cannot tell you much of anything, except for which layer you like the best!

Planning and Carrying Out Investigations

Scientific research involves conducting investigations. Scientists use many different methods for planning investigations, but every method has common elements. One method is outlined here. The elements in this method are common to other methods that a scientist might use. What things should you consider when planning an investigation, and what might happen when carrying out an investigation?

The steps in planning and carrying out an investigation can happen in any order and can be repeated multiple times.

Identifying Evidence Identify what evidence you need to answer your question; only some evidence will be useful. If you were investigating why birds sing in the morning, you might observe birds in the morning and also at other times of the day to see what else they do.

Identifying the Phenomenon

The subject of your investigation might be a phenomenon to be explained, a question to be answered, or a design to be tested. You might try to answer the question, "Why do birds sing in the morning?"

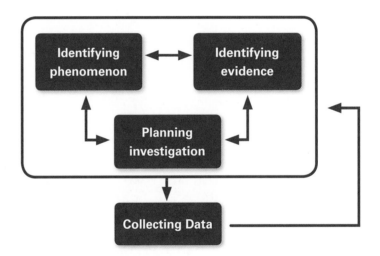

Planning the Investigation

Describe how you will gather data that will serve as evidence toward a claim. Create a specific list of steps to follow. For example, you could set up a camera in a park. Then, you could watch the video, marking down bird activity such as singing, feeding, and flying.

Collecting Data Collect your data by following the steps outlined in your investigation plan. Be sure to keep your data organized. For an investigation about birds singing, you could make a table with rows marked with time of day and columns marked with various bird behaviors.

Refining the Plan Refining your investigation plan means making changes to improve it. Ask yourself questions such as: Was the data accurately and precisely collected? Does the data support a claim about the phenomenon that I am investigating? If the answers are "no," then you need to change the investigation's plan.

Your science class is having a toy car race to investigate forces and motion. Each team of students is given a kit with which to build a toy car, but the design of each car is up to the team members. What plan do you come up with for your investigation?

Identifying the Phenomenon Together your class brainstorms factors that may affect the speed of a toy car. The class decides to investigate how a car's shape affects the car's speed.

Identifying Evidence Your class identifies the data to collect: which car shape wins each race. These data can then be analyzed to find evidence for which shape is best for a fast car.

Specifying the Steps The class comes up with the following steps:

1. Each of the 15 teams will make a car, and each car will have a different shape.

2. Cars will race on a track that has five lanes.

3. In preliminary rounds, five cars will race at least two times. The first car to win twice will advance to the final round.

4. In the final round, the preliminary round winners will race. The first car to win twice will be declared the best shape.

Collecting Data The winners of the preliminary rounds include your wedge-shaped car, a minivan-shaped car, and a car shaped like a cone. However, you notice that the car in the leftmost lane always finishes last.

Scientists plan and carry out investigations to gather evidence to support their explanations. You can gather evidence about which toy car design is fastest by holding a series of races and recording which design wins each race.

Refining the Plan Because the leftmost car always loses, the answer to the question, "Were the data accurately collected?" is "no." The class runs trial races, which show that cars run slower in the outside lanes. The class revises the investigation plan. Instead of racing five cars, you race three cars using only the center lanes. Then you will have two semifinal rounds and one final round.

Your wedge-shaped car wins its preliminary round and its semifinal before barely losing to the cone-shaped car in the final round. The race is so close that some classmates think the investigation may need more revision to be sure of the winning design. What other revisions could you make?

Analyzing and Interpreting Data

Scientists and engineers collect data in many different ways. In order to connect data to their investigation, scientists and engineers have to analyze and interpret the data. How can you think like a scientist or an engineer to make sense of data you collect?

Analyzing and interpreting data involves organizing the data, identifying relationships within the data, and then interpreting the data based on the relationships found.

Organizing Data Scientists and engineers organize their data in tables or graphs to help them make sense of it. Data that include written descriptions might be organized in data tables, while data that show changes over time might be organized in a line graph, bar graph, or pie chart.

Identifying Relationships Scientists and engineers identify relationships by looking for patterns in the organized data. They ask themselves questions such as: What parts of the data show changes? Are there data that change in regular ways? Do two different kinds of data change in similar ways?

Interpreting Data Scientists and engineers interpret data by drawing conclusions from the relationships identified. They may ask: What could be causing the patterns in the data? What could happen if the patterns continue? Could the patterns have more than one explanation?

Your science class is studying a nearby lake. You collect measurements of air and water temperature at the same place at the same time every day for a year.

Organizing Data You divide the measurements into air temperatures and water temperatures for each month. Then you find the average air temperature and water temperature for each month. Finally, you organize the average temperatures into a data table.

Both air temperature and water temperature change throughout the year. But you are not sure how the temperature changes are related. So, you graph the temperatures over time.

Identifying Relationships You can see a relationship between air and water temperature in the graph. The changes in temperatures follow similar patterns, but the patterns do not line up. The water graph is about a month behind the air graph. The air graph reaches its highest temperature in July, but the water graph does not reach its highest temperature until August.

Interpreting Data After studying your graph, you propose an explanation for why air and water temperatures follow a similar pattern. You propose that the changing air temperatures cause changes in water temperature. That is why the temperature changes follow similar patterns. Furthermore, you suggest the patterns do not line up because water changes temperature slower than air does.

The data in this table are organized using a line graph. You can see a relationship in the data on the graph; the changes in air and water temperature follow a similar pattern. How would you interpret this relationship?

Average Lake Air and Water Temperatures

Month	Air Temp. (°C)	Water Temp. (°C)
Jan (1)	-5.6	6.1
Feb (2)	-4.4	3.3
Mar (3)	-1.1	1.7
Apr (4)	7.2	2.2
May (5)	12.2	3.3
June (6)	18.3	6.7
July (7)	21.1	10.0
Aug (8)	17.8	16.7
Sept (9)	12.8	15.6
Oct (10)	4.4	13.9
Nov (11)	-0.6	10.0
Dec (12)	-2.2	7.8

Using Mathematical and Computational Thinking

Scientists use mathematical and computational thinking in many ways. They might use math to analyze data, make predictions, or build scientific models. Furthermore, some scientific laws and principles can be expressed as equations. For example, Newton's second law of motion can be expressed as force = mass × acceleration. In each of these situations, scientists use math to represent observed systems. How can you use math to represent systems you encounter in science and your everyday life?

When scientists use math to describe a system, they state what parts of the system are represented, describe how numbers and symbols are used to model the system, and then use math to analyze the system.

Representation In math, representation means to use symbols (such as letters) to stand in for variables in a system. For example, Newton's law describes the relationship between three variables: force, mass, and acceleration. These variables are represented by the letters F, m, and a, respectively.

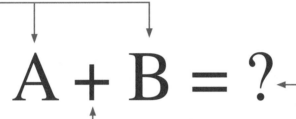

Mathematical Modeling Mathematical modeling means to find how the variables in a system are related mathematically. For example, the relationship between the variables in Newton's second law is represented mathematically by the equation $F = m \times a$. You could use graphs to find relationships or you could see if the variables are related by an equation. Scientists sometimes build computer simulations that connect many different variables.

Analysis Analyzing a mathematical system means to find patterns in the system. The pattern can be used to make predictions or support claims. Analyzing a system might involve solving equations, finding trends in graphs, or using a computer simulation. For example, you can use the equation for Newton's second law to analyze how a change in force affects acceleration. If a force on an object is doubled, the acceleration of the object will also double.

The equation for Newton's second law of motion, like many equations in science, can be applied in many situations. However, scientists sometimes develop equations that describe only the situation that they are studying. How can you develop an equation to describe the change in a rabbit population in an ecosystem?

Representation The first step in developing a rabbit population equation is to identify and represent the variables in the system. You might pick the following variables and representations:

- b represents the number of rabbits born

- e represents the number of rabbits eaten by predators

- d represents the number of rabbits that died of natural causes

- Δp represents the change in rabbit population (The Greek letter delta (Δ) often means "change in," so Δp means change in p, the rabbit population.)

Mathematical Modeling To mathematically model the change in rabbit population, you have to decide how each variable affects the population. Does the variable increase or decrease the population? What mathematical operations are the equivalents to increasing and decreasing a value? An increase in population would add to the population, and a decrease would subtract from the population. Births increase the population and deaths decrease the population. So an equation for the change in population would be:

$$\Delta p = b - e - d$$

Scientists often use math to represent the systems they are studying. An equation can be used to find the change in a rabbit population in an ecosystem. The equation can be analyzed to predict how the rabbit population might change under various conditions.

Analysis To analyze the accuracy of your equation, you might solve the equation to see how the number of rabbits changes each month. Then you might draw conclusions, such as the rabbit population increases in the summer months due to a rise in births. You could also analyze the equation by using it to make predictions. What would happen if the predators in the ecosystem died? What would happen if a disease spread throughout the rabbit population?

Constructing Explanations

As they work, scientists construct explanations of phenomena. Constructing explanations is similar to engaging in argument from evidence but has key differences. When scientists engage in argument, they are using evidence to defend an idea. When scientists construct explanations, they are using evidence and reasoning to build an idea. How can you learn to think like a scientist when constructing explanations for the phenomena you experience?

Scientists construct explanations by using reasoning to describe the connections between phenomena and evidence.

Phenomenon When scientists construct explanations, the phenomenon is the event or observation that they are explaining. For example, scientists might try to explain why honeybees are dying off.

Arguments for the Explanation Scientists use arguments to support their explanation. An argument is made up of a claim, evidence for that claim, and reasons why the evidence supports the claim. For example, scientists might claim that more flowering plants are sprayed with pesticides now than ever before. Evidence supporting that claim may include data about historic and present day sales of pesticides.

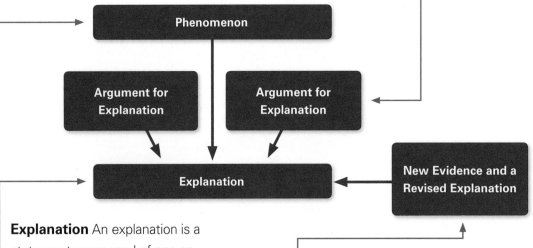

Explanation An explanation is a statement composed of one or more arguments that describe how or why the phenomenon happens. An example explanation might be: Honeybees are dying off because of the use of pesticides on flowering plants.

New Evidence and a Revised Explanation After scientists have proposed an explanation, new evidence may arise that makes the scientists change their explanation. Perhaps scientists studying honeybees learn that a disease is spreading throughout honeybee populations. They may revise their explanation to include the disease as a reason why the bees are dying off.

You can construct explanations for phenomena that you observe in your everyday life. For example, suppose you have a banana bread recipe that you make successfully all the time. Your friend who lives in Denver, Colorado tries to make the bread, but the batter overflows and the bread is gummy. What causes the differences?

Phenomenon Your friend says that he followed your recipe exactly. You determine that the only variable that changed between your loaf and his loaf was where the loaves were made. So, the phenomenon that you are trying to explain is why the same recipe produces a nice loaf at your home but makes a mess at your friend's.

Explanation You and your friend talk to figure out the differences between your homes. You know some differences, such as the number of bedrooms in the homes, will not cause changes in how bread bakes. You rule out those differences as factors. Eventually, you come up with an explanation. The recipe failed because your friend in Denver lives at a higher altitude than you do.

Arguments for the Explanation The main argument for your explanation is that the higher altitude in Denver causes the banana bread batter to rise too much during the baking process. You learned that the air pressure at higher altitudes is lower. When the air pressure that is pushing down on the batter is lower, the air bubbles produced by the baking soda in the batter can get bigger. The bigger bubbles cause the batter to rise too much and overflow the pan.

New Evidence and a Revised Explanation You tell your friend your explanation, and he has another idea. He explains that the lower pressure in Denver allows liquids to evaporate more quickly. This new evidence causes you to rethink your explanation.

Your explanation is not completely wrong, but it needs to be improved. Your explanation accounts for the batter overflowing but does not explain why the loaf was gummy. You cut yourself a piece of banana bread while you think about how quicker evaporation of liquid in the batter might affect the bread's texture. Hopefully, the snack will help you come up with a more complete explanation!

Scientists construct explanations of phenomena and use arguments to support their explanations. An explanation as to why a banana bread recipe fails in Denver is that the city is at a higher altitude. Therefore, Denver has a lower air pressure.

Designing Solutions

An engineer's primary job is to design solutions to problems. You use these solutions all the time. For example, an engineer designed the calculator you use in math class. Engineers have also designed bus routes, airplane seats, and water treatment plants. How do engineers come up with their solutions? And how do they know which solution is best?

Engineers generate a lot of ideas for solutions. They then narrow down those solutions to find the best one to a given problem.

Possible Solutions Engineers think of many different solutions to a single problem. All the possible solutions should be based on scientific knowledge. They may ask themselves: What scientific ideas are related to the problem? What scientific ideas will help or hinder finding a solution to this problem?

Evaluating Solutions Evaluating solutions is the process of comparing the solutions to the criteria and the constraints. In this step, engineers determine how well each solution meets the criteria and fits within the constraints.

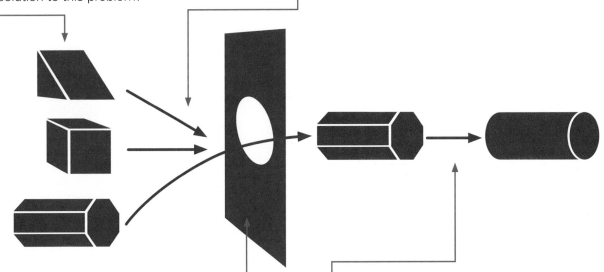

Criteria and Constraints Criteria are the requirements that must be met for an engineering solution to be successful. Constraints are limitations on an engineering solution. Criteria and constraints describe which possible solutions are good and which are not as good. Criteria and constraints may be redefined based on things learned during the designing process.

Optimizing the Best Solution Even after picking the best solution to a problem, engineers need to refine the solution. During this step, engineers test their solution and make changes based on the results of the tests. The solution may need to go through several iterations to make it the best possible solution.

Suppose that your class is having a fundraiser, and the class decides to sell cookie cutters in the shape of the school's logo. Before you can sell the cutters, you have to make them. And before you make the cutters, you have to decide what material to use.

Criteria and Constraints The criteria for the material include that it has to have the ability to be shaped in the form of your school's logo, and it has to hold its shape. Other criteria are that the material has to be able to cut cookie dough and last a long time.

Some of the constraints for the material are that the students in your class have to be able to make the cutter from the material and that the material is not too expensive.

Possible Solutions Science can help you come up with possible materials to use for the cookie cutters. Copper is a possible material because it is a malleable metal. It can be bent into the right shape. Stainless steel is another malleable metal.

Evaluating Solutions You use the criteria and constraints to evaluate the solutions. Copper fits the following criteria: It can be shaped, it can hold its shape, and it will last a long time. It fits the constraint that students can shape it, but it is relatively expensive. So, it does not fit within the inexpensive constraint. Stainless steel fits the following criteria: It can be shaped, it can hold its shape, and it will last a long time. It fits within the constraints that students can shape it, and it is inexpensive. You decide to use stainless steel.

Optimizing the Best Solution Using stainless steel, you make a prototype cookie cutter. The prototype is made out of a 1-cm wide strip of steel. You make cookies using the prototype and find that it does not hold its shape. The narrow strip bends too easily.

You make a second prototype that is made out of a 2.5-cm wide strip of steel. You test the second prototype and find that it holds its shape well. This prototype is determined to have the best design.

You and your classmates make 200 cookie cutters that are identical to the second prototype. You sell the cutters and raise enough money for a field trip to a science museum.

Engineers compare solutions to the criteria and constraints to determine which solution is most likely to solve the problem. The best solution is then optimized through testing and refining. You can use a similar process when designing your own solutions.

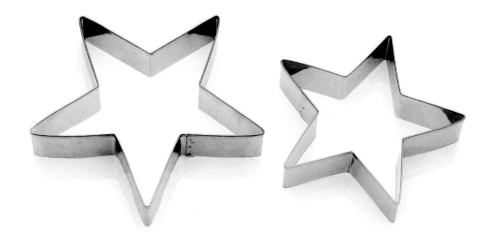

Engaging in Argument from Evidence

Engaging in argument is a key element of scientific practice. However, the arguments that scientists and engineers have with each other are not like typical arguments. They are not trying just to prove each other wrong. Rather, they are trying to collaboratively find the best explanation or model, or design the best solution. What kinds of thinking and statements are needed for a strong argument?

Strong scientific arguments have three key components—a claim, evidence for that claim, and reasoning as to why the evidence supports the claim.

Claim The claim is the statement that the argument is attempting to convince people to believe. Scientists might make claims about an explanation of a phenomenon, such as why snowflakes are always symmetrical. Or, they may make claims about a model, such as a food web. Engineers might make claims about which material is best for their design.

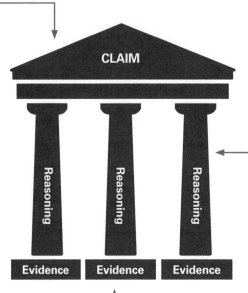

Reasoning Evidence alone is not enough to convince people of a claim. Reasoning shows how the evidence is connected to the claim, using logic or scientific concepts. The reasoning might, for example, explain why a diagram of the structure of water molecules supports the claim that all snowflakes are symmetric.

Evidence Evidence is the data or observations that support a claim. Relevant measurements, tables, and graphs can often be used as strong evidence for a claim. Generally, the more evidence there is for a claim, the stronger the argument is.

Refutation Of course, no argument is one sided. There is often an opportunity for someone to refute an argument. A refutation provides new evidence, which, along with reasoning, shows that the claim is incorrect. A refutation may also provide a different interpretation of the evidence, showing that it does not support the original claim.

Your friend Jerome sent you a photo with his phone. "Check out this great rainbow!" Look at Jerome's photo, and make an argument about the weather Jerome is experiencing. Try asking yourself questions as you develop your argument.

To make your claim, ask yourself, "What kind of weather is in this photo?" Next, identify your evidence by asking, "What specific things do I see in this photo that support my claim?" Then develop your reasoning by asking, "How do the things I pointed out as evidence support my claim?" Your argument might look something like this:

Claim Jerome took the photo while weather was clearing up after a rainstorm.

Evidence There are no visible raindrops in the photo, and the ground does not look wet. However, there is a rainbow in the sky. There are also dark clouds on the right side of the sky, but not on the left side of the sky.

Reasoning Since there are no visible raindrops in the photo and the ground does not look wet, it was probably not raining right when the photo was taken. However, rainbows only form when there are water drops in the sky, and usually form immediately after it has been raining. Also, dark clouds like the ones in the photo usually produce rain. But since the clouds only cover half of the sky in the photograph, the storm seems to be moving away from the place the photograph was taken.

Do you agree with this argument? If not, come up with a refutation. Then, the next time you make a claim, do it like a scientist or engineer—back it up with evidence and reasoning.

Your friend sends you a photo of a rainbow. You can develop an argument of what the weather was like at the moment the photo was taken by asking yourself a set of questions.

Obtaining, Evaluating, and Communicating Information

Scientists spend a lot of time obtaining, evaluating, and communicating information. In fact, most people use this process every day. For example, when you read, you are obtaining information. You then evaluate the information you read by determining if it is accurate and important. You also might communicate this information by talking about it with a friend. How does obtaining, evaluating, and communicating information help scientists do their work?

A scientist may obtain, evaluate, and communicate information during any point in an investigation.

Obtaining Information
When scientists gather information, they may ask: Where can we find information about this topic? What different kinds of information are available?

Evaluating Information
Scientists evaluate information by asking questions like these: What does this information mean? Is this information reliable? Is this information relevant?

Communicating Information Before scientists share information, they must decide how to communicate it. They may ask themselves: What is the best way to communicate this information? Should we give lectures, or should we write about it? Should we make a video? Or will a graph, photo, or mathematical equation better communicate the information?

Although scientific research is generally thought of as being a good thing, it can be controversial. One controversial topic in astronomy is the placement of telescopes on a dormant volcano in Hawaii named Mauna Kea. Some of the world's best telescopes are already on Mauna Kea. Astronomers consider the volcano to be one of the best places in the world for telescopes, and they would like to build additional ones there. However, some Hawaiians consider the volcano to be sacred and do not want any more telescopes built on it. Do you think astronomers should put more telescopes on Mauna Kea? How would you decide?

Obtaining Information *Where can you find information about this topic?* Probably the easiest place for you to get information is the Internet. You can also check specialized resources at the library. *What different kinds of information are available?* Scientists, the Hawaiian government, and Hawaiian residents are some of the groups that provide information on this topic.

Evaluating Information *What does this information mean?* Some information will tell you why Mauna Kea is such a great place for telescopes, while other information will explain the negative impact of telescopes on the volcano. *Is this information reliable?* Consider where the information is from. Websites from universities, the government, and major media outlets tend to be reliable sources. *Is this information relevant?* Once you have information from reliable sources, think about whether the information supports either side of the Mauna Kea controversy. If the information does not help one side or the other, the information is probably not relevant.

Communicating Information *What is the best way to communicate this information?* If you are communicating your opinion about telescopes on Mauna Kea to your class, you might make a poster or explain your reasoning in a class discussion. But if you are a Hawaiian citizen, you might want to write a letter to the state governor that could influence the future of Mauna Kea.

People obtain, evaluate, and communicate information all the time. Scientists and the public need to obtain and evaluate reliable information when making decisions on controversial topics, such as the placement of telescopes on Mauna Kea.

Patterns

Patterns play a key role in many scientific investigations. Scientists make sense of data they have collected by trying to recognize and analyze patterns. Often, noticing a pattern in nature will spark a series of questions. All patterns have an underlying cause, which can be uncovered by a scientific investigation. What patterns can you recognize in the following natural phenomena?

How can the different patterns in finches' beaks help you understand how a species can adapt to its environment? When Charles Darwin discovered different species of finches on the Galapagos Islands, he noticed that each species had a beak that was well-suited to its diet. The differently shaped beaks led Darwin to discover the pattern that exists between the shape of a finch's beak and its individual diet. This pattern seemed to point to a species' ability to adapt to its environment.

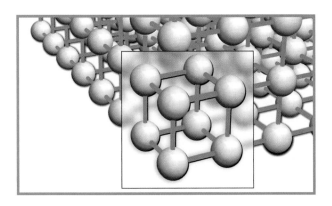

How is the microscopic pattern of table salt related to the macroscopic, or easily visible, shape of a salt crystal? You can see that each individual crystal has a cube-like structure. On the atomic level, sodium and chlorine atoms are arranged in a regular, repeating pattern that is shaped like a cube. The way a substance appears to the human eye is often determined by its atomic level structure.

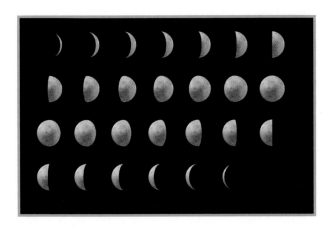

How can understanding patterns help you predict the different shapes of lunar phases? The apparent shape of the moon from Earth is determined by the positions of Earth, the moon, and the sun. Over the course of about a month, the moon transitions from a new moon to a full moon and back to a new moon in a repeating pattern. Because the apparent change in the moon's shape always follows the same pattern, you can predict when the next full moon will take place!

Cause and Effect

Looking for cause-and-effect relationships can help immensely when you are designing experiments to answer scientific questions or testing engineering solutions. Think about these three questions from different areas of science. What experiments might people design to test them?

Do magnetic fields cause compass needles to rotate? Suppose you measure the direction a compass needle points under normal conditions. Then you could add a magnetic field and look at the change in the behavior of the needle. Identifying cause-and-effect relationships allows you to make predictions about related situations. You could predict that a compass needle will always point north because Earth's magnetic field prompts the needle to point in a consistent direction.

Does the introduction of wolves cause elk populations to decrease? Biologists might measure the size of the elk population before and after wolves settled in an area. While cause-and-effect relationships may seem obvious, they are not always true. For example, climate change could have resulted in the loss of nutrient rich grasses for elk to eat, leading to a decrease in the elk population.

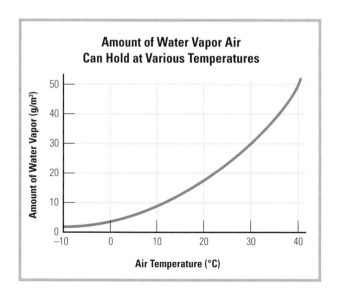

Amount of Water Vapor Air Can Hold at Various Temperatures

Does an increase in temperature indoors cause humidity to rise? First, you could measure the current humidity in a room. Then you could increase the air temperature of the room and measure if there was a change in humidity. It is important to only change the air temperature so there is only one cause to observe the effects of.

Scale, Proportion, and Quantity

Systems occur at different measures of size, time, and energy. Part of science is recognizing that different objects and situations occur at different scales, in different proportions, and in different amounts. Something that can be observed at one scale may not be observable at another scale. How can scale, proportion, and quantity help you understand phenomena in science?

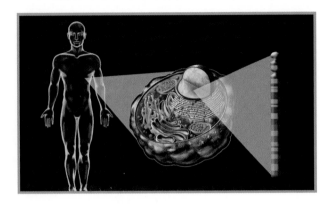

How can you describe the functions of the human body at different scales? Your whole body functions to eat, breathe, and move. At a smaller scale, cells, which can only be seen with a microscope, are the building parts for tissues and organs. Inside these cells is a nucleus, which contains chromosomes on an even smaller scale. Chromosomes are structures that contain instructions for how your body should grow.

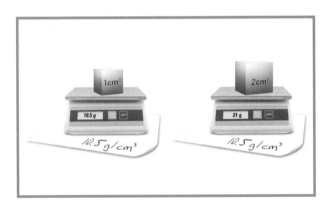

How can proportions be used to identify materials? Density is a proportion that can be used to identify materials. Here, there are two different cubes on a scale. The mass of each cube is different, just as the volume of each cube is different. However, the density of the two cubes is the same. Though the cubes are a different mass and volume, their density allows you to identify them as the same material.

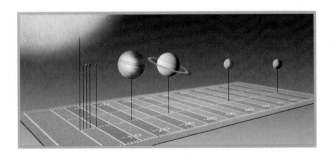

Why are different measurement units used to measure quantities in space? Within the solar system, scientists use astronomical units (AU) in which 1 AU is the average distance between the sun and Earth. However, the distances between stars are so far apart that scientists use a different unit of measurement—light years.

Systems and System Models

Systems occur in the natural world and in objects that are engineered by humans. Many systems interact with other ones, are parts of a larger complex one, or have subsystems of their own. How can you use the concept of systems to understand different phenomena such as the human body, a motor, and the motion of planets in the solar system?

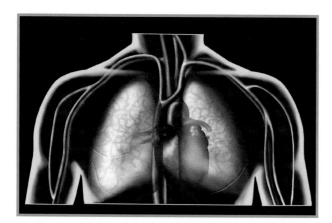

How do subsystems interact within the human body? Your whole body is composed of subsystems that work together to allow you to function. As your respiratory system draws in oxygen through your lungs, it sends oxygen to your bloodstream that is then carried through your body by the circulatory system. Both of these systems work together to help fulfill the body's needs. This is an example of two naturally occurring subsystems interacting as part of a complex whole.

How does a model of a motor represent the way energy and matter flow through a system? This model of an electric motor shows that there is an energy input into the system from the battery. The energy is transferred to electrically charged particles in the motor's wires. The particles begin to flow, forming an electric current that flows past a magnet. The forces between the wires and the magnet cause the motor's shaft to spin, outputting energy.

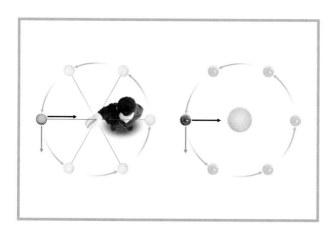

How can you use a model to represent the Earth-sun system? Suppose you swing a ball tied to a string around your head, causing it to move in a circle around your head. The string exerts a force on the ball, but the ball is moving fast enough to keep it from falling back into your hand. In this model, the string represents the gravitational force between the sun and Earth. Using a model allows you to understand how gravitational force functions in the Earth-sun system.

Energy and Matter

Systems can be described in term of energy and matter. Matter is anything that has mass and volume. Energy is the ability to cause motion or change. Energy takes two forms—kinetic energy, which is energy due to motion, and potential energy, which is stored energy. If you can track the energy in a system, you can use it to explain or predict motion and other changes. How does the transfer of energy drive motion or changes in each of the following systems?

How does a food web describe the transfer of energy and matter in an ecosystem? Energy can come from different places and is introduced into the food web when producers, such as plants, absorb energy from sunlight. Other organisms, called consumers, eat producers and other consumers to obtain their energy. Organisms use the energy they obtain to do things like move and stay warm. When they use this energy, they transfer energy to the environment.

Matter follows a path similar to energy in the food web. A consumer will eat an organism lower in the food web, consuming that organism's matter. However, unlike other organisms in the food web, producers get their matter from a different place than where they get their energy. Producers get matter from air, soil, and water, rather than sunlight. The matter from the air, soil, and water comes from decomposers that get their matter from the dead matter and wastes left behind by other organisms in the food web.

Matter and energy follow similar, but different paths. Matter is constantly being cycled through the ecosystem, while energy will flow in one direction.

How does a snowboarder transform potential energy into kinetic energy? Suppose a snowboarder was at the top of a hill, waiting to glide down to the bottom. A chairlift used energy from electricity to lift her up the mountain. That energy is stored by the snowboarder as potential energy. Since the mountain is so tall, she has a large amount of potential energy stored up.

Once the snowboarder tips over the ledge and glides down the hill, her potential energy begins to transform into kinetic energy. Kinetic energy is the energy an object has due to its motion. As the snowboarder is moving down the hill, not only is she moving herself, she is also moving the snow beneath her board. So, she is transferring some of her energy to the snow, giving it kinetic energy.

After the snowboarder glides to the bottom of the hill, nearly all of her potential energy has become kinetic energy. In order to stop, she must transfer all of her kinetic energy to her surroundings. Her board slides across the snow, spraying some of the snow forward and heating it up.

How does the transfer of energy drive the motion of matter in the water cycle?
Water particles are always moving, so they always have some kinetic energy. Water particles near the surface of water with a lot of kinetic energy evaporate off of the surface. When they do, they carry energy away from the water.

Since the particles that escaped the surface of the water have a lot of kinetic energy, they also have a high temperature. Their high temperature causes them to rise into the atmosphere. As they rise, their kinetic energy is converted into potential energy. Since the particles are losing kinetic energy, they also cool.

High in the atmosphere, slow-moving particles condense to form water droplets and clouds. These droplets are held high in the atmosphere due to updrafts of air.

During the precipitation stage, the water particles become too heavy to be held in the atmosphere by updrafts. They begin to fall, and their potential energy is converted back into kinetic energy. Even after reaching the ground, they continue to convert potential energy into kinetic energy as water flows down rivers and into the ocean.

Structure and Function

The structure and properties of a natural or engineered material often determine how that material will function. If a scientist or engineer can understand the structure of that material, then they can also determine how it should function and what may cause it to function improperly. How can you use the concept of structure and function to understand the behavior of natural and engineered materials?

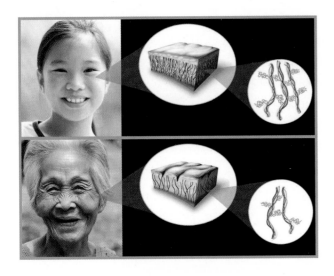

How do changes in the structure of skin tissue affect its function? Two of the proteins made by skin cells, collagen and elastin, help determine the skin's traits. When you are young, your skin continually replaces its collagen and elastin, which keeps your skin strong but flexible. Young skin is very good at protecting the underlying tissues of the body. Over time your body produces less of these proteins, resulting in more wrinkles and reduced protection, strength, and flexibility. The skin's functioning is directly related to the structural components that make it up.

How does the molecular structure of plastic affect its function? Plastics, such as the ones that make up water bottles, are polymers that are made of long flexible chains of molecules. Their structure allows them to retain their shape while remaining flexible. Biodegradable plastics are made of polymers that easily break down into smaller molecules over time. This allows the plastics to break down when buried in a landfill.

How do engineers use the properties of light and glass to design camera lenses? The structure and shape of the glass lens determines how well it functions as a medium for light waves. Glass can be shaped to refract the right amount of light, minimize absorption and reflection, and transmit light to the camera sensor. Once the structure is designed to be just right, the camera can get the perfect shot.

Stability and Change

Scientists can measure the behavior of systems by their stability, or resistance to change, and how they respond to change. Systems, whether small or large, will respond to any amount of change in different ways. How can you observe the way that systems respond when different amounts of change are introduced on different scales?

How can an ecosystem adjust to a change and reestablish its stability? When beavers construct a dam on a stream, they cause changes in the nonliving parts of the ecosystem. These changes in the nonliving parts of the ecosystem do not destroy the system but instead change which species can live there. The ecosystem adapts to changes over long time scales so that it is not completely disrupted. The ecosystem is able to reach a new state of stability.

How do stability and changes in your motion affect you when you ride in a car? If you are moving, you will continue moving at the same speed and in the same direction unless unbalanced forces are acting on you. In a car crash, this stable motion can be very dangerous. Unbalanced forces on the car cause the car to stop suddenly. If you are not wearing a seatbelt, there is no force pushing you back, so your motion will remain stable. You will keep moving forward.

How do different amounts of change over time effect the stability of Earth's system? The amount of carbon dioxide in Earth's atmosphere took millions of years to slowly reach a level that supports animal life on land. But starting about 150 years ago, people have been adding large amounts of carbon dioxide in the air. This fast change caused many destabilizing effects to Earth's system, which causes changes in stability to subsystems such as weather and climate systems.

Analyzing Text Structure

After watching a television program about space, you decide to do some reading about our solar system. You have already found a long online article and a couple of books at the library, but there is a lot of information to read through. How can you get the most out of your reading in the least amount of time?

Reading scientific texts can seem like a difficult task, but when you identify the structure and organization of the text, it becomes much easier to understand the topic you are reading about.

Identifying the Purpose of the Text One way to make sense of a text is to identify the author's purpose. An author may be writing for many different purposes, including any one of these three:

- **Persuasive Argument** The author tries to convince the reader that his or her argument is correct.

- **Tell a Story** The author informs the reader about a process or explains why something came to be.

- **Explanation of Facts** The author informs or teaches the reader about a subject or topic.

Identifying Text Structures Another way to analyze text is to figure out how the information is organized, or structured. Authors may use many different text structures, including the following:

- **Cause and Effect Structure** The author attempts to answer a question about what causes something to happen.

- **Chronological Structure** The author explains a series of events in order.

- **Compare and Contrast Structure** The author compares two or more subjects to argue or clarify facts.

Identifying Organizing Elements Look for specific features of the text that you can use to preview or review the text. A piece of text may have one or more of these organizing elements.

- **Table of Contents** The table of contents helps you identify where information is located in certain lessons or sections.

- **Introductions and Summaries** An introduction can provide previews of the text and explain the structure, while a summary can provide main ideas and a conclusion statement.

- **Headings** Reading headings provides information about the topic of a particular section of text.

- **Graphic Organizers** Visual aids organize large amounts of data into charts and graphs that are easy to understand.

Common Roots, Prefixes, and Suffixes in Science

While reading, you come across the word *exoskeleton*. You know what *skeleton* means, but you wonder what *exo-* means. Knowing common roots, prefixes, and suffixes, and how they combine, can make unfamiliar science words easier to understand! Here is a list of some of the common roots, prefixes, and suffixes you may encounter when you are reading science related texts:

Root, Prefix, or Suffix	Meaning	Examples
astro-	pertaining to stars or celestial bodies	astronaut, astrophysics
bio-	life	biofuel, biomass, biome, biosphere
chem-, chemo-	chemical	chemical, chemistry, chemotherapy
eco-	environment, nature	ecology, ecosystem
endo-	within, inside	endoskeleton, endothermic
exo-	without, outside	exoskeleton, exothermic
gene-	pertaining to heredity	genes, genetics, mutagen
geo-	the earth, pertaining to Earth	geography, geology, geosphere
hyper-	over, above	hyperthermia
hypo-	under, below	hypothermia, hypodermic
macro-	very large in scale, scope, or capability	macroscopic
micro-	extremely small	microscope, microscopic
-ology	a science or branch of knowledge, the study of something	archaeology, biology, geology
poly-	many, several, more than one	polymer
-sphere	spherical shape, supporting life	atmosphere, biosphere, hydrosphere
therm-, thermo-	heat, hot	hypothermia, thermodynamics, thermometer

If you can recognize a common root, prefix, or suffix, you can identify the meaning of unfamiliar words. Insects commonly have exoskeletons. The prefix *exo-* means "without" or "outside."

Writing Scientific Arguments and Explanations

After making observations and conducting an experiment, your teacher gives you an assignment to write a scientific argument about your experiment. It may sound simple, but where do you start?

Scientists do a lot of hands-on experimentation, but they also write arguments that convince people their claims are true. Writing is very important to the scientific process—well-written observations and notes will help you write a strong argument.

Claim The claim is where you introduce your hypothesis or the answer to a question you are trying to solve by gathering data. This is also where you would establish a formal style. You can do this by using full sentences and scientific terms you may have learned in class.

Evidence Your evidence is specific scientific data that supports your claim. You can also use charts and graphs to communicate your findings. They make it easy to see and compare evidence, which can make your argument stronger.

When writing scientific arguments, it is useful to organize your data into charts or graphs and ask a peer to review your work. Doing these simple things will help to make your argument stronger and more convincing.

Reasoning After providing your evidence, you need to convince the reader that the evidence supports the claim. If your classmates have different claims, you can point these out and use evidence to tell the reader why your claim is correct. You may also write a concluding statement to refresh the reader's memory and summarize the evidence and related reasoning.

Before you finish writing a scientific argument, read it for any spelling and grammatical errors. It also helps to have a peer read your argument. If your peer does not understand your argument, you may need to rewrite it until how you came to your conclusion is clearer.

Writing Investigation Procedures

The steps needed to carry out an investigation are called a procedure. Scientists write a procedure as part of the process of designing an investigation and use the procedure as a guide during the investigation. Scientists also record a procedure so that their fellow scientists can follow the investigation easily and confirm results. How can you write a good investigation procedure?

A good procedure organizes steps and data easily so you can complete your experiment without running into problems or danger. A procedure should also be written so anybody can repeat your experiment and obtain an identical result. Use this checklist as a guide when writing your procedure and to evaluate your writing when you are done:

☑ All of the necessary steps are included and clearly labeled.

☑ The tools and materials for each step are listed.

☑ Each step is clearly written using precise language and vocabulary so that a classmate or any stranger can follow it.

☑ The steps are in the correct order.

☑ Safety notes are included for any steps that require them.

☑ The type of data you will collect in each step is clearly described.

☑ If necessary, a data table is prepared to record data in.

☑ The language of the procedure is unbiased and something a fellow scientist would be comfortable reading.

Once your teacher has reviewed your procedure, you are ready to conduct your investigation!

When writing an investigation procedure, it is important that the steps are clearly written, are in the right order, include the materials needed, and have identified safety precautions.

Communicating with Graphic Organizers

Your teacher divides the class into teams and gives you all an assignment to build a protective structure for an egg out of simple materials. Afterwards, you work together as a class to create a graphic organizer to explain all the information and see why different teams got different results.

Scientists use graphic organizers to visually communicate complex ideas or large amounts of data. If you can read a graphic organizer, you can explain the results you see. When gathering data, it is useful to take the information you have and sketch a graphic organizer by hand. Once you decide how to present the information on paper, you can create your graphic organizer on the computer. Many software programs have the tools you need to create graphic organizers, like flow charts, Venn diagrams, and tables.

Flow Chart Flow charts are useful for displaying processes. In this case, the flowchart is explaining the process your team used to build your egg protector. You can add more detailed information to each box, but the chart should be a step-by-step explanation of each stage of your work. Computers have many applications that can be used to create flowcharts, including word processors or paint applications. The flowchart you see here is a good reference for the process you should follow when designing a solution to a problem.

Defining the Engineering Problem
- Clearly state the problem to be solved
- Define criteria for egg container
- Define constraints of egg container

Developing Possible Solutions
- Develop egg container designs
- Narrow down egg container designs
- Design egg container
- Test egg container

Optimizing the Design Solution
- Optimize design of egg container
- Retest egg container
- Optimize container more if needed

Tables Tables group information into various categories by columns and rows and are useful for displaying large amounts of data. Scientists use tables to help them observe patterns in their data. In this case, the table displays the different materials used by the teams in your class to create their egg protectors. You can create a table by using spreadsheet software and inputting information into cells or by hand-drawing rows and columns on a sheet of paper. Look at the table below. Can you see any patterns in the materials used by the teams to create their egg protectors?

Team 1	Team 2	Team 3
Tissue Paper	Tissue Paper	Tissue Paper
Wooden sticks	Cotton Balls	Paper cup
Tape	Plastic Bag	Tape

Venn Diagram Like flowcharts, computers have applications that can be used to create Venn diagrams. Venn diagrams are used to show similarities and differences; each circle lists the traits of an object, and the overlap is used to list similarities. They are useful when comparing the traits of two or three different objects or ideas. Consider the Venn diagram below. Which material was used by all teams? Which materials were only used by one team? What conclusions would you be able to draw from this based on the results of the experiment?

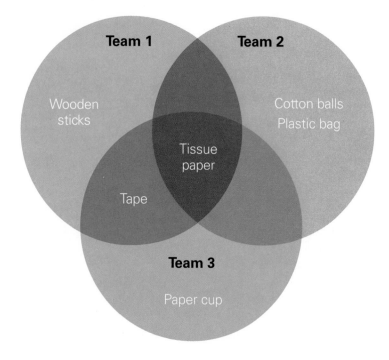

Research Project Tips

After reading about the periodic table, you decide you want to research it as a research project topic for your science class. One of the first things you need to do is find sources. With so many different places to look, including online and print sources, how do you even know where to begin?

How to Find Sources

- **First, go to the library.** The reference librarian will be able to point you in the right direction and teach you how to use the online catalog to find books, magazines, and journal subscriptions.

- **Find reliable sources.** Government and university websites, scientific magazines and journals, and other major magazines can be valuable sources of information that are easy to access.

- **Start general with search engines.** When using search engines, use words you would expect to find in your source. You do not need to worry about capitalization. Most search engines are able to understand what you are trying to find.

- **Try an advanced search tool.** Many search engines have a button for an "advanced search." Here, you can tell the search engine which kinds of websites you are looking for. If you want to find a government website, you can type "site:.gov" into one of the search fields.

The library is one of your best resources for research. Not only does it have books, it also has subscriptions for online magazines and journals that have current information on scientific advancements.

How to Evaluate Sources

- **Evaluate whether a source has bias.**
  Consider whether the source has arguments
  that are either supported by widely accepted
  facts or available data. If you find information
  on a website that is very different from
  some of your other sources, you may want
  to reconsider using that source.

- **Evaluate the source of your source.**
  Unofficial websites that are not supported
  by scientific, government, or academic
  institutions are probably not good sources
  to use. Check the URL for clues. Websites
  that end in .gov or .edu tend to be more
  reliable than general .com sites. You can also
  read a source's "About" page to see what
  their intention is for the information they
  provide.

- **Evaluate the quality of your source.** One
  source that has a lot of information about
  one topic can be more useful than several
  sources that have a little information about
  one topic.

How to Cite Sources

- **Keep track of which sources you use.** Keep notes as to
  which sources you use and where you use them in your own
  work. It helps to use bookmarks that you can label to mark
  which pages you draw information from. Another easy way to
  keep track of your sources is to make a copy of the first page of
  a book or article, or take a screenshot of a webpage. You may
  also want to create a spreadsheet or document that keeps track
  of the name of a source, its title or URL, and the information you
  took from the site.

- **Use a style manual.** There are several guides that teach you
  how to cite sources. The APA Style Manual, MLA Handbook,
  and Chicago Manual of Style are good places to start.

- **Avoid plagiarism.** When you quote a source or use
  information you got from a source, you need to give the source
  credit. The style manuals will have instructions on how to give
  credit for different kinds of sources.

As you gather information from
sources, it is very important to keep
track of which sources you use. Keep
organized notes for online sources by
creating a document or spreadsheet.
Label paper bookmarks or sticky notes
for print sources.

Positive and Negative Numbers

Positive and negative numbers are used together to describe quantities having opposite directions or values. Positive numbers represent values greater than zero, while negative numbers represent values less than zero. How can you use positive and negative numbers to describe changes in temperature?

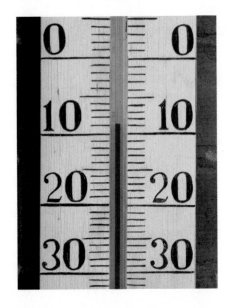

Thermometers display temperatures on a vertical number line. Numbers below zero on the number line are negative temperatures, while numbers above zero are positive temperatures.

A weather report says the temperature is –5°C. A negative number is a number that is less than zero. A number line represents numbers in relation to zero. On a horizontal number line, negative numbers are to the left of zero and positive numbers are to the right of zero. So, –5°C is five degrees below zero, which is five degrees to the left of zero. Likewise, 5°C would be five degrees above zero which is 5 degrees to the right of zero on a number line diagram.

During the afternoon, the temperature rises. The weather report says that the temperature increased by 7°C. What is the temperature now? To add a positive number, move right along the number line.

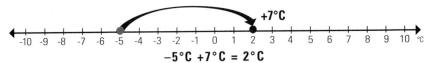

$$-5°C + 7°C = 2°C$$

After sunset, the temperature drops, or decreases in value. The weather report says the temperature dropped 10°C after sunset. What is the temperature now? When you subtract a positive number, you move left along the number line.

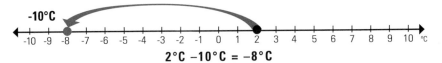

$$2°C - 10°C = -8°C$$

What is the difference between the temperature in the morning (–5°C) and the temperature after sunset (–8°C)? To find the difference, subtract the morning temperature from the current temperature. To subtract a negative number means to add the positive of that number, so move right on the number line, just like adding a positive number.

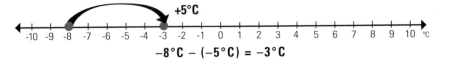

$$-8°C - (-5°C) = -3°C$$

Exponents and Scientific Notation

Scientists often need to represent very small numbers and very large numbers, which have many digits. These numbers can be so long that they are difficult to read. So, scientists developed a simpler method to represent these numbers, called scientific notation.

Scientific notation requires the use of exponents. An exponent is a number or symbol indicating how many times a base number should be multiplied by itself. For example, the "5" in 8^5 is an exponent, and 8^5 can also be expressed as "eight to the power of five" or $8 \times 8 \times 8 \times 8 \times 8$.

When you write numbers using scientific notation, 10 is the always the base number. Each time you multiply by 10, you move the decimal point one place to the right. So, multiplying by 10^6 moves the decimal point six places to the right. Scientific notation takes a number between 0 and 10 and multiplies it by a power of 10. This calculation moves the decimal point to the left or right the correct number of places.

Scientists use scientific notation to represent very small and very large numbers using powers of 10. Neptune is approximately 4,700,000,000 km from Earth, which can be written in scientific notation as 4.7×10^9 km.

Scientific notation is useful for writing very large numbers that represent distances in space. For example, engineers designing a probe to send to Neptune would often need to refer to the distance between Earth and Neptune, which is 4,700,000,000.0 kilometers. 4,700,000,000.0 can be expressed as 4.7 with the decimal point moved to the right nine places.

$$4.7 \times 10^9 \text{ km} = 4,700,000,000.0 \text{ km}$$

Very small numbers can also be written using scientific notation. For example, the diameter of a hydrogen atom is approximately 0.000000000106 meters. To write small numbers, you divide by 10 instead of multiplying by 10. You can represent this in scientific notation using negative exponents. 0.000000000106 meters is 1.06 meters with the decimal point moved to the left 10 times.

$$1.06 \times 10^{-10} \text{ m} = 0.0000000000106 \text{ m}$$

Dependent and Independent Variables

Scientists use dependent and independent variables to describe the relationships they measure in their investigations. Independent and dependent variables are used in equations to represent two different quantities that change in relationship to one another.

A commercial airplane has a cruising air speed for long-distance flights of 900 km/hr. In this relationship, the distance the plane travels depends on how long the plane has been flying. However, the time it has been flying does not depend on the distance it has traveled. So, time is the independent variable (x), and distance is the dependent variable (y). The relationship between kilometers traveled and the time in hours can be represented between two variables using an equation, a table, or a graph.

An equation that represents the relationship between the distance the airplane has traveled and how long it has traveled is:

$$y = 900x$$

The letter x represents the independent variable, which is the time the plane has been flying. The letter y is the dependent variable, which is the distance the plane has traveled.

The second way to represent the relationship between variables is with a table. The table on this page uses the equation $y = 900x$ to calculate the dependent y value that matches each independent x value in the table. It represents the relationship between x and y.

The third way to represent the relationship between two variables is with a graph. You can use either the equation or the table of values to represent the relationship in a graph. The graph both shows the equation and plots the points from the data table.

Equations, tables, and graphs are three ways to represent the relationship between an independent variable x and a dependent variable y. For a plane flying at 900 km/hr, the independent variable is flying time, and the dependent variable is distance traveled.

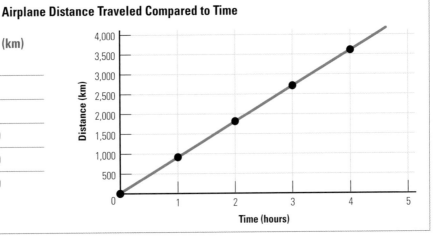

Airplane Distance Traveled Compared to Time

Time (hours) x	Distance (km) y
0	0
1	900
2	1,800
3	2,700
4	3,600

Chance and Probability

Some events scientists study involve things that definitely will happen or will not happen. However, most events might happen but will not happen for sure. How can understanding probability help predict how likely events are to happen?

Every year, sugar maple trees produce many seeds, which are carried away from the trees by wind. Many of the seeds germinate, or sprout into a seedling that can grow into a new tree, but not every seed does. A scientist decides to study how likely it is that a maple seed will sprout. That is, she will study the probability that a seed will germinate.

The scientist randomly collects a sample of 1,000 seeds from trees in a 1 km × 1 km area. She and her team plant the seeds in a large field. They return in the spring to determine how many of the seeds germinated into new maple trees. She might find that 910 of the seeds germinated. The proportion of seeds that germinated was $\frac{910}{1,000}$, or 91%.

Her team repeats the experiment several more times in different years and finds that in one year, 97% of the seeds germinated. In the second year, 94% germinated, and 95% germinated in the third year. From this data, she finds the average proportion of seeds that germinate and concludes that the chance of a maple seed germinating is about 95%.

A 95% probability means that each seed has a 95 in 100 chance of germinating. If you looked at 100 seeds, you would expect 95 of them to germinate. If you looked at 1,000 seeds, you would expect 950 to germinate. However, 950 seeds would not germinate every time. For example, sometimes 962 seeds would germinate, or 935 seeds, or 900 seeds, or even all 1,000 seeds. A probability describes the chance that something will happen, but it does not predict exactly what will happen every time.

Sugar maple trees produce many seeds, but some seeds do not germinate. By collecting data on how many seeds germinate, a scientist can estimate the probability that each individual seed will germinate.

Representing and Interpreting Data

Scientific investigations produce a lot of data, but it is often difficult to make sense of the data the way it is recorded during the investigation. Scientists carefully choose how they will represent data to make it easy to analyze, interpret, and communicate its meaning to others.

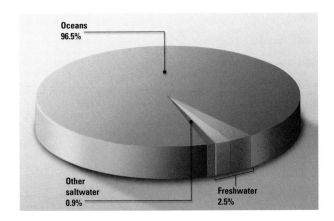

Pie Graphs A comparison between the amount of freshwater and saltwater on Earth is best represented using a pie graph. Scientists use pie graphs to display data with percentages. A pie graph, also known as a pie chart, divides a circle into sections to show the relative sizes of data and how a part relates to the whole. A pie graph can effectively show how one variable is divided between different categories. They often show the percentage of a variable in each category. For instance, the wedges on this pie graph show how the water on Earth is divided into three categories: water from oceans, fresh water, and other saltwater.

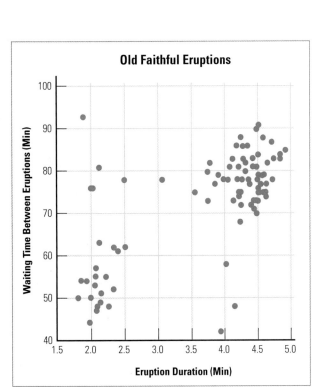

Scatter Plots Scientists use scatter plots to show repeated measurements of a similar phenomenon, such as the relationship between the waiting time between eruptions of the geyser Old Faithful and the length of the eruptions. Each measurement of an eruption is one point on the graph. The x coordinate of the point shows the duration of the eruption. The y coordinate shows the waiting time before the eruption. Scatter plots are effective for comparing two variables that do not fall into specific categories. There are many patterns in data that scatter plots can reveal.

The scatter plot shows that Old Faithful eruptions fall into two main groups: a short wait between eruptions (45–60 minutes) followed by a short eruption (2 minutes), or a long wait between eruptions (70–90 minutes) followed by a long eruption (4–5 minutes).

A scatter plot that compares shoe size to height would probably form a line, indicating that people who are taller usually wear larger shoes.

Bar Graphs This bar graph of earthquakes in Oklahoma shows how many earthquakes occurred in Oklahoma in each year between 2000 and 2015. Scientists use bar graphs, or bar charts, to represent the relative sizes of data values in different categories, such as years, months, colors, or cities. They use horizontal or vertical bars to represent the size of the value in each category. Larger bars represent a higher value, and smaller bars represent a lower value. The bar graph of earthquakes in Oklahoma shows a huge increase in earthquakes in 2014 from previous years since the bar for 2014 is much larger than any of the previous bars.

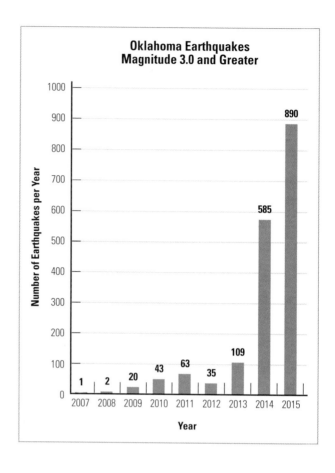

Line Graphs Scientists use line graphs to show how a dependent variable changes as an independent variable is increased. In many cases, the independent variable is a measure of time, so the graph shows how a dependent variable changes over time. For example, the average global temperature over time can be shown using a line graph. Like in a scatter plot, each data point has an x coordinate (time) and a y coordinate (average temperature). Unlike a scatter plot, each data point is connected to the last one with a straight line. Following the line shows how the average temperature changed over time.

This line graph shows many patterns about how the global average temperature changed between 1880 and 2000. The temperature was lowest between 1900 and 1920 and highest after 2000. What other patterns do you see in the graph?

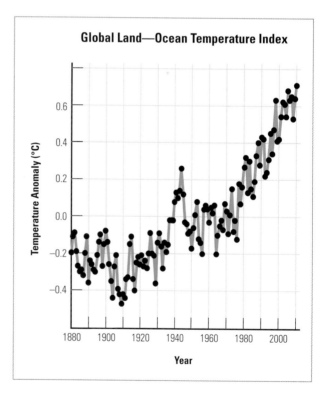

Ratios, Rates, Percents, and Proportional Relationships

When scientists collect data involving numbers, quantities are often compared. You can compare quantities using ratios, percentages, and unit rates. How are these mathematical concepts useful in understanding one of the most important scientific investigations related to changes in species?

Scientists have been observing and studying dark peppered moths near Manchester, England, since 1848. More than 70 species of moths in England have undergone a change from light to dark, with similar observations in the United States.

Expressing Ratios as Percentages To study this change, a scientist named Henry Bernard Davis Kettlewell released light and dark colored moths in polluted and unpolluted woods. He then recaptured as many of the moths as he could over the next week. In the unpolluted woods, he released 496 light colored moths and captured back 62 of them. So, the ratio of captured moths to released moths is 62:496. By finding an equivalent ratio with 100 as the number of moths released, you can find what percentage 62:496 equals.

$$62:496 = 12.5:100$$

Kettlewell recaptured 12.5% of the light moths he released. Similarly, he released 488 dark moths into the unpolluted woods and only recaptured 34. That is 34:488 as a ratio, or 7.0% as a percentage.

Kettlewell released light and dark colored moths and then recaptured them to study how well each type of moth survived in polluted and unpolluted woods. He used the ratio of moths captured to moths released, expressed as a percentage, to support his findings.

Using Unit Rates Scientists often compare quantities using unit rates. A unit rate is the number of one quantity there is for every one unit of another quantity. If Kettlewell wanted to know how many moths he needed to release in order to capture one moth, he would calculate the unit rate. He would do so by starting with the ratio of moths released to moths captured (496:62 for light colored moths). Then he would find an equivalent ratio where the number of moths captured is one. Unit rates are usually written as fractions.

$$\text{Unit rate} = \frac{8 \text{ moths released}}{1 \text{ moth captured}}$$

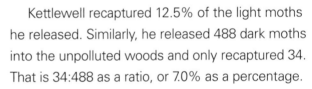

So, for every eight light colored moths Kettlewell released, he captured one light colored moth back.

Graphing and Interpreting Proportional Relationships

Scientists and engineers look for proportional relationships to better understand and predict how two variables are related. In a proportional relationship, the ratio of one variable to the other is always the same. How can using proportional reasoning make someone a better bowler?

An engineer wants to improve her bowling score, so she decides to study the relationship between the mass of the bowling ball she uses and the kinetic energy of the ball. She builds a machine that throws a bowling ball down the lane at exactly 8 m/s. Then she tests a variety of bowling balls. She makes a table of her data and finds the ratio of energy to mass of the balls. She sees that the ratio is the same for every ball moving at 8 m/s. She discovered a proportional relationship between the bowling ball's energy and mass.

She makes a graph of the data in her table and sees that the data points form a straight line. The line passes through the origin (0, 0). She calculates that the slope of the line is 32 J/kg. The line's slope is the same as the ratio of energy per unit mass in her table.

To make predictions, the engineer writes an equation to describe her data. The equation of a straight line is $y = mx + b$. The y-intercept (b) of her line is 0 J. The slope (m) of her line is 32 J/kg. So, the equation for her line is:

$$y = 32x$$

In this equation, y is energy of the ball, and x is mass of the ball. The engineer now knows how the energy of the ball depends on its mass. But she still has more questions. How does the energy depend on the speed of the ball? And how much energy should the ball have to knock down all the pins?

Mass versus Kinetic Energy With Constant Velocity

Mass (kg)	Energy (J)	Ratio: energy/ mass (J/kg)
4	128	$\frac{128}{4} = 32$
5	160	$\frac{160}{5} = 32$
6	192	$\frac{192}{6} = 32$
7	224	$\frac{224}{7} = 32$

Angles, Perpendicular and Parallel Lines

Scientists use angles as well as parallel and perpendicular lines to describe how objects are oriented relative to each other. How can using these mathematical ideas help when explaining how light rays interact with a glass slide?

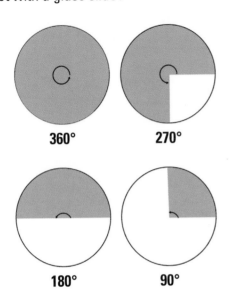

360°   **270°**

180°   **90°**

Angles Light travels in a straight line as long as it is not changing the material, or medium, it is traveling through. When a beam of light enters a glass slide, it bends. The amount that the beam bends depends on the angle between the slide and the beam of light. An angle is a shape formed by two rays that begin at the same endpoint, and the size of the angle can be changed by rotating the two rays. Angles are measured in degrees (°). Rotating 360° is rotating in a full circle, returning the object back to where it started. Rotating by 180° is rotating through half a circle, and rotating by 90° is rotating a quarter circle.

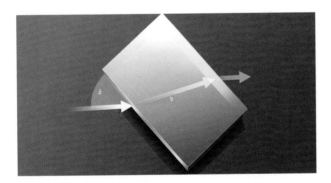

Parallel Lines The beam of light meets the glass at a 51° angle. As it enters the glass, it changes direction, turning 14° counterclockwise. When the beam of light leaves the glass, it rotates back, turning 14° clockwise. The beam of light leaving the glass is parallel to the beam of light entering the glass. Parallel lines are lines that, if you extend them out infinitely in both directions, will never cross.

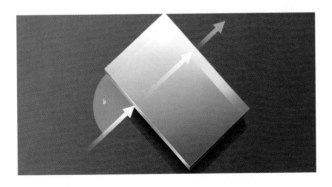

Perpendicular Lines A beam of light will not always bend when it enters a glass slide. If the beam of light is perpendicular to the edge of the slide, the light will pass straight through without bending. Two lines are perpendicular if they meet at a 90° angle.

Area, Surface Area, and Volume

Scientists use area, surface area, and volume to describe the sizes of various objects they study. Area describes the size of a two-dimensional surface. Surface area describes the total size of the surface of a three-dimensional object. Volume describes the amount of space a three-dimensional object takes up. How could a scientist who wanted to explain why cells are so small use the concepts of area, surface area, and volume? He investigates simple cube-shaped cells in the human body.

Area The scientist knows that for a cell to survive, enough nutrients have to pass through its cell membrane to supply the needs of the cell. The larger the area of the membrane, the more nutrients can pass through it. So, the scientist calculates the area of one square-shaped side of the cell.

$$\text{Area} = s^2$$

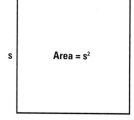

Surface Area But the scientist knows that nutrients can pass through any side of the cube, not just one side. So, he needs to calculate the surface area of the cube. The surface area is the total area of the surface of the cube. The cube has six sides, so its surface area is six times the area of one side.

$$\text{Surface Area} = 6s^2$$

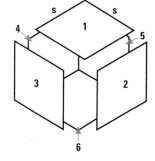

Volume However, the scientist knows that volume of the cube is important too. The volume is the total amount of space that the cube takes up. Generally, the larger the volume is, the more nutrients the cell needs to stay alive and the farther the nutrients have to go after entering the cell. The volume of a cube is the side length cubed.

$$\text{Volume} = s^3$$

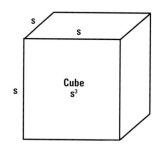

The scientist sees that as the cube gets larger, the volume grows much faster than the surface area grows. So, he decides that the cells he is studying are all very small because a large cell would not be able to take in enough nutrients through its membrane to support its volume. Cells need a large surface-area-to-volume ratio to survive.

Metric System Units

Throughout history, people around the world used different measurement units for trading goods and building objects and structures. Body parts were used to measure length. Grains of wheat were poured into containers to measure volume. Notches on a burning candle measured time. What problems did these customs cause, and how were they solved?

Traditional measurement units were awkward. It was difficult to compare one unit to another. Even when the same unit was used, there were often variations in how the unit was applied from place to place. In the late 1700s, that all changed. Scientists began to develop new units that were easy to use and accepted by scientists everywhere. Many of those units are part of the metric system.

The units you choose are determined by the goal of your investigation. If you want to measure the amount of matter in a rock, you would choose grams, a measure of mass, as your unit. If you want to measure how warm water is, you would use degrees Celsius. Other metric units are a combination of two units. For example, to describe the speed of a toy car rolling down a ramp, you would record the speed as meters per second.

Some Common Units of the Metric System

Measurement	Unit Name	Symbol
length	meter	m
mass	gram	g
time	second	s
temperature	degrees Celsius	°C
area	meter squared	m^2
frequency	hertz	Hz
force	newton	N
volume	meter cubed	m^3
density	kilogram per meter cubed	kg/m^3
speed, velocity	meter per second	m/s
acceleration	meter per second squared	m/s^2
energy	joule	J
power (energy per second)	watt	W
energy	watt hour	Wh
electric charge	coulomb	C

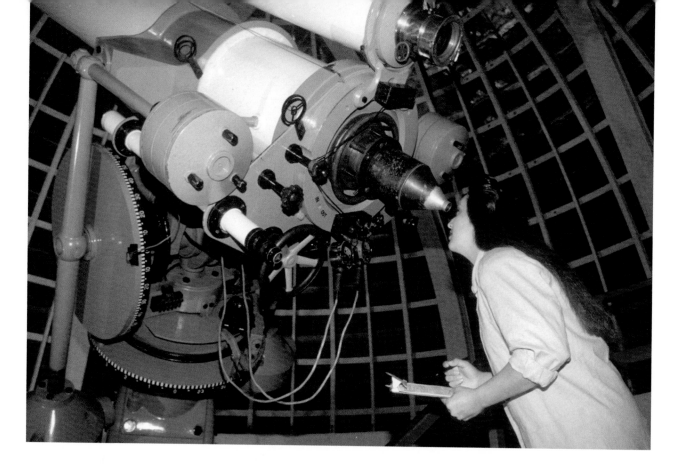

Some units were not developed as part of the metric system, but are still used by many scientists and engineers around the world. For example, if you want to compare distances of objects in the solar system, meters or even kilometers make the numbers difficult to communicate. Astronomers prefer to use astronomical units for this purpose. Similarly, when you need to describe distances between two stars or two galaxies, astronomical units are difficult. The distances are so great that astronomers use a unit called a light year, which is the distance that light travels in one Earth year.

Several measurement units are not part of the metric system, yet they are widely used by scientists and engineers. Two of these units, astronomical units and light years, are essential for communicating data to scientists such as this astronomer.

Some Common Units Outside the Metric System

Measurement	Unit Name	Symbol
time	minute	min
time	hour	h
time	day	d
angle size	degree	°
liquid volume	liter	L
distances inside the solar system	astronomical unit	AU
distances between stars	light year	ly
energy	calorie	cal
digital information	byte	B

Metric System Prefixes

A base unit can be modified using prefixes that indicate different amounts of each unit. Let's say you are investigating plant species to determine how much variation there is among their flower sizes. Some plant species have flowers that are so tiny that they can only be seen with magnification. Others have flowers as wide as a human's arm length. How can understanding measurement prefixes help you?

This flower is produced by plants called *Rafflesia* and is about 1 m across. Most plants have flowers that are much smaller, so smaller units are more useful for describing them.

Using prefixes with base units allows you to choose the unit that is simplest to communicate. Adding a prefix to a base unit makes a new unit. The new unit is made larger or smaller than the base unit by multiplying the base unit by a certain factor of 10. Each prefix represents a different factor of 10.

Here is how it works when measuring length. Meters are the base unit for length and are suitable for describing the size of the largest flowers in the plant kingdom. Millimeters have the prefix *milli*, which is 0.001. So a millimeter is 0.001, or 1/1,000, times the amount of one meter. There are 1,000 millimeters in one meter. Millimeters is a suitable unit for measuring the smallest flowers in the world. Now, suppose you were to travel around the world touring exotic flowers. A larger unit for length would be helpful to describe the distance you traveled. There are 1,000 meters in a kilometer. The prefix *kilo* means 10^3, or 1,000. So a kilometer is 1,000 times the size of a meter.

Many base units can be changed to easier-to-use units by adding a prefix. Start by choosing a base unit. Move up to get larger units and move down to get smaller units.

Some Common Units of the Metric System

Prefix	Symbol	Word	Decimal	Factor of 10
tera	T	trillion	1,000,000,000,000	10^{12}
giga	G	billion	1,000,000,000	10^9
mega	M	million	1,000,000	10^6
kilo	k	thousand	1,000	10^3
hecto	h	hundred	100	10^2
deka	da	ten	10	10^1
Choose a base unit.		one	1	10^0
deci	d	tenth	0.1	10^{-1}
centi	c	hundredth	0.01	10^{-2}
milli	m	thousandth	0.001	10^{-3}
micro	μ	millionth	0.000001	10^{-6}
nano	n	billionth	0.000000001	10^{-9}
pico	p	trillionth	0.000000000001	10^{-12}

Converting Measurement Units

You can also find equivalents of measurements that have the same base unit but different prefixes. One method is to divide or multiply by the number of one unit in the other unit. Another method is to use a metric "staircase" to decide how many places, and in what direction, to move the decimal point.

You can convert a larger unit to a smaller unit using multiplication. To do so, multiply the original measurement by the amount that the new unit differs from it. For example, to convert 9 kilometers to centimeters, you would multiply 9 (the number of kilometers) times 100,000 (the number of centimeters in one kilometer). So, 900,000 cm is equivalent to 9 km.

A smaller unit can be converted to a larger unit by using division. To do so, divide the original measurement by the amount that the new unit differs from it. For example, to use division to convert 900,000 centimeters to kilometers, divide 900,000 (the number of centimeters) by 100,000 (the number of centimeters in one kilometer). As before, 9 km is equivalent to 900,000 cm.

Another way to convert units is by picturing the metric "staircase" shown here to decide how many places to move the decimal point. For example, to convert 1.1 kilograms to milligrams, take six steps down the staircase and move the decimal point six places to the right. There are 1,100,000 milligrams in 1.1 kilograms.

In the United States, certain non-metric units are used in everyday situations. For this reason, you may sometimes need to convert non-metric units into metric units. Luckily, there are many websites and apps that will do conversions for you!

To convert to a larger unit, move the decimal point to the left for each step up the staircase. To convert to a smaller unit, move the decimal point to the right for each step you take down the staircase.

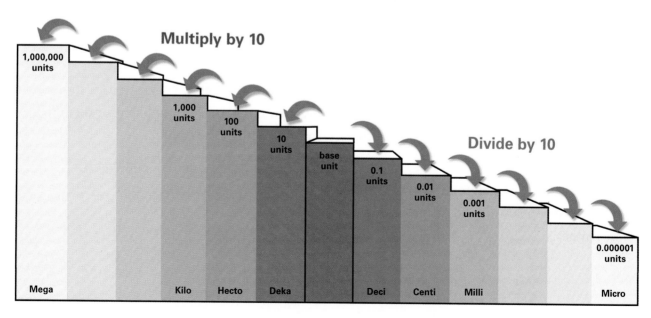

Multiply by 10

1,000,000 units

1,000 units

100 units

10 units

base unit

0.1 units

0.01 units

0.001 units

Divide by 10

0.000001 units

Mega   Kilo   Hecto   Deka   Deci   Centi   Milli   Micro

GLOSSARY

B

biodiversity   the variety of organisms on Earth or in a particular habitat or ecosystem

biofuel   a material that is made from biomass and releases energy when it is burned

biomass   the combined mass of the bodies of organisms, which collectively represents stored energy

biome   a large area of Earth characterized by certain physical conditions and the living things that are found there

biosphere   the parts of Earth in which organisms are able to live

C

carbohydrate   a molecule used to store energy

carbon cycle   a model that describes how carbon-based molecules move among Earth's ecosystems and atmosphere

carnivore   an organism that mainly eats animals

cellular respiration   the process that cells use to release the energy stored in sugars

cellulose   the material that forms the rigid walls and support for plant cells

chlorophyll   a green pigment that is important in photosynthesis

chloroplast   a cell structure that uses the sun's energy to make sugar through the process of photosynthesis

climate change   a long-term change in climate patterns on Earth, including changes in average global temperatures and the frequency of severe weather

commensalism   a relationship between two species in which one species benefits and the other is unaffected

competition   an interaction between living things that need the same limited resource

constraint   a limitation on an engineering solution

consumer   an organism that gets energy and matter by eating or absorbing other organisms as food

criteria   the requirements that must be met for an engineering solution to be successful

D

decomposer   a kind of consumer that uses the wastes or dead remains of other organisms as a source of energy and matter

direct effect   an interaction in a food web where one population affects the abundance of another

disease resistance   a characteristic of organisms that makes it unlikely for them to be infected with or die from diseases

dynamic system   any system that is characterized by constant change

E

ecological succession the predictable way that ecosystems change from one type to another over time

ecosystem a group of populations of living things and the nonliving parts of their environment that support them

ecosystem service a natural process humans rely on that healthy ecosystems provide, such as cleaning water and conserving soil

emerging disease a disease that has recently appeared in human populations, often as a result of new interactions with species in ecosystems

evidence information obtained by observation or experimentation

extinction when all of the members of a species die and the species no longer exists

extirpation when all of the members of a population die and the species no longer exists in that place

F

fat a molecule that is used to store energy in the form of oils and is important in forming cells

food chain an individual path in a food web

food web a model that shows feeding relationships between organisms in an ecosystem

H

habitat degradation changing or destroying natural ecosystems in ways that disrupt their healthy functioning

herbivore an organism that mainly eats plants or plant parts

I

indirect effect an interaction in a food web where one population affects the abundance of another through its effect on a third population

invasive species a species that has been introduced to a place where it is not naturally found and causes ecological or economic harm

K

keystone species a species that affects the diversity of an entire ecosystem

L

law of conservation of matter a scientific law that states the amount of matter in a closed system stays the same, although the forms of that matter may change

M

matter anything that has mass and volume

mitochondria structures in cells that convert energy in sugar molecules into usable energy

mutualism a relationship between two species in which both species benefit

GLOSSARY

N

natural resource   a material or source of energy found in nature that benefits humans

niche   the ecological role that a species plays in an ecosystem

nitrogen cycle   a model that describes how nitrogen-based molecules move among Earth's ecosystems and atmosphere

O

omnivore   an organism that eats both plants and animals in similar amounts

organism   an individual living thing

over-exploitation   harvesting species from the wild faster than those populations can recover, resulting in population decline

P

parasitism   a relationship in which one species benefits while the other is harmed but not usually killed

per capita   a measure of something per person; for example, per capita income is the ratio of total income to people

photosynthesis   the process of using energy from the sun and matter from the environment to produce sugars that store energy in chemical bonds

population   a group of individuals of a species that lives and reproduces in the same area

predation   a relationship in which one organism, the predator, benefits by eating another organism, the prey

producer   an organism that captures energy and matter from its surroundings to produce sugars and other molecules

proportion   the relationship between a part and a whole

protein   a type of molecule that makes up much of an organism's structure and helps it function

R

reforestation   the re-planting of forests that have been cut down

resource   any material or energy needed by living things to survive, grow, and reproduce

S

scavenger   an organism that eats other organisms that are already dead

species   a group of living things that share traits and can breed successfully with each other, but not with other groups

T

trophic pyramid   a model that shows how much energy is transferred from one stage to the next in a food chain

W

water cycle   a model that describes how water molecules move among Earth's ecosystems and atmosphere

*Page numbers in **bold** indicate definitions.*

A

abalones, 116

acorns, 71

algae, 28, 48, 57, 94, 95

American cockroaches, 34

amoebas, 72

analyzing a mathematical system, 190, 191

anemones, 21

angler fish, 98

angles, 224

Año Nuevo State Park, 171

anteaters, 129

antelope, pronghorn, 12, 41

ants, 30, 114, 129

aphids, 30

aquatic biomes, 13

aquatic ecosystems, 57, 131

Long Island Sound's ecosystem, 167–168, 169

aquatic "farms," 152

aquatic plants, 53, 59

aquatic producers, 57

Arctic foxes, 125

Arctic Ocean, 131

Arctic tundra ecosystems, 124–125, 130, 135

area, 225

surface area, 225

arguments

claims, 196, 197, 210

from evidence, 196–197, 210

for explanations, 192, 193

persuasive, 208

reasoning in, 196, 197, 210

refutation of, 196, 197

writing scientific arguments, 210

Asian carp and the Great Lakes, 165, 169

asking questions, 180–181

Atchafalaya River, 44

B

bacteria, 53, 88, 99, 105, 113–114

cyanobacteria, 57

denitrifying, 107, 109

nitrifying, 106, 108

nitrogen cycle and, 106

nitrogen-fixing, 106, 108

badgers, 41

Baja Peninsula, 171

bananas, 145

bandages, super, 134–135

bar graphs, 221

barnacles, 29

beach grasses, 149

bears

black, 43

grizzly, 30

polar, 7, 125

beaver dams, 42

beavers, 42

as a keystone species, 127

bee(s)

bumble bees, 37

pollination, 113, 143

populations, 114

beetles, 37, 87

dung beetles, 88

beets, 62

"Beware Bilharzia" sign, 161

bilharzia infections, 161

biodiversity, 121, **122**, 130–131

human benefits of, 132–133, 135

importance of, 122–123, 134–135

in tundra ecosystems, 124–125

in kelp forest ecosystems, 126–127

in tropical rainforest ecosystems, 128–129

scientists, 136–139

biofuel(s), 55, **64**

biomass, 55, **63**

as an energy source, 64–65

in a food chain, 90

in food webs, 90, 92–93, 95

biome(s), 7, **12**

aquatic, 13

grassland, 12–13

limited resources, effect of, 12–13, 15

terrestrial, 13

biosphere, 7, **14**

earth's, organization of, 14–15

Biosphere 2 mission, 112–115

birds

Arctic, 125

black-and-white warblers, 164

eagles, 41

hawks, *see* hawks

owls, *see* owls

pigeons, 19

rock doves, 19

CREDITS

Lesson 5

70: Thinkstock 72T: Shutterstock 72B: Thinkstock 73L: Shutterstock 75: Thinkstock 77: Mint Images Limited/Alamy 78: Thinkstock 80: Shutterstock 81: Shutterstock 82: Thinkstock 83: Shutterstock

Lesson 6

84: Shutterstock 86: Shutterstock 87T: Shutterstock 87TC: Shutterstock 87C: Shutterstock 87BC: Shutterstock 87B: Shutterstock 88TL: Scimat/Science Source 88TR: Shutterstock 88BL: Shutterstock 88BR: Shutterstock 92-93: Shutterstock 94: Shutterstock 94 inset: Shutterstock 95: David Hay Jones/Science Source 96: Shutterstock 97T: Image courtesy of NOAA Okeanos Explorer Program, MCR Expedition 2011. 97B: Steve Downer/Science Source 98L: Nature Picture Library/Alamy 98R: Karen Kaspar/Alamy

Lesson 7

100: Thinkstock 102: Shutterstock 104: Thinkstock 106: Shutterstock 108-109: Shutterstock 111: Shutterstock 112: ASSOCIATED PRESS 113: Wikimedia 114T: Wikimedia 114B: Shutterstock 115: NASA/Wikimedia

Unit 3 Opener

116: Chuck Place/Alamy 119TR: National Geographic Creative/Alamy 119B: William D. Bachman/Science Source 119TL: Matthew Oldfield/Science Source

Lesson 8

120: Shutterstock 122: Shutterstock 123T: Rolf Nussbaumer Photography/Alamy 124: Shutterstock 125: Shutterstock 126: Shutterstock 126 inset: Shutterstock 127: Frans Lanting Studio/Alamy 128: Avalon/Photoshot License/Alamy 129T: Rolf Nussbaumer Photography/Alamy 129B: Shutterstock 130TL: Shutterstock 130TC: Thinkstock 130TR: Thinkstock 130BL: Thinkstock 130BC: Thinkstock 130BR: Getty Images 131TL: Shutterstock 131TC: Thinkstock 131TR: Thinkstock 131BL: Shutterstock 131BC: Christopher WATERS/Alamy 131BR: Thinkstock 132: Frans Lanting/MINT Images/Science Source 133: Michael J. Tyler/Science Source 134T: Nature Picture Library/Alamy 134T: H Lansdown/Alamy 134C: Shutterstock 134B: Country girl/Alamy 134B: Shutterstock

135: Thinkstock 136: Frans Lanting Studio/Alamy 137: Shutterstock 138: National Geographic Creative/Alamy 139T: NPS 139B: Indraneil Das/Alamy

Lesson 9

140: imageBROKER/Alamy 142: Shutterstock 143: Shutterstock 144C: Shutterstock 145TL: Nigel Cattlin/Alamy 145TR: Nigel Cattlin/Alamy 145B: Shutterstock 146: GaryRobertsphotography/Alamy 147: dbimages/Alamy 148T: Shutterstock 148B: Thinkstock 149TL: Martin Shields/Alamy 149TR: Pat Canova/Alamy 150T: Getty Images 150B: Thinkstock 151: Mauro Fermariello/Science Source 152: Shutterstock 153: Shutterstock 154: National Geographic Creative/Alamy 155: William D. Bachman/Science Source

Lesson 10

156: Matthew Oldfield/Science Source 158T: Getty Images 159T: NASA Earth Observatory image by Robert Simmon, using Suomi NPP VIIRS 159B: Shutterstock 161T: Ulrich Doering/Alamy 161B: Chris Howes/Wild Places Photography/Alamy 162T: BIOSPHOTO/Alamy 162B: Steve Trewhella/FLPA/

CREDITS

Science Source **163T:** Thinkstock
163B: Getty Images
164T: Shutterstock **164BL:** Getty
Images **164BR:** Thinkstock
165T: U.S. Fish and Wildlife
Service **166T:** Shutterstock
167L: Ted Kinsman/Science
Source **167R:** Thinkstock
168: Terese Loeb Kreuzer/
Alamy **169:** Getty Images
170: Shutterstock **171:** David R.
Frazier Photolibrary, Inc./Alamy
172: WILDLIFE GmbH/Alamy
173: Chuck Place/Alamy

Back Matter
174: Reto Stöckli, Nazmi
El Saleous, and Marit
Jentoft-Nilsen, NASA GSFC
176: Corbis Premium RF/
Alamy **177:** iStockphoto
178: Image Source Plus/Alamy
179: Thinkstock **181:** Shutterstock
183: Shutterstock
184: Shutterstock **185T:** Karin
Hildebrand Lau/Alamy
185B: A.J.D. Foto Ltd./Alamy
187: Thinkstock **191:** Shutterstock
193: Shutterstock **195:** Thinkstock
197: Shutterstock
199: Shutterstock
200T: Wikimedia
201T: Thinkstock
201C: Thinkstock
205T: Thinkstock
205C: Thinkstock
206B: iStockphoto
207T: Thinkstock **207C:** Getty
Images **207B:** NASA
208: Thinkstock **209:** Borislav

Toskov/Dreamstime **210:** Image
Source Plus/Alamy **211:** Hero
Images Inc./Alamy **214:** Blend
Images/Alamy **215:** iStockphoto
216: Thinkstock **217:** NASA/JPL
219: Thinkstock **222:** Wikimedia
227: Ted Foxx/Alamy
228: iStockphoto